Creating A Successful Family

Here is a comprehensive guide for dealing with and preventing the problems and difficulties families often encounter in everyday life. As we approach the twenty-first century, creating a successful family requires new skills and a commitment to equality which encourages communication and mutual trust, respect and affection between husbands and wives, parents and children. In this positive and optimistic book the authors offer practical guidance for shared decision-making and problem-solving, stress management, nurturing the unique qualities of each child, and developing the emotional support that can bring to the family a major source of enrichment for all its members.

Khalil A. Khavari is Professor of Psychology at the University of Wisconsin-Milwaukee. He has served as Director of the University's Institute on Drug Abuse and in 1986 received the State of Wisconsin Outstanding Research Award in the field of Alcoholism. Professor Khavari has served as consultant, reviewer, and editor to numerous national bodies and scientific journals. He was adopted by the Raven Clan of the Tlingit Indian Tribe of south-eastern Alaska for the services he rendered to them. His given name in their language is 'Father of Many Leaves'.

Sue Williston Khavari received her Master's degree in Library and Information Science in 1972 and subsequently served as the Director of Technical Services at the Law School Library of Marquette University until 1985. She now works as a freelance writer. They have two adult children.

Creating A Successful Family

KHALIL A. KHAVARI, Ph.D

and

SUE WILLISTON KHAVARI, M.A.

ONEWORLD

Books for Thoughtful People

Creating A Successful Family

Oneworld Publications Ltd
1c Standbrook House, Old Bond St, London W1X 3TD

British Library Cataloguing in Publication Data
Khavari, Khalil A.
Creating a Successful Family
1. Family
I. Title II. Khavari, Sue Williston
306.8'5 HQ734

ISBN 1–85168–014–4 (hardcover)
ISBN 1–85168–008–X (softcover)

Typeset by DMD Ltd., St. Clements, Oxford

Printed and bound in Great Britain by
Biddles Ltd, Guildford and King's Lynn

Dedication

To our children, Paul and Katherine

Preface

Our aim in writing this book has been to provide information and advice to families who wish to achieve a higher level of unity and psychological well-being – the key components in creating a successful family. Learning new ways is not easy, but neither is living in a state of disunity and conflict.

We have drawn on a variety of psychological, sociological, historical and other sources, our own research, and the observation of many families. We have incorporated moral and ethical teachings, as well as experiences from our own family life over the last twenty-nine years.

Our primary concern in this book is with those issues which face the entire family as we approach the twenty-first century; readers will find a more detailed discussion of the various aspects of marriage, building up a strong partnership, and the changing roles and expectations of both husbands and wives in our forthcoming book, *Creating a Successful Marriage*.

How do authors begin to acknowledge the people who have contributed to the thoughts and ideas which eventually appear in print? Every lecture, conference, friend, book and article we have encountered has had some influence on us – and we are grateful. We owe much to our students in the many classes, workshops and institutes we have given over the years. Sharing their insights and problems challenged us to find sound, practical solutions. We would particularly like to thank our publishers, Juliet Mabey and Novin Doostdar.

Milwaukee, Wisconsin
June, 1989

Khalil A. Khavari
Sue Williston Khavari

Contents

1

Introduction

THE SUCCESSFUL FAMILY

To us, success does not mean material affluence, but rather an affluence of the heart, spirit and mind. We believe that with the proper motivation, training and the efforts of all its members, every family can successfully become more unified and loving. In a thriving family, not only do the members get along well together, they encourage each other's accomplishments and allow everyone to be successful – the mother as much as the father, the children as well as the parents. Productive and confident, each family member is happy and the source of happiness for others.

In these families, a balanced interdependence exists as the children grow up, where no one is either overly-dependent and clinging, or aloof, lonely and independently solitary. Children and parents have room to explore and grow towards self-development and self-fulfilment while at the same time feeling securely bonded to the others and able to count on an ever-present network of family psychological support and love.

One secret of a successful family is its ability to solve problems together. But even more important is learning how to foster those positive conditions that prevent problems from arising in the first place.

We live in a highly stressful time of incessant technological and social change affecting every aspect of life. The sheer number and rapidity of these changes call for stable and supportive families to provide the necessary emotional strength to deal with them. Yet, just when the need to rely on them is greatest, we find that contemporary families are vulnerable, even fragile. Because personal interactions between husbands and wives, parents and children are fragmented as never before, special efforts must now be made to learn how to form and maintain the loving relationships found within a well-functioning family. In the forthcoming chapters we will explore many topics to help achieve this:

- How family relationships are changing in response to the global rise in the appreciation of individual human worth.
- How children can form a comprehensive view of life that can best serve them in adulthood, one that gives them a sense of identity and security through humane and responsible personal values.
- How to release the day-to-day tensions inherent in raising children, even when both parents work.
- How to prevent problems through the use of psychologically-sound methods of discipline and emotional nurturance.
- How to establish effective communication and joint decision-making.
- How to solve problems, deal with the family's finances, manage stress, handle sibling rivalry, and co-operatively share in household maintenance.
- How to teach children the social and intellectual skills essential for the workplace of the future.

Recent research on these and many other subjects will be presented along with some down-to-earth advice − a mixture of the theoretical and the practical that reflects the dynamics of family life itself. We will provide suggestions not only on *what* to do, but *why* it should be done. You must, however, only do what feels right for your own situation. While keeping your mind open to potentially useful guidance, ultimately you must trust your own judgement – it is you, after all, who are the real expert on your particular family. Having said that, we welcome you to join us in learning to make family life the emotionally and intellectually exhilarating experience it can and should be.

The methods and suggestions in this book will work for many different types of families. Today's households may be headed by one parent or two; they may contain one child or many, including step-, full- and half-siblings; they may have one or more grandparents permanently living in the same home. The basic principles and skills discussed in this book apply equally well to all these household situations, and we use the word 'family' to embrace them all.

LEARNING NEW SKILLS TOGETHER

Whenever possible, the entire family should read and discuss the ideas and information together. If you have children over eight or nine, you may want to read some sections out loud to them. If the vocabulary is a little difficult, you can supply the definitions and explain the ideas. They will probably enjoy this chance to feel grown-up and to be involved. You may want to ask an older child to browse through the book, choose a section to study, and to lead a family discussion on it.

In this way each person is provided with a common background from which to learn the necessary skills and attitudes for improving family life and especially for learning consultation, an innovative process for planning, day-to-day decision-making and conflict resolution. It does not replace or undermine parental authority but instead informs it with the thoughts, feelings and suggestions of all family members. Consultation is collective thinking which encourages emotional as well as intellectual input; the decisions which result from it are often more inventive and relevant than the dictates of a single authority imposed from above. Consultation allows family decisions to be reached co-operatively; it promotes true consensus by ensuring that every member's thoughts and feelings are considered, for at the heart of the decision-making process is the affirmation of each participant's dignity, worth and welfare. In a family which consults together regularly, honestly and in good faith, everyone wins. Consultation is discussed in depth in Chapter 5 because it forms the cornerstone of healthy modern family relationships. To develop your expertise and practise your new skills in consultation, we have included games and exercises.

All these subjects are presented within the framework of the changing times in which we live and will give your family not only insight into current challenges, but guidance for creating a family equipped to deal successfully with the future. We hope that the book will serve as a congenial way of introducing your family to a continuing habit of sharing feelings and ideas, a habit that will draw the family closer through many years of preventing and solving problems together.

In order to understand what is happening to contemporary families, we need to take a look at the social setting of the late twentieth century, a time of whirlwind changes. As the next century approaches, major transformations are occurring in the workplace and throughout our political, economic and social institutions. Nowhere are these changes literally being 'brought home' to us so intimately as in the sphere of family life.[1]

THE FAMILY REFLECTS
THE LARGER WORLD

Families are not isolated islands, remote and unaffected by the society in which they live. One reason why problems arise may be a failure to recognise how deeply changes in society as a whole affect relationships within the family. Some of these changes are comprehensible, some are puzzling; all have a greater and lesser impact upon us. If we look at things from a wider, more historical perspective than the newspaper headlines and news broadcasts offer, it is possible to make sense of what otherwise seem to be random, illogical events.

Families everywhere have been influenced by rising educational levels, industrialisation and increased life spans. Electronic communication and modern transportation systems have demolished the barrier of distance that separated the flow of ideas between peoples of different cultures in the past. Furthermore, insights from research in psychology, sociology and anthropology have influenced popular conceptions of thinking and behaviour patterns. All this has led to profound differences, especially in the developed nations, between our own lifestyles and those of our ancestors. Ervin Laszlo of the Club of Rome writes: 'All societies in the world today are in a process of transformation. Technologies and institutions, as well as values, beliefs, and goals are changing.'[2]

But we know that old ways and old ideas have always given way to new ones before – why should this be so difficult for us now? One clear answer is the increased speed at which scientific research, inventions, new products, and ideas are affecting us – we have seen more changes in just one generation than used to occur in centuries. Not only does this process show no sign of slowing down, it gives promise of even swifter acceleration. The social historian Alvin Toffler writes: 'Throughout the past, as successive stages of social evolution unfolded, man's awareness followed rather than preceded the event. Because change was slow, he could adapt unconsciously, 'organically'. Today unconscious adaptation is no longer adequate.'[3]

We must come to terms with the fact that change is, and will continue to be, the pattern of our lives, and that to cope effectively with it we will have to see it in a positive light. To resist the process of change, to dig in our heels and brace ourselves against it will only sap our energies and block our attempt to understand it.

Change is not our enemy. When we look at it from a certain perspective, we can see that many of these technologies and the new ideas that accompany them are pulling us towards a more unified, more humane world. What we are seeing unfolding before our eyes is the 'planetary development process of humankind'.[4]

> The scientific and technological advances . . . portend a great surge forward in the social evolution of the planet, and indicate the means by which the practical problems of humanity may be solved. They provide the very means for the administration of the complex life of a united world.[5]

For some nations, science and technology have provided the resources to end the severe poverty and early death that had always existed and we can hope that, before long, these benefits will be extended to the remaining members of the human race. With the coming of higher standards of living beyond mere subsistence and with universal education to release the potential of the individual, we now have a new vision of what it means to be a human being. We can scarcely yet imagine the possibilities which lie in each person should his or her capabilities and talents be developed to their fullest expression. The prospect of what the world's people will achieve in the future is indeed exciting.

THE RISING APPRECIATION OF HUMAN WORTH

In today's enlightened society there is a growing interest in the idea of individual human worth, a belief that people have certain inalienable rights because of the simple fact that they are human beings. Another aspect of this concept can be called 'the oneness of humanity' which means that all human beings belong to one physical species and are of equal value and dignity regardless of gender, age, race, religion, nationality, ethnic group or any other consideration. Accordingly, every man, woman, and child is not only valued, but should be given the opportunity to become the best human being possible, using all potential abilities to the fullest extent. Documents such as the Universal Declaration of Human Rights, officially signed by governments all over the world, are only the first step in the process of making these rights a reality. Once such ideas are diffused, they become the common property and agenda with which society can reshape and renew itself. Even though there are still many violations of human rights and dignity throughout the world, these beliefs have a persuasive force which is impossible to deny or reverse.[6]

For instance, the old traditional social model that existed in the western world was that of an aristocratic hierarchy with access to literacy, politics and economic power concentrated in the hands of the few. This model is, thankfully, defunct. It is as if a switch had suddenly been flipped; what has always been taken for granted has become no longer acceptable, as the impetus for valuing human life grows stronger. We see these changes taking place more dramatically in the developed countries, but it is happening everywhere, especially as the new technology continues to draw nations together, economically and through the exchange of ideas.

For us, the following historical events are landmarks of the growing influence of the universal theme of the rise in human dignity:

- The extension of the right to vote to all races, social classes and genders in virtually every nation.
- The emergence of new nations from former colonies.

- The enactment of laws in many countries against child labour, child abuse and neglect.
- The increasing availability of public-funded education all over the world.
- The initial stages of equal educational and occupational opportunity for women in all countries.
- The increasing number of voluntary donations, in yearly amounts of millions of dollars, and its equivalent in other currencies, for the relief of the needy and victims of disaster around the world by ordinary people whose only return is the knowledge that they have helped to alleviate the suffering of their fellow human beings.

Such enormous differences in the way of life and thinking on our planet during the last few generations indicates that a fundamental alteration is taking place in the conduct of human existence. Unconnected as these changes may seem superficially, they have a common universal theme.

But how, you may wonder, does all this affect the family?

The family is the smallest social unit affected by the swiftly evolving changes related to the pivotal concept of human worth and, not surprisingly, it is currently a focus of drastic transformation.[7] The notion of equal rights, worth and dignity for all has profound implications for marriage and the family. Many of the old practices and expectations in family life are simply no longer workable because they conflict with the new thinking and social realities of our time. All around us we see evidence of this as families struggle and often fail to remain intact.

Family patterns can and must change when necessary. By becoming aware of how the new social context affects us, we can rethink our ways and consider readjusting our own family patterns to meet current needs. In the next chapter we will look at many of the issues facing contemporary family life which are rooted in the rising appreciation of individual human worth.

2
Human Rights at Home

Where, after all, do universal human rights begin? In small places, close to home – so close and so small that they cannot be seen on any maps of the world . . . Such are the places where every man, woman and child seeks equal justice, equal opportunity, equal dignity without discrimination. Unless these rights have meaning there, they have little meaning anywhere.

Eleanor Roosevelt[8]

How do we bring human rights into our family life? In this chapter we will first examine past and present gender roles and attitudes to children. Then we will discuss the structure of family authority and how it is changing. The more information families have on these topics, the better equipped they will be to understand their own situations.

THE ROLES OF WOMEN AND MEN

A good example of how change has affected families is the new status of women. Under the concept of the oneness of humanity, women are equal to men for a logical and simple reason: both are human beings. Uncomplicated as this sounds, it has complex ramifications for the traditional role of women in family life.

Consider the choices facing late twentieth-century women in the developed nations. It is now possible for a young woman to completely reject the role of wife and mother. She can be trained, enter a profession, and earn her own living: she does not need to marry in order to eat, and her pension and savings will support her in old age. All the decisions concerning spending money, where to live and how to use leisure time are controlled by her alone – she is fully independent.

Contrast this with a woman's traditional role. First her father, then her husband made important decisions for her. She was given little education, had few marketable skills, generally earned no money that she could keep for herself, and had no right to decide where or how to live. In theory, she was required to obey an all-powerful husband who could even beat her, if he wished, with little interference from the law. This child-like dependency stifled talents and frequently produced resentful wives. In modified forms, this condition still survives in many places, even in so-called advanced societies. For some women, male dominance continues to include physical abuse.

The independent and dependent models of womanhood described above represent the ends of the spectrum, the extremes of choice available today: both models are unacceptable. At first glance, the independent model, completely free of marital and parental responsibilities, would seem to be far more attractive. Yet how would the human race survive into the future if every woman chose this path and no one took the responsibility for bearing and raising children? The old dependent model looks more attractive, perhaps, to a man looking for a wife. Yet, with economic independence possible, what woman would willingly place herself in such a repressed role?

In our view, the high rate of divorce partly stems from this basic contrast in available alternatives. With their new earning capacity, women no longer have to put up with their traditionally powerless role in marriage, yet many men have unreasonable expectations of retaining undisputed, unshared power. Some couples are able to compromise and strike a balance between the two models, but a great many unhappy couples are at an impasse; they cannot mesh new realities with old traditions.

Since most women are not likely to give up their newly-won progress towards equality and go back again into subservient dependency, the problem of sharing family power and decision-making must be dealt with; it will not go away by itself. It is critical that a solution be found soon for this unresolved conflict – the number of families that are breaking up is alarming, and has serious ramifications for the stability of all societies.

WOMEN, WORK AND MOTHERING

A glance backwards in history is useful for understanding the present difficulty in adjusting to gender equality. Most societies have been dominated by men with little recognition of the rights of women. The basic women's work of creating a home, bearing and raising children, and processing the raw products of the hunt and farm was rarely given the credit it deserved. At best, there was a tacit acknowledgement that women discharged certain important functions, but these were deemed secondary to what men did.

Females were often considered dispensable. Infanticide, practised in ancient Greece, Arabia, China, and many other societies, was directed primarily at baby girls.[9] In some cultures, women's value was largely based on their capacity to bear sons. Women were generally considered less competent and important than men, except in their 'natural' domestic sphere.

Only a few generations separate the developed world from the time when women were permitted neither to vote nor to enter most professions. Until the last century in England and America, married women could not sign

contracts or own property. Even the money they earned
or inherited from their fathers legally belonged to their
husbands. Nor could they seek recourse in the courts,
because women could not bring lawsuits; they lost their
legal identity as a separate individual when they married.
The common-law tradition in England and its colonies
was reflected in the old adage, ' "My wife and I are one,
and I am he," said the Englishman.'

Gender prejudice has deep roots that permeate virtually
every society. All kinds of traditional assumptions, made
by men and women alike, help maintain this error.
Freud's seemingly innocent three-word slogan 'anatomy
determines destiny' both summarised and perpetuated
the long-standing justification for condemning women to
second-class status.

Why was the fact that women bore children such a
hindrance to equality? It is hard for those of us who live
in developed countries in the late twentieth century to
imagine what life was like for women in the past and is
like for some women in undeveloped countries even
today. Because of the lack of effective birth control, the
typical woman was pregnant, nursing babies, or caring
for children through most of her adult life, that is, if she
lived through the dangers of successive births.[10] Poor
sanitation and ignorance caused the common and often
fatal disease of 'childbed fever' which made women's lives
precarious. After much suffering and personal risk
bearing their infants, mothers frequently had to watch
helplessly as their young children died from infectious
diseases and other causes; if seven children were born in
a family, perhaps two or three might live to adulthood.

Practically speaking, implementing the concept of the
equality of men and women remained impossible until
the progress of medical science in the nineteenth and
twentieth centuries brought about safer childbirth, an
increase in the rate of child survival, and reliable
methods of birth control. The high birth rates and high
infant death rates of the past have now been replaced by

low birth rates and low infant death rates in the developed nations. The demographic transition, as this change is called, means that fewer children are born to individual mothers and that a much larger proportion matures to adulthood. Mother mortality has also decreased dramatically. In other words, mothers can and do have fewer, but far healthier children than before. Sheer quantity is rapidly being replaced by quality, as health and education levels for children continue to rise.

Another factor in reducing the birthrate is that children are no longer the economic assets they used to be in pre-industrial societies where large numbers of children could work in the fields or in cottage industries. Industrialisation has taken primary production away from the individual family.

These significant changes plus an increased life span have freed women from their all-consuming reproductive and domestic roles. They can now begin to plan for longer lives in which raising a small number of children may form a delightful part, but not the entire reason for existence.

In the past, one major advantage that favoured men over women was a physical one: men generally have stronger muscles capable of delivering greater force, and this was significant when it came to subjugating the adversary, whether it was animal prey, an enemy – or a woman. The advent of machines, however, has placed a man's muscles in the same cateogory as those of a horse; today it is mechanical, not biological, horsepower that does the heavy work. What really counts is brain power and in that both sexes are indeed equal, as has been shown indisputably over many decades by intelligence tests.[11]

If it is true that women have always been equally intelligent, then why have they not accomplished more? There are, after all, few women's names among the lists of great historical figures. One answer is that, generally, women have been perceived as being less competent than

men because, by both law and custom, they have never
been permitted to develop their potential.

> Woman's lack of progress and proficiency has been
> due to her need of equal education and opportunity.
> Had she been allowed this equality, there is no
> doubt she would be the counterpart of man in ability
> and capacity.[12]

Culture also plays a part in denying women opportunity.
Even in those societies where there are equal educational
opportunities, women themselves often accept their
secondary role because it is so strongly emphasised as
'normal' in their culture and is continually reinforced
through today's mass media. For example, girls usually
receive better marks than boys all through school, yet
they usually underestimate their own intellects and
perceive boys as more able. In college, women have less
confidence in their abilities to perform their assigned
tasks well.[13] From childhood on, women seem to accept
society's view of their inferiority, even in the face of
strong evidence to the contrary.

Gender prejudice harms every society. Governments
should ensure that men and women have the same
inalienable right to choose any profession, to be trained,
and to have an equal chance at getting any job for which
they qualify. More and more women around the globe
are determined to take their rightful place in society;
they are proving themselves capable of working in all
occupations as the barriers to equality are coming down.

MEN, WORK AND FATHERING

Men are understandably confused by the disparity
between traditional views of women and contemporary
realities. Raised to be solely responsible for providing for
their children, to be undisputed decision-makers and
heads of households and, most of all, to have 'women's

work' done for them, many men find themselves disorien-
ted in a time when these long-standing verities are being
questioned. They ask, 'Why do women no longer find
complete satisfaction and fulfilment in being wives and
mothers? Why are women no longer the way that women
have always been, since time out of mind?' Bewildered
about it himself, Freud once asked, 'What do women
want?' The answer is not difficult to understand; women
simply want:

> What men had – the power to achieve financial
> independence, the self-esteem which comes from
> highly regarded work, and the opportunity to engage
> in work which provides challenge, expansion
> of skills, and recognition and reward for one's
> abilities.[14]

The truth is that the emancipation of women is not only
good for women, it is good for men as well. Wives can now
become full financial partners with their husbands, just
as they once contributed their unpaid work in the home
and on the farm. Now they are simply going to where the
work is, outside the home. Instead of remaining in a state
of dependency, a wage-earning wife can be respected as a
colleague by her husband and appreciated for proving
competence in the work-a-day world.

Half of the world's most intelligent people are women –
we need them to occupy the top positions in science,
commerce, industry and government along with the
other intelligent half. This will benefit everyone: 'The
happiness of mankind will be realised when women and
men co-ordinate and advance equally, for each is the
complement and helpmeet of the other.'[15]

Women are just beginning to taste the delicious fruit of
economic self-sufficiency. But the price of independence
is often unacceptably high. No society, as yet, has made
the essential adjustments to fully accommodate the

modern woman. Many young women are rightfully concerned that the demands of motherhood may seriously interfere with, if not totally disrupt, their professional plans, leading to dissatisfaction and outright resentment of the unshared burdens placed on them. While some women have exceptional drive and energy, the over- whelming majority find it extremely difficult to combine family and job responsibilities. For many women, the dilemma is whether to forgo motherhood, or even marriage, to have a career.

A real choice now exists for women – they can easily decide not to marry and have a family. At this time, few men seem to have grasped the full implications of this possibility.

If men want to have the joys of having a wife, children and the comforts of a happy home life they will have to change their expectations about continuing the old ways. The wife should not have to struggle with the double burden of doing a 'man's job' all day and yet be expected to face a full quota of 'women's work' at night as well. Nor should a woman, taking care of very young children at home and expending the time and great energy that good parenting skills now demand, be expected to carry in addition the whole burden of housework 24 hours a day, 365 days a year. *If men want a family life, they will have to view themselves as equal partners with their wives in child-raising and household management.*

There is no reason for a woman to be forced to choose between having a family and a career when adjustments can be made in the family power structure through the use of joint decision-making and other measures. Husbands will eventually find that the new way is better, and not only for reasons of justice. A much more loving and rewarding relationship will be established with their wives and children when the internal workings of the family are more in tune with the realities of a broader society moving towards equality.

We generally think of sharing power as something that men give to women, but there is another way of looking at it. What power men had came from outside the home: the power of making money, the legal powers of property ownership and contracts, and the power of voting and political participation. We can call this 'macro-power'. But there is another kind of power, just as potent in human life.

This is the great fundamental power that women have always had – to bear, nourish and mould the personality, values and beliefs of every new human being. Each person is educated and shaped by his or her mother, that first teacher whose power in influencing the character and life of each individual is unparalleled, generation after generation.[16] Traditionally managed by women, the home was the one place where they were perceived to be both competent and sovereign. Let us call this power within the home and family 'micro-power'.

And just as men must yield macro-power to women in the workplace and in the realm of legal rights and politics, so must women permit men access to micro-power by sharing their dominance in their children's lives and the central role in maintaining the home.

This is not as easy for women as it would seem. It is hard to yield the only power ever fully granted to women. To change the primary role for which women had been trained since childhood, when they played with dolls and imitated their mothers, goes against all cultural assumptions. Unconsciously, a woman may feel that her femininity is threatened when she sees her husband doing 'her' dishes or mopping 'her' floors. There is a tug at the heart when a mother notices a child running, not to her, but to Daddy for a kiss when a knee is scraped.

A woman may unwittingly sabotage a well-meaning husband's first attempts at taking on domestic responsibilities. Untaught and clumsy, the husband may feel not only awkward, but absurd. And if the wife, who secretly feels proud of her own competence, betrays the slightest hint of disdain for the attempt, it can blight a budding new era of co-operation. As one man said poignantly, 'I tried to braid my daughter's hair one morning; it wasn't quite perfect. My wife glared at me and rebraided it. I resolved never to try it again.'

There are other ways that a father may be denied access to micro-power. Often, when the mother and children are closely bonded, the father is excluded from the central core of the family and feels left out, a peripheral figure to the children, relegated to the fringes of family life. Moreover, when a father can only relate to his children in a coldly remote, authoritarian way, he loses out on much of the satisfying joy and companionship in the family. Sometimes the husband may focus all his time and energy on his job, depriving himself of the company of his wife and children and the emotional support that rightfully belongs to him. When this happens, he may become alienated and find solace in alcohol or other harmful things.

The mother is the focal liaison between the parent-child bond and the husband-wife bond. When she makes sure that the father is included within the family circle and yields some of the central power of the home to him, everyone benefits. The father gains a deep sense of being needed and loved, the children gain another adult willing to share time, wisdom, and affection with them, and the mother gains a unified home with a full partner to help shoulder the task of raising the children. Permitting the father to share in the joys and sorrows of the most intimate aspects of parenting and caring for the household neither feminises the man nor defeminises the woman. When we struggle with these new roles, we should not be surprised at the difficulty of adjustment, for the ingrained habits of many centuries die hard. But we will succeed because we must; family life is too precious for men to risk becoming excluded from it, as lonely divorced fathers come to know through sad experience.

In the successful family, both macro-power and micro-power are jointly held by mother and father, neither one is constricted by a specialised gender role. The two powers merge in each individual parent who is truly a whole human being, competent and essential both for the outer world of society and within the inner sphere of the household.

Sharing power in the family does not mean dividing it, like cutting a loaf of bread, where giving more to one side means taking away from the other. Not at all, because it actually results in *multiplying* the powers of the two individuals. The new egalitarian family life does not decrease the husband's manhood, it increases the wife's personhood; it does not make the woman less of a devoted mother, it allows the father to fully bond with his children in the same intimate, loving way that mothers have always done.

When a father becomes more involved in caring for his child, he will find a whole new world of fulfilment in the endless fascination of witnessing and contributing to a child's developing capabilities. The freshness and excitement of seeing commonplace objects through a child's eyes can renew a sense of wonder in the father, which would have been denied him if he were not so closely involved with the day-to-day experience of his child's life.

When a mother encourages her husband to fully integrate into the family circle by giving him time alone with the children and relinquishing her constant watchful supervision, fathers develop more nurturing relationships with their children. The whole family becomes more harmonious, a supportive network able to make the tensions and frustrations of rapidly changing life in the late twentieth century more bearable. Love flows more tenderly from father to child, and child to father.

The title of this section includes the word 'fathering', which at present generally has a very different meaning from 'mothering'.[17] To father a child means to be the biological father, whereas to mother a child means to care for it, to succour and watch over it for an extended period of time. We believe that fathering will someday have the same meaning as mothering, that children will think of their fathers as having raised them with as much devotion and loving concern as their mothers.

Today, the larger society needs those very qualities that women have developed over millennia of personal sacrifice to raise the world's children: compassion, unselfishness, nurturance, and above all, conciliation and peace-making. Like all human qualities, these are not inborn, but must be learned from others. Men can learn them from women and from the experience of caring for children just as women are now learning from men how to operate tall construction cranes, teach chemistry, and run for political office.

There is an unforgettable image that conveys the concept of the equality of men and women: humanity is like a bird with two wings, one male and the other female; both must be strong. With two vibrant wings working in harmony, to what heights will the bird of humanity soar?[18]

A NEW ATTITUDE TOWARDS CHILDREN

Another fundamental change in families is the growing belief that children should be included in the concept of the oneness of humanity, with certain rights of their own, such as the right to be educated during their childhood years. In the past, a child was often treated like a small adult and put out to work in the fields or apprenticed to a master craftsman at an early age. Children commonly earned their own living before they were ten or eleven.

In the developed nations of our time, laws require children to stay in school for many years at public expense because the entire society benefits from having an educated population. But when children must be dependent on their parents' support for such a long period of time, problems arise. Parents often find it difficult to control the behaviour of adolescents who not only look and feel grown-up, but feel entitled to the privileges of adulthood while still at home in a highly dependent situation. Adjustments are often required to ease the tensions which arise when the methods used for controlling small children no longer work for adolescents. Family life must accommodate the need for these near-adults to share in making decisions that affect them.

The present recognition of the value of human life means that child abuse and neglect, in spite of its long, harrowing history[19] and persistent prevalence, can no longer be officially tolerated by any society. We have seen some progress in this area. In earlier times, children were generally treated as the parent's property, with little interference from others. In the last few decades, however, laws have been passed which finally recognise that parents are to be held responsible for violent acts towards their children. Nevertheless, in spite of a heightened awareness that children have the right not to be beaten and neglected, abuse in families of all social and economic levels appears to be increasing along with family stress in general, particularly in times of financial hardship.

Mothers and fathers in this age of change and complexity need training in newer skills of child-raising. The former, more authoritarian ways of their own childhoods are no longer either suitable or effective during the present age when the status of children, along with all formerly oppressed people, is rising. Methods of discipline which are more humane – and much more effective – are available; a great deal of research in child development and parenting techniques has been done and parents can and should use this information.

Parents must also learn how to help their children

prepare for the rapid changes occurring in the workplace. In the past, daughters were almost always limited to doing the kinds of work their mothers did. Many sons followed their fathers in the family farm or business; class distinctions often limited the types of occupations open to them. In the last few generations, however, the number and variety of occupations has greatly multiplied and there has been more specialisation in the work force. The continuing automation revolution, the use of more sophisticated computers, and technological advances such as the development of superconductors promise even more occupational diversity. New types of employment are being created as old ones become obsolete: indeed, many of the occupations for which children will need skills do not exist yet. How can parents prepare their children for the future in such circumstances? They can enhance their children's natural ability to learn new things by encouraging creativity and flexibility. By learning to think for themselves, these future adults will stand a better chance of acquiring the initiative and self-directedness future jobs will require.

Most important of all in this time of rapid change and its accompanying social confusion, parents should ensure that their children acquire a solid foundation of ethical and moral values to provide them with the guidance they need in making the difficult daily choices they will face in both their professional and personal lives. When parents provide standards to live by, at the same time assuring them of their unconditional love and acceptance, these well-balanced, psychologically healthy children can, in turn, reach out to love others. As they mature, they can then forge those vital personal connections through marriage and friendship that will allow them to withstand the many changes in ways of living and thinking that are coming in the years ahead. These issues are examined in more detail in later chapters.

THE CHANGING FAMILY

Family stability is currently being undermined for many reasons, including unrealistic personal expectations on the part of the marriage partners, inadequate interpersonal skills and a traditional family governance structure which does not satisfy the needs of our time.[20] At present, the divorce rate in the United States is extremely high and even in countries where it is lower the effects of the destabilisation of the home are all too apparent. As a result there has been a marked increase in the unhappiness of men, women, and, saddest of all, their children. We are moving from the old to the new. Still in motion, we find ourselves caught in the turbulence between eras.[21]

If the old patriarchal, authoritarian pattern of family life is no longer working, clearly a different family structure is required which would retain the effectiveness of the old ways yet accommodate the new realities of our time. In order for it to do this, it should have an egalitarian approach to sharing power, planning, communication, nurturing and mutual need-fulfilment. Such a structure also needs a method of interaction that protects the rights of all family members. Consultation, a tool for discussion and decision-making, fits these requirements exactly; when skilfully used it has the potential to establish and maintain family harmony. Moreover, it fully accommodates the new roles of men, women, and children. Consultation is effective because it is consistent with the concept of the oneness of humanity which, as we have seen, is at the centre of many changes both in the family and in the wider society. We will discuss it in detail in Chapter 5.

In thinking about the differences between the old era and the new, we can visualise the gradual modification of power and decision-making from authoritarianism to a more egalitarian system by picturing two geometric shapes. The old autocratic model can be thought of as a pyramid, with power and authority flowing in one direction only, down from the one or few at the top to the many below. The new egalitarian model, however, is like a circle, with each point on the circle equally important, with power and authority flowing freely to and from every point. Authority is held in common, and both rights and responsibilities are shared. In this egalitarian system, oppression by the few is replaced by the consent of the governed. The responsible freedom that accompanies it releases the creative powers of all participants.

In authoritarian families, the father was unquestionably at the top of the pyramid with the mother ranked below him and the children far below them both; orders were handed down and unquestioning obedience was enforced. In the egalitarian family, the mother and father are equally empowered, with the children participating more and more fully in the circle of family decisions as their gradually maturing capacities allow, until they reach adulthood and leave home.

Engendering good-will and co-operation, the new structure of family authority is based on the inherent dignity and worth of each person. It strengthens the family because it is based on the stable foundation of justice.

THE ENDURING FAMILY

The institution of the family has endured throughout the ages because it is a sustaining shelter in which to conduct our lives in the close company of those we love. The technology of modern times which has transformed so much of our traditional life will not do away with this shelter. It will last because no one has found a better way to organise human society at this most fundamental level.

Marriage and the raising of children within a family has proved to be very flexible by adapting itself to new requirements when necessary over the last several thousand years. We should not forget that it has already survived drastic transformations brought about by once-new technologies before. For example, families adapted when they changed from a nomadic way of life as part of hunting and gathering tribes and settled in permanent agricultural villages as farming became a reliable source of food. The institution of the family survived again when people moved from farms to towns and eventually to highly industrialised urban centres. During the coming years, the resilient institution of the family will again readjust the delicate relationships between men and women, parents and children; this time it will be done with an eye to equality.

In spite of its current problems, we believe that marriage and the family will remain the unassailable and enduring bedrock of human love because no other substitute provides so richly and fully for our physical, emotional, spiritual and companionship needs – for the total well-being of all of us.

3

Foundations of Child-Raising

One of nature's kindnesses is that first-born babies are unaware of their new parents' amateur status and will, without criticism, benignly beam at them even when they are completely befuddled and inept. Parents and new babies study each other's faces intently as part of a process known as bonding, which is essential in establishing the close relationship between them. Holding up the infant in the *en face* position, a parent marvels at the whole miracle of birth and ponders the profound question: What is a child?

Before we can discuss the practicalities of how families can function more positively through consultation and other ways, we need to consider some key concepts about human nature, the innate worth and uniqueness of every child and the physical, mental, and spiritual factors that form a child's own individual point of view or frame of reference. Finally, we will look at the way in which positive and negative influences can add up to a child's total sum of developmental experience. Once these fundamentals of child-raising are understood, the chapters in the remainder of the book can be read as components of a unified approach to family life.

UNDERSTANDING HUMAN NATURE

Belief in the intangible, higher faculties of the human spirit has been eroded by the modern emphasis on experimentally verifiable observation as the sole means of discovering 'truth'. With all due respect to what constitutes empirical evidence, some things are beyond the scope of the scientific method. Ideas such as the Creator and the soul are not subject to dissection or direct observation – we cannot take such abstract concepts and weigh or measure them in the same way we ascertain physical properties.

Without physical proof of the existence of the human soul, some people may ask such questions as: 'Are humans merely sophisticated animals with larger brains? If so, are they captives of nature, with predetermined patterns of behaviour based on instincts? Is the principal task of parents to "tame" an inherent wildness, subduing aggression and selfishness with a thin layer of civilised control?'

A closer examination of the facts does not support the position that human beings are animals. It is true that humans and animals have certain physical characteristics in common. But unlike animals, humans do not have the in-born behaviour patterns called instincts which are common to the whole species: scientists have never found 'instinct genes' which children everywhere invariably inherit. They come into the world with a few reflexes, such as those for sucking, swallowing, and breathing, but beyond the reflex level, human behaviour is almost entirely the result of learning.

So prevalent is this public misconception that humans have animal instincts which require them to behave in certain ways, that some of the world's leading psychologists, neurophysiologists, ethologists and others from the natural and social sciences gathered in Seville, Spain in 1986 to formulate a statement on the issue which was subsequently endorsed by the American

Psychological Association and the American Anthropological Association, among other organisations. They all agreed that it was scientifically incorrect to say that we have inherited aggressive tendencies from our animal ancestors; neither war nor any other violent behaviour is genetically programmed into our human nature.[22]

How else can we account for so many varieties of behaviour within our species *Homo sapiens* except that we have no instincts to predetermine our actions? A recent study of 110 nations found that one country had 50 times the murder rate of another otherwise similar society. From the evidence of research about homicide gathered over many years from around the world, psychologist Dan Archer concluded that human violence is not the direct result of a biological drive but a product of social forces.[23] Animals of one species basically behave the same way wherever its various members live. If people were animals, human behaviour would also be similar throughout the world – clearly it is not.

Although it is true that humans share certain biochemical and physical characteristics with animals, they also have other capabilities which are far more complex, such as rational minds and the ability to modify conduct in accordance with accepted codes of behaviour. We see this in the observable fact that humanity has attempted to organise its social life around intangible concepts, such as justice, compassion, and mercy – humane qualities that do not exist among animals.

Animals are not held rationally or morally accountable for their actions; we say they are simply acting according to their instincts. We do, however, hold human beings responsible for an enormous range of behaviour, from theft to truth-in-advertising, to child neglect, cheating on taxes, violating tribal taboos – the list is very long and anyone who does not learn to act according to societal expectations soon gets into serious trouble.

If people are required to act according to the accepted behavioural and ethical standards that all societies everywhere have incorporated into their written or unwritten codes of law, it follows that humans, of necessity, must have a special dimension beyond that of animals: the ability to develop a sense of morality or conscience and learn that it is wrong to kill, to steal and to lie. There are many uniquely human qualities, and to some people, the existence of the human soul is proved through the evidence of such spiritual attributes as unselfish love, kindness, charity, justice, forgiveness, generosity, empathy, trustworthiness and others.

When taught these values, people can put their distinctly human gifts of high intelligence and reasoning power to work for good purposes and in beneficial ways. But when a sense of morality or conscience is not learned in the family, the results can be disastrous not only to the one deprived of it, but also to society. Many criminals were emotionally and physically abused as children; many were denied the patience, time and attention necessary in the crucial early years when ideas about right and wrong are most easily implanted. Without a commitment to obey the laws of human behaviour, the talents of such people are misspent and wasted in anti-social conduct, lost to the world at large. Experts who try to rehabilitate criminals note that early family and pre-school programmes are far more rewarding areas in which to spend money on crime prevention than the usually futile rehabilitation programmes aimed at the nineteen- or twenty-year-old veteran criminal.[24]

Human intelligence is like a two-edged sword. If it is not tempered by the knowledge of ethical standards and spiritual values, it may be used in an inhumane way against others, creating havoc and destruction. History shows us that people can learn to behave like angels or worse than beasts.

> The inner reality of man is a demarcation line between the shadow and the light . . . With education it can achieve all excellence; devoid of education it will stay on, at the lowest point of imperfection . . .

Every child is potentially the light of the world —
and at the same time its darkness; wherefore must
the question of education be accounted as of primary
importance.[25]

Attitudes towards human nature affect parenting

The examination of our personal beliefs and perceptions
about human nature is crucial since these attitudes will
inevitably affect how we raise our children.

Some parents believe that children are fundamentally
evil and animalistic: such parents play a police role,
always expecting the worst. The children of such parents
never feel that they are trusted. Accepting their parents'
view of their inherently evil natures, they behave exactly
as expected, a classic case of self-fulfilling prophecy.
Psychologists have established that expectation has an
important influence on the behaviour of others. If
children are expected to be bad, they will be.[26] When
constantly told they are naughty and treated with
impatience, the children will not be given the chance to
learn and develop the human values that rightfully
belong to them. They may grow up lacking self-esteem
and good social skills, handicapped in their relationships
with others as surely as if they had been born without
hands.

Unlike animals, human behaviour is largely the result
of a person's own will, a will which has been shaped
by learning from others and by life experiences. Bad
behaviour is not, we believe, the result of any 'inborn
evil', but usually reflects ignorance resulting from a lack
of clear guidance. It is unreasonable to expect a child to
'behave' when he or she doesn't know what the correct
behaviour might be. It is the task of the parents to assist
the child in understanding what having a good character
means and how to acquire it. This objective is best
achieved by both pointing out the desirable from
the unacceptable, and noticing and encouraging good
behaviour.[27]

If parents believe that human beings are fundamentally good and capable of developing the higher qualities, such as compassion and kindliness, they will treat their children with psychologically-healthy expectations. They will try to serve as examples to show them how these virtues may be translated into everyday living. When trusted and respected, a child will not be seen as an enemy with a stubborn will that needs breaking, but as a valued small friend who needs careful guidance and patience to learn what it means to be a compassionate, upright, responsible human being.

THE UNIQUENESS OF EVERY CHILD

Each newborn child carries within it the genetic heritage of thousands of generations of its ancestors; it is the latest link in an unimaginably long family chain stretching back to the dawn of human development. Each link represents a person who was born, grew to maturity and produced a child. In a sense, each one of us is the self-evident proof of the success of our family line in surviving the great dangers and hardships present in all ages.

A unique blending of the two long lines of inheritance from its mother and father, a baby has hundreds of thousands of genes which make up its one-of-a-kind, highly personalised genetic code. Never before and never again will this particular genetic combination exist in all creation. Recognising this inborn uniqueness, parents must love their baby for itself, without undue comparison to other children or even to themselves.

Such genetic uniqueness extends beyond physical features and includes temperament, which consists of the emotional and personality predispositions and tendencies of the individual. Although these predispositions can be modified by training and experience, they cannot be completely changed. Family members may resemble each other physically, but they do not always have similar temperaments, and this can lead to problems.

One study that followed children from birth found that it was not children with difficult temperaments or children whose parents had maladaptive styles who needed psychiatric help, but children whose temperaments did not match their parents' styles. Disturbances arose when parental demands ran head on into children's temperamental characteristics, placing the children under heavy stress.[28]

It is important to remember that it is not necessarily a bad thing if your child's temperament and personality are different from your own, even though you may have day-dreamed that your child would turn out to be an improved copy of yourself. It is a great mistake to try to strip a child of his or her personality and temperament and impose your own version instead. Chances are that you will fail and all kinds of problems will result.

Parents generally accept their children's physical features and wouldn't seriously consider changing them to suit their fancy. Would you want to permanently dye your child's hair because you preferred another colour? Of course not. Although you can help your children improve their temperaments and develop their personalities, neither can be replaced. A child's nature is not like a lump of clay to be forced into a mould any way the parent wishes. From the first, each person has a character and individuality which can develop to the best advantage only in a particular way. As a result, no two people should be raised exactly alike.

Parents should care for their children like wise gardeners, who tend different plants by giving each the particular treatment and encouragement it needs, knowing that one plant likes bright sunshine, another shade; one likes to be near the water's edge and another on a dry hill. Only when each plant has its needs appropriately supplied will its potential perfection be revealed.[29]

Sensitivity to the individual differences between children even within the same family is necessary for communicating, instilling good habits, and handling discipline. It does not always come from experience, however, because many parents never acquire the ability to recognise the special needs of each child. But sensitivity can be learned and practised if parents are willing to increase their awareness and powers of observation.

Today the world is slowly becoming more and more aware of the principle of the oneness of humanity which affirms that, as a basic human right, every individual should be valued, educated, and given the opportunity to achieve just as much as their talent and hard work allow. Consciously or unconsciously, parents should not restrict the ambitions of their child. Whatever their own social and educational limitations or ambitions may have been, their child is not condemned to duplicate them. Sometimes parents can become too possessive; they must always realise that children are independent beings, even when they are dependent on adults for their survival. They are not cute little toys, pets, or playthings that 'belong' to the parents. Excessive possessiveness is common and lies at the root of many problems.

What is needed first and above all is the acceptance of the child's uniqueness in all his or her aspects – physical, intellectual and temperamental. The parents' task is to help the child to become the best he or she can be, consistent with this personal uniqueness. In addition to personality and temperament, all children have their own special talents and capabilities, like rough gems waiting to be discovered in the mine of their intellectual and emotional potential. One child may have mathematical talents, another artistic gifts, still another an unselfish capacity for caring for others. Finding and polishing each child's special gems is a task entrusted to parents.

No one in the world is exactly like any other individual, not even a twin brother or sister. A child who is raised in a family where a certain amount of uniqueness is not only tolerated but encouraged is fortunate. Such a child will feel truly accepted. Love is one of the most essential ingredients for well-being. When a child knows deep down in his or her heart that the parents' love will not be withdrawn, that child can feel safe and genuinely secure. Parental love is as permanent as it is profound. More than anything else, it allows the child to flourish. This form of love is not eroded by every little failure or misbehaviour of the child. On the contrary, it is this solid bond of support that serves as a long-enduring source of strength. We want our children to feel this continual love flowing from us, surrounding them, filling up the deepest wells of their beings, enabling each one to grow and become a fountain of love to others. The emotional bond between parents and child should be guided by the twin forces of love and wisdom. It is as if a parent were extending two hands to a child; one hand gently prods the child along the long path to full independence. At the same time, the child clings to the other hand for assurance and never-failing support.

THE FRAME OF REFERENCE

How does a person learn to think and act in his or her own way? What are the factors which enable us to make sense out of the great quantity of sensory perception and information that bombards us?

Through a long and elaborate process in which learning plays a key role, each maturing individual puts together his or her own personal system of values, opinions, beliefs, attitudes, knowledge and skills which enables one to deal with the demands of life. Together these form the frame of reference, or 'framework', through which each of us looks at the world and decides how to deal with it.

It is this frame of reference that tells us about ourselves, other people, the physical universe, and the Creator. It determines our understanding and behaviour by functioning as perceiver, master file, analyser, interpreter, and decision-maker all rolled into one. We act and react from perceptions as they are filtered through it. Our well-being, happiness and successful negotiation through life all depend on a healthy frame of reference.

Each person gradually builds a frame of reference, piece by piece, beginning at birth. Throughout childhood the building process gathers momentum until at adulthood it is basically complete, though major and minor repairs and some remodelling of the frame of reference go on throughout life. Clearly then, a solid and healthy foundation is critical to the superstructure that we continually build upon.

When a baby is born, she enters a world of total mystery, hardly aware of who she is. Oblivious to the rest of the universe, she has no means to explore and sort things out for herself. Images, sounds and physical sensations do not form themselves easily into comprehensible patterns.

It takes the child a long time to realise that there is a difference between beating a toy teddy bear with a stick and using it on herself! Gradually she makes the distinction that 'she' is a separate entity. What lies beneath her skin is part of her, while what lies beyond is 'not her'. Even after realising that it hurts her to use the stick on herself but doesn't hurt the teddy bear, she still has to learn that the stick can also hurt the family dog, Daddy, or an unsuspecting visiting child. She hits others not out of maliciousness but to gather information or simply to exercise her muscles. In each case, the consequences of her action will teach her a lesson.

As the baby grows, her sensory system becomes more

functional, her muscles develop and her world expands. People, animals, objects and events assume considerable significance in her life. Knowingly or unknowingly she spends her waking hours learning, organising, classifying, testing her universe, acquiring new skills and refining the old ones.

Early in life, the powerful forces of reward and punishment, love and hate, joy and sorrow, pain and pleasure begin to shape her attitudes, skills and behaviour. She experiences various degrees of hunger, cold, loneliness, fear, pain, and other discomforts. She may also receive varying amounts of love, assurance, warmth, and affection. Soon she becomes more adept at enhancing the chances of being rewarded and reducing the likelihood of being harmed. She eventually sorts out the confusing fact that different people and situations require different responses and strategies and that she needs to make a speedy assessment of each case before deciding how to behave.

Uncertainty about what to do and when to do it increases as time goes on. A lack of consistency on the part of a volatile, emotionally immature parent can seriously interfere with the development of a healthy frame of reference. The challenge becomes even greater as the child's circle of social contacts expands to include relatives, friends and neighbours with various backgrounds and ages. Each will have different likes and dislikes with contradictory expectations and values; they may also have various levels of mental health. The child tries hard to make sense of the apparent chaos of this perplexing thing called 'life'. The fortunate child becomes adept at working things out as best she can do to minimise her hurt and maximise her gain. It is a tribute to human resilience that most people survive, thrive even, in the face of such heavy odds. Many people succeed in developing a coherent, flexible, comprehensive frame of reference that will effectively guide them for the rest of their lives.

Yet not everyone makes it; some people 'hang loose', remaining uncommitted to much of anything, always prepared to shift in response to each person or situation, always hoping that they might just be lucky enough to do the 'right' thing. Others may eventually give up the struggle altogether. There are casualties of emotionally-disturbed people at all ages. Unfortunately, some will never understand what life is all about, partly because they lacked the guidance of a mature, patient adult who taught them to see the relationships between things, to grasp the idea of cause and effect, and to understand why people act as they do. No one was there to tell them that the behaviour of others need not be copied blindly; no one was there to explain the higher laws that determine how one should behave and other basic skills needed to function adequately.

Trying to figure out the rules of the game of life without good parental guidance is like attempting to navigate in the desert by relying on ever-shifting sand dunes as landmarks. One may end up spinning one's wheels, going round in circles, unsure which way to turn, and eventually giving up hope altogether.

With few exceptions, almost all children are capable of acquiring a healthy and functional frame of reference. Early on, the child draws heavily on his or her parents' frames of reference. Later on, school, religious training, playmates, people, and personal experiences also influence a child's personal outlook. What makes a person decide to adopt some types of behaviour and shun others? The primary factor is what is already in his or her frame of reference. All of us tend to believe and value ideas which are generally in accord with our personal preferences and temperament. We also learn what works for us through trial and error; if one type of behaviour is ineffective, it is likely to be replaced with a more successful one.

What comprises a healthy frame of reference? The five major components are knowledge, realism, vision, optimism, and spirituality. Let us now consider each of them in turn.

Knowledge

The only true wealth is knowledge, and someone who has done little to acquire it is impoverished indeed. We gain knowledge in all kinds of ways: through experience, from books or school, or simply by observation and conversation. It enables us to tap into the wisdom of other people, multiplying and expanding our own limited understanding. Knowledge gives us a base from which to begin seeing with our own eyes and not just through the eyes of others. It frees us from blind imitation of the ideas, thoughts and conduct of others. Knowledge permits the independent investigation of truth, whether that truth be in the physical or social sciences, the arts, religion or in the day-to-day business of living, and liberates us from old prejudices and from being imprisoned by outworn traditions. It is central to the advancement of humanity.

When children are enlightened through both formal and informal education, they can weigh and sift the opinions of others with confidence in their own judgement; at the same time, a frame of reference firmly anchored to human values gives them standards by which to measure and adjust their decisions and actions.

Realism

Our children need to develop the capacity to accurately assess things and situations for what they actually are, rather than what they might wish them to be. While maintaining a long-term perspective and a sense of idealism, they must also be in close touch with the immediacies of everyday life. A faulty sense of realism means that mistakes are made, energies wasted and valuable time and opportunities lost. It is foolhardy to indulge in wishful thinking to avoid perceiving an unpleasant reality or to try to transform an ordinary situation, through fantasy, into what it is not. Absence of a sense of realism can lead to disappointment, even heartbreak.

A realistic frame of reference enhances the chances for taking effective measures when possible; it teaches children that an instant solution does not exist for every difficulty – some things simply must be accepted and endured either temporarily or permanently.

Vision

Being visionary is just as important as being realistic. There is a crucial difference between being a dreamer and a visionary. The dreamer spends time fantasising about the impossible, whereas the visionary works towards a lofty and attainable goal. Without the directing force of vision, there would be little to buoy the spirit, fuel human progress, and give us hope for a better future. It is vision that energises a scientist's long search to find a cure for a disease, that sustains an artist's pursuit of excellence, that motivates parents to spend many years patiently loving and nurturing a child into a fine human being.

Optimism

Optimism allows a child to regard people, things and events in an open-minded, positive light by looking beyond the immediate and obvious to see the potential for good in every situation and person. Pessimism narrows the perspective into a perpetually dissatisfied negativism; the pessimistic child remains critical, suspicious, unready to concede even the smallest benefit of a doubt.

It is easier to be pessimistic and distrustful, just as

impulsiveness and selfishness come more naturally to us than wise caution and generosity. Optimism represents a higher level of development and should be deliberately cultivated. Mothers and fathers can transmit it through their own enthusiastic attitudes and love of life; it must be caught from others, not just talked about. Children will learn it if they see models of optimism at home.

The value of optimism lies in its capacity to release positive energy, to impart the strength to overcome defeat and refuse to surrender to surmountable difficulties. Where the pessimist sees an overwhelming problem, the optimist sees an opportunity. Someone with this trait is always looking for even the faintest ray of hope. Friends are easily attracted to and warmed by this ability to see the good in life – we would all prefer to spend time with an enthusiastic person rather than with a chronic complainer.

An optimistic frame of reference is not naive: it is healthy, creative and sustaining, protecting us from despair as well as enriching the lives of others. Realism and optimism are not opposites. We can learn to see the positive side of any realistic situation, to feel a sense of confidence in the future and to look for the worthy qualities that exist, no matter how deeply buried, in every individual.

Spirituality

In our view, an essential element of a healthy frame of reference is a belief in a Supreme Being or Creator. This provides children with a sense of identity and individual permanence through an understanding of their possession of an eternal soul; it engenders feelings of self-worth as the receiver of the Creator's love and helps them to be caring, sensitive and tolerant towards others. It also gives children a realisation that there is a profound, spiritual purpose and meaning for life. Psychological studies have shown that people who live without the benefit of the moral and ethical standards usually acquired through the various religions, experience more uncertainty and confusion, and are consequently more susceptible to anxiety and stress. The use of drugs and alcohol has also been linked to a lack of firm commitment to a religion or set of moral standards. A three-year study of 4,853 people of various occupational, age, ethnic and religious backgrounds concluded that:

> In general, people who viewed themselves as 'very religious' drank less and used less psychoactives, [i.e. alcohol and drugs of abuse] when compared to those individuals who considered themselves 'not religious at all'. Significantly elevated use of alcohol, tobacco products, marijuana, hashish, and amphetamines was associated with the 'not religious at all' group.[30]

Without spirituality, the individual's frame of reference lacks a steering mechanism. Why is this so? Why do we need guidance from the Creator? Because it takes a higher form of existence to know the reality of a lower form. Humans can study, classify, and understand the behaviour of animals better than the animals themselves can. In the same way, the Creator comprehends the human condition far more profoundly than any mortal and can provide us with those distinctly human moral and ethical ideals with which to conduct our lives, both personally and in a social community – if we ignore them, it is to our own detriment. It is our belief that as surely as there are physical laws, such as gravity, there are also spiritual laws or universal standards of human conduct that bring order, virtue and happiness to one's life. When a connection is made with these spiritual principles, the child's frame of reference becomes reinforced with a feeling of certitude and a firm set of principles on which to base thought and behaviour.

What parents can do

What can we do to help our children form a healthy frame of reference? First, we must be thoroughly convinced of the innate value of each child. It is this conviction that makes all our efforts meaningful and worthwhile. Second, we need to improve our own frames of reference in order to become better examples. Third, to aid this process, there must be unity and love between the parents as a couple. If there is marital disharmony, parents will find their energies diverted and sapped by the friction of their personal lives and will be unable to give the children the full measure of the attention they need. Also, the children are less likely to be as receptive to their parents' help and advice if they see parental immaturity and discord, with neither side willing to forgive or compromise. When this happens, both the parents and children are deprived of a reciprocal enrichment. Therefore, the mother and father must establish and maintain a mature and unified bond between themselves as a couple. Even if they are no longer married, the mother and father can still have some degree of courteous unity between them.

Parents should do this for their children's sake, if not for their own. In these times of great social and moral upheaval, it is extremely difficult for children and youth to form their individual frames of reference. They must pick and choose from a multitude of contradicting alternatives currently offered. The result is that more and more young people are growing up without a firm grasp of how to conduct their lives.

Unfortunately, many parents are not helping for several possible reasons: a cynical abandonment of some of the high human ideals, a lack of independence of mind to set standards for their own family, or being overly centred on themselves with little concern for their children. It has been said that we grow up twice: once in passing from childhood to adulthood and again when our children do the same. The parent's own unfinished business of maturing often takes place during these years of raising children, and it is never easy.

POSITIVE AND NEGATIVE EXPERIENCES

In the long run, a child who eats good meals, gets plenty of sound sleep and exercise, and is protected from toxins and harmful things, is likely to grow up healthy. If he misses a few hours of sleep one night or if he eats a bag of sweets for dinner on a rare occasion, his health is not likely to suffer permanent damage. In much the same way, a child's psychological development is the net result of exposure to various positive and negative experiences.

For the sake of illustration, let us suppose that a theoretically perfect child, as graded by a panel of qualified judges, receives a score of 100, representing total success. How does he manage to score 100? Through a process of addition and subtraction; the final score is what remains after the positives and negatives have cancelled each other out.

For instance, enlightened, loving parents may contribute the most to the child's imaginary total score, let's say 55 points over the years. An older sibling who is jealous and aggressive may make a negative contribution of -10 points. A marvellous aunt who spends a lot of time with the child contributes 12 points. A crotchety, neurotic neighbour a -4, and so forth.

Good experiences bolster the child, bad ones deplete the reserve. A problem child may have a net score of only 30. This score indicates that at this point in his life, the child has accumulated only 30 per cent of the optimal 100. But a child who is raised in a loving, supportive environment will probably grow up psychologically healthy and close to the 100 total points. Occasional lapses in his support system are not likely to damage him for life.

When we were trying our hardest to be adequate parents we took comfort in the thought that perfect parents would not prepare children to face an imperfect world. So, when the inevitable slip up happens, we should just forgive ourselves, try not to do it again, and go forward! Remember the old saying that the neurotic builds a castle in the air, the psychotic lives in it, and the therapist collects rent on it. Make sure that you don't build any castles in the air by an excessively active imagination or paralysing guilt feelings.

Even though children are resilient, however, we should not rely too heavily on this adaptability. Certain traumatic events in childhood can seriously affect a person's development. The best thing we can do is to expose children to as many positive opportunities and experiences as possible, building up an abundance of plus points as a hedge against the eventual time when some negative ones will be deducted. In many ways, children accurately reflect the amount of parental time and emotional energy that have been invested in them. If the investment is generous, especially during infancy and the early years when nurturing is most essential, it will be evident as the child grows up.

One way we can tell how things are going in a child's life is to observe whether the child is usually happy or unhappy. A child who is frequently sad, sullen or angry is showing that something is wrong and help from the parents is needed. A happy child usually feels good both physically and emotionally. Bright eyes, smiles and laughter are eloquent signs of health in body, mind and heart.

Now that we have discussed some of the fundamental concepts of child-raising – this exciting challenge which uses all our emotional, intellectual, and spiritual resources – we are ready to consider the valuable skill of family communication.

4

Communication

When the members of a family communicate with each other, much more than just an exchange of information takes place; ties of affection can also be either strengthened or weakened. Understanding not only what is being said, but the feelings behind it makes real communication possible. In this chapter, we discuss the components of communication and suggest exercises which teach both parents and children the techniques of more sensitive interaction.

COMPONENTS OF COMMUNICATION

As important as communication is, most people have a poor understanding of what it actually involves. When asked to define it, people say things like, 'It's getting ideas across, informing others, giving a message.' A common tendency is to consider mainly one side of communication: the 'I' or 'my' component, the personal and often egotistical aspects. This inadequate understanding makes many of us poor communicators. There are three equally important parts to any communication.

- The person who generates the message
- The message itself
- The person who receives the message

If any of these three parts is absent or not working properly, communication cannot take place. The third component, though often overlooked, is just as necessary as the originator of the message – there must always be a tuned-in receiver, someone able (and willing) to understand the message.

Verbal communication

Before people learned to control fire over a million years ago, human jaws were massive because all food was eaten raw. After fire began to be used for cooking and food was more easily chewed, the large, heavy jaws evolved into smaller, lighter ones. Anthropologists surmise that this structural change allowed for the refinement of the speech mechanism so that eventually verbal language developed. Over the centuries, words and their meanings multiplied as the human family dispersed throughout the world. Every language has its own cultural heritage which is handed down primarily through the agency of the family as each new generation learns its mother tongue.

The ability to generate messages comes naturally and early; shortly after birth, a baby begins to make all kinds of sounds and enjoys exercising his vocal chords. By the second or third month, parent and child take turns, exchanging cooing, babbling, and nonsense sounds. Although the content of these exchanges is baby-talk, the turn-taking itself is as well ordered as that between adults.

Dr Jerome S. Bruner, Professor of Psychology at Oxford, has written that parent and infant participate jointly in solving the problems in language acquisition. The initial control of the dialogue is dependent on the parent, who continually interprets the child's responses and updates the level of interaction, guided by a sensitive awareness of the youngster's growing competence. Acquiring a language is a series of closely tuned transactions between an active learner and an equally active teacher.[31]

Although a child usually starts to talk during the second year, understanding the meaning of words begins much sooner. Parents can do a great deal to increase a child's verbal competence by patiently pointing out things in the environment and naming them as the baby learns that sounds refer in some way to objects or events. Pictures add to what is available in the immediate surroundings and enrich the number and variety of objects that can be named. A mother or father may introduce the child to brightly illustrated books at seven or eight months.

Sitting with the child on the lap, the parent turns the pages, points things out and teaches labels for the things that are pictured. Dr Bruner observed that the mother or father drastically limits speech to a steady regularity in a strikingly fixed pattern and word order. To get attention, the parent first says, 'Look!' Next, with a rising inflection, 'What is that?' Then, 'It's a (whatever)!' When the child responds, usually with a verbalisation, the parent says an encouraging, 'That's right'.[32] We have personally observed mothers using precisely this same pattern of 'Look, what's that', and so on in a different language and in a non-western culture with the same kind of voice inflections described by Dr Bruner.

Another researcher studied the interaction between mothers and infants from nine to thirteen months old. He found that the mothers of competent children talked or made other sounds when interacting with their babies more often than did the mothers of less competent infants.[33] Some psychologists are so impressed by the importance of verbal stimulation that they give it a pre-eminent role in development. The most consistently favourable kind of learning for a child between eleven and sixteen months old is 'live' language directed to the child by another person. Hearing language from a radio, television or even conversation directed at someone else benefits the child little, if at all.[34]

Language development is a remarkable process. A baby is fascinated by her own utterances and loves to make the same sound over and over. Later, she particularly delights in saying a new word and observing her parents' excited reactions. Going on to form an immense vocabulary, the child makes liberal use of a well-developed signal-generating capability. Parents are amazed at how rapidly words and sentences are acquired; they rejoice in the thought that they will no longer have to go through agonising guesswork when their loved one is crying in pain. Soon the child can talk about all sorts of things, sharing thoughts and feelings in a two-way exchange.

What happens if children do not receive this encouragement? Parents, frequently pressed for time, stressed, and distracted, do what they can, not necessarily what they should, in nurturing the communication skills of their children. This approach is likely to produce poor results. For instance, a mother in the middle of reading a newspaper may respond harshly to her child who is trying to say something. She may shout, 'Quiet, not now, please. Can't you see I'm reading?' The child persists. This time the mother rebukes even more harshly. Or the fledgling speaker struggling with words may be interrupted by an older sibling in mid-sentence. As life goes on, the child may be subjected to ridicule by well-meaning and not-so-well-meaning elders such as parents, teachers, and others for opening his mouth and saying something labelled as 'stupid'.

Negative experiences of this kind, when repeated many times, can lead to the development of speech impediments and mannerisms such as stuttering or saying 'um' and 'ahh' between words. These are a way of saying, 'Please don't interrupt me, I'll come up with my next word or sentence, soon . . . give me a chance, I'll say it yet.' All these experiences add up in some mysterious manner and people emerge from the pressures of childhood socialisation in different ways. Some become the silent types who say little or nothing. Others totally ignore social constraints and become domineering talkers. Most of us fall somewhere between the two extremes.

What about grammar? Should parents correct a child's grammatical errors? Yes, but not by saying 'That's wrong' and embarrassing the child. It is preferable simply to repeat the phrase in its correct form without any tone of disapproval in your voice. This restatement will provide an appropriate model without belittling the child's efforts at speaking.

When children are carefully taught to use spoken language proficiently as pre-schoolers, they will learn to read and write more easily. If children are listened to and encouraged to speak fluently at home, they will have a highly developed verbal skill to help them throughout their lives, greatly increasing their chances of success in any profession they choose and, just as important, in their personal relationships.

Inarticulate people with poor language abilities will have a difficult time in the decades to come, because the trend in every occupational field is away from low-skilled labour. The repetitive, manual jobs in industry and agriculture are being replaced by robotic and other machines. Working people at all levels need more education to enable them to quickly re-train as technological changes continually occur. Parents have a responsibility to ensure that their children grow up with a good command of their language in reading, writing and speaking. The old saying that children should be seen but not heard is now clearly obsolete.

Bodily communication

Verbal communication, although important, is not the

only way we send out information about how we think and feel. Facial expressions, body postures, and gestures are types of bodily communication also used extensively. These often have culturally determined shades of meaning. In one part of the world, nodding one's head means 'yes'; in another, it signifies an emphatic 'no'. We learn our own culture's code of gestures in childhood and, if we travel widely enough or work for a multinational company, we may need to become informed of the meanings of body language and gestures in other countries.

Within families, non-verbal cues can be eloquent messages. A smile may be more informative than a thousand words; a grimace may reflect pain without any need for further elaboration. A clenched fist can convey a good deal, as can the gentle squeeze of a hand. A look of shyness in someone's eyes, the way a child slams school books down when arriving home, the tender touch of a spouse soothing an aching head – these are also communications to a sensitive receiver.

Behavioural communication

Actions really do speak louder than words; in fact, it can often be the most powerful and effective form of communication of all. Words may be empty promises, but deeds, such as doing difficult chores for a dear one without being asked, speak for themselves and reveal true feelings and values.

Sometimes, words and behaviour are at odds and send out contradictory signals. For instance, one may profess loyalty, allegiance, and love to someone while doing things which indicate otherwise. A parent may promise to spend time with a child and then always break the promise by finding other, 'more pressing' things to do. A spouse may speak of undying love, yet consistently make plans for activities that do not include the partner.

Message content

The way the content of a communication is phrased and presented makes a great difference: the same message may be thoughtlessly blunt or it may be carefully expressed with a considerate concern that the receiver 'takes it the right way'. One should always think about how a message will affect the hearer's feelings; the art of communication is to convey the message with as much tact and sensitivity as possible. There are always at least two legitimate ways of saying the same thing, probably more. Why not choose the one that will do the job with the minimum harm and without being negative and critical? As long as one is truthful and honest, why not say things in a way that will make others feel encouraged and happy?

Receiving the message

Sometimes a family member may generate a message without even once considering whether the third component, the receiver, is getting (or even wants to receive) what is being sent. For example, one day a parent motioned a child to come near. In an authoritarian tone of voice, the parent issued a series of rapid-fire instructions. The parent then dismissed the child, confident that the duty had been well discharged; the child was now to be held accountable for any infraction of these instructions. After all, the child was now informed of them, wasn't he? In the meantime, the child was blissfully unaware of the message. He had not listened to his parent's harangue since the second word was uttered because his gaze and his mind had wandered to watch his friends through the window.

By not paying attention to each other, both parent and child contributed to this missed communication. Later, when the child unwittingly disobeyed the lost message, further communication was muddled when both sides blamed each other, saying simultaneously, 'But (I told you) (you never told me) about it!'

Unfortunately, some people never fully develop the more difficult talent of listening, but only act as generators. They spew out a non-stop barrage without ever pausing to flip their switch to become receivers. If they are not generating meaningful signals, they just produce noise and jam the other signals. A kindly grandfather once pointed out that nature itself shows us the proper ratio between talking and listening: 'We have two ears, but only one tongue. Therefore, we should listen twice as much as we speak.'

Becoming a sensitive receiver is a difficult task. It does not come easily because it takes considerable maturity and selflessness to harness one's natural tendency to do all the talking and instead listen with interest and sympathy to others. By inclination, people don't particularly care to listen – what they like to do is talk. All you have to do to verify this statement is to watch a group of young children at play. It is true chaos. Each one is talking at the same time, happily uninterested in what anyone else might have to say. Eventually a child must learn to listen so that communication can take place. It requires great patience on the part of parents and older siblings to teach a child to listen, and perhaps one of the most important methods is by example!

Parents often complain that their older children, especially adolescents, seldom talk to them; this may be because the parents have not learned to listen in an encouraging and effective way. You may want to take the following steps:[35]

- **Listen with your body** by turning it fully towards the person speaking; put down whatever you are doing or remove distractions to give the person your full attention. No one feels like chatting with someone who says absently, 'Oh, I can hear you', while busily hammering nails or rattling pots and pans. It's better to say, 'I'd rather talk to you than read this newspaper, let me get it out of the way. Sit down, I'm glad you're here.'

- **Listen with your eyes** by establishing eye contact which conveys trust and gives the speaker confidence. Look for non-verbal cues in facial expressions, gestures and posture.
- **Listen with your ears** for the content of what the speaker is saying, and for the intensity and tone of the words.
- **Listen with your heart** for the emotions of the speaker – is he or she angry, pleased, disappointed, fearful, frustrated?
- **Listen with your mouth closed** as the most effective way to encourage the speaker. Refrain from offering instant solutions. Other people do not always want advice; in fact, they seldom do. Nor do they want to hear about a similar experience that happened to someone else – they want you to listen, acknowledge their feelings and, above all, *understand*.[36]

When the speaker is through, you may want to confirm your perception of the situation to be certain it is correct by saying, 'You seem so happy about your plan', or 'I can see that this is making you frustrated and angry', or 'Am I right in thinking that you really don't want to go?'

Many times the speaker will think of a solution to a problem unaided simply by talking it out with someone who makes no judgemental remarks, but serves as a sounding board and empathises with the emotions expressed. The act of expressing the problem requires the speaker to organise thoughts and analyse feelings; this alone may clarify the situation enough to think of a way to work through it.

When feelings are revealed, take care to avoid saying such contrary things as, 'Your teacher doesn't really dislike you', or 'You're too big to worry about being afraid of the dark'. These kinds of statements will make the child angry at your attempt to minimise or even deny the feelings. Contradicting someone's feelings makes for arguments; opposition creates an antagonistic relationship that blocks communication.

Allowing feelings to be expressed without throwing up barriers creates a sense of companionship – you have understood and you communicated that understanding by being an ally, not an adversary or opponent. Say instead, 'You must feel worried to think your teacher doesn't like you – what makes you think she doesn't?' 'Does being afraid of the dark keep you from going to sleep? What do you think we can do about it?'

Parents should realise that although all *behaviour* is not acceptable, all *feelings* are legitimate. To accept another's feelings is to acknowledge their worth as human beings. Having emotions is normal and healthy; children should not have to suppress them when interacting with a parent for fear of being scolded or ridiculed for having them.

If your child has scraped a knee and feels pain, don't belittle it, but sympathetically agree that all scrapes can hurt for a time. If your child wants something wonderful that you can't afford, don't try to make him feel bad about wanting it by saying something deriding like, 'That's not for the likes of you' or 'You're always wanting something, what's the matter with you?' Instead of making him sorry he told you about it, you can sympathise with the desire and his feelings without committing yourself further. 'That's a lovely thing to wish for', conveys empathy and affection at the same time.

When your children know deep down that you listen with respect and a sincere effort to understand their feelings, they will not shut you out, but will want to share with you their experiences and thoughts. Being well understood makes a person feel worthy and beloved. Parents should also disclose some of their own feelings and be ready to receive empathy from their children as well.

If you really want your spouse or your children to 'open up' and talk to you, you must listen quietly *and*:

- **Don't interrupt**; allow for the completion of the thought. Wait patiently until you receive a subtle indication that you should speak.
- **Don't contradict**; allow others to have their own opinions. There is no need for everyone to think alike, nor must everyone agree in their opinions and preferences. Making a judgement about what someone else thinks is seldom necessary. Respect your own opinion, but don't insist that anyone else must agree with it.
- **Don't criticise or lecture about past behaviour**; if a mistake was made, allow others to see it for themselves during the conversation. This will enable them to learn their own lessons from the experience with much less embarrassment. Try to preserve their self-esteem as much as possible.
- **Don't nod your head constantly to hurry them along**. Nodding in approval once in a while is encouraging, but doing it too often can be annoying and even disruptive.
- **Don't assume that what they are talking about is the total content of their message**; watch carefully for clues in tone and body language for what might be really bothering them. With a few carefully worded comments or a gentle question, the underlying reason why they are feeling this way may come tumbling out, to their own surprise.
- **Don't interrogate** by asking questions requiring yes or no answers such as, 'Did you have fun in school today?'; 'Have you had a good day?' Instead ask open-ended questions such as, 'What kind of day have you had?' or 'What's the best thing that happened in school today?'
- **Don't use the occasion for self-aggrandisement** or soliciting admiration. Avoid the temptation to top

their story with a better one from your own past. Don't try to improve on their jokes – just enjoy being their audience.

When we invest time in patiently listening to others, we build up credit against the day that we will need a sympathetic ear ourselves. Besides, listening is not necessarily always an act of suffering and sacrifice; by being a receiver, from time to time we might just learn something ourselves.

GOOD FAMILY COMMUNICATION

Family members should always feel that they are each other's greatest public and will never be refused a hearing. With opportunities to speak one's mind at home without fear of recrimination, members serve as loving and sympathetic confidants. Such open communication within the family, however, is a privilege which should not be abused. It is all too easy to become a constant complainer, pouring out all your real and imagined troubles in endless tales of woe. After a while, others may stop caring and may even think that you deserve them! Try to handle the smaller difficulties on your own and save your family's patience for the major ones you really need to share.

Let us return to our example of the parent who blithely gave instructions to the unhearing child. How can we avoid this typical family non-communication? First, the parent catches the child's attention by saying, 'I have something to tell you that you need to remember. After I tell it to you, then you'll repeat it back to me so I know you've understood it. Then we can discuss it.' By alerting the child to the importance of the message and requiring some 'feedback', the parent gives fair warning that remembering it will be expected. Patiently repeating the message if necessary until the child knows it thoroughly, the parent is teaching the youngster the habit of listening carefully.

The parent and child then go on to discuss the reasoning behind the message, thus enabling the child to learn to articulate ideas as well as to practise rational thinking. Certainly this takes more time and energy than merely opening one's mouth and issuing an imperial decree, but it is well worth it.

Keeping the lines open

Parents must never shut off communication, either between themselves or with their children. Saying, 'I don't want to talk about it', only delays resolving the situation until it festers and becomes worse. Whatever the grounds for a quarrel, there is no justification for refusing to talk, since apart from signifying anger or hurt, 'not speaking' does nothing to eliminate the cause.

> It is absolutely essential that husband and wife take the risk of bringing their feelings out into the open if they are to find successful ways to deal with the inevitable differences in even the best of marriages ... Never assume that your partner knows what you are feeling. Even people who have lived together for years can be amazingly unaware of things that are bothering their mates or of changes in values and needs with the passing years. Keep the lines of communication open to allow closeness to continue to grow.[37]

Weighing our words

Keeping the lines of communication open should not be taken to mean spewing out anything that comes to mind at any time. We should think about what we want to say, particularly when it is a message out of the ordinary. An ordinary message is one with no significant consequence to a person's well-being, such as routine 'small talk'. For instance, when someone says, 'Hello, how are you?', we respond without having to give it much thought. On the other hand, when we are annoyed or in a bad mood, wisdom dictates that every word should be thoroughly weighed and examined in our minds before it is spoken. It would be a good idea to develop a verbal 'quarantine' in which most words and statements should spend some time before they are allowed to be blurted out. One should never be too hasty with words, particularly when they are likely to hurt someone's feelings.

Talking things over openly is crucial to a successful relationship, but a tedious monologue or spending endless hours rehashing things and talking issues to death is not good communication; it can become a source of alienation. Be sensitive to your hearer and talk only as long as the other person wants to listen.

Good timing

Good timing can often be as important as the message itself. Certain messages can be exchanged at any time, while other communications are best done at specific moments. Unfortunately, one consequence of our busy way of life today is that much of our family communication is hurriedly sandwiched between other things, occurs at the wrong time, or does not take place at all.

In some families, all the members have their daily 24 hours parcelled out in a way that suits them best as individuals, with little regard for the schedules of the others. The home then resembles a hotel. At any given time, some are checking in for rest, recreation, and re-fuelling, while others are dashing off into the big world. They run into each other in the doorway and may exchange perfunctory greetings.

More commonly, members of a family with older children come together only at the dinner time and, as a result, a great deal of important communication takes place under less than ideal conditions. Parents may find that a mealtime is just about the only occasion to ask questions, share news, issue new regulations and repeat the frequently ignored old ones. The children may present their own new list of demands and share brief glimpses of what is going on in their lives. But even mealtimes are hurried and people are in a rush.

Unfortunately, open communication never really develops in this type of family setting, which resembles a household of convenience rather than a true family. Mealtimes, which should be occasions for peaceful nourishment, sometimes become an arena for venting frustrations and abusive exchanges. Parents may feel compelled to lecture and reprimand their children at these times or even to argue between themselves. This type of chaotic 'non-communication' is not seen in the houses of families which we would call successful, who devote a generous part of their free time to the all-important matter of interacting with each other in a comfortable, relaxed and intimate atmosphere.

When the children are small, their lives centre on the home. As they grow, activities after school and on weekends can pull them away. It is all too easy to let communication lapse, to let everyone go their separate ways. It is up to the parents to make sure that time is spent together because family life is too precious to be handled in a haphazard way.

Where are you going to get more time? Perhaps by regularly turning off the television, video machine, stereo, or radio and just filling up the silence with your own conversation! When families find pleasure in talking and listening to each other, they will make the time for it, just as they do for other things they enjoy.

COMMUNICATION EXERCISES

As we have seen, messages about thoughts and emotions can be conveyed in words, through our faces and bodies, and by our behaviour. There are two main categories of emotion: pleasant or unpleasant. Each emotion varies in intensity; for example, the difference between being pleased and ecstatic, or between being afraid and terrified, is one of degree.

If family members are to start becoming sensitive to underlying feelings in communication, they need to know what to look for. The following exercises are designed for the whole family, from the pre-schooler to the grandparents, and should be done with appropriate courtesy and respect for each person. We suggest that you find an hour when everyone is home and wants to have fun doing a little 'acting' and learning at the same time. The exercises will teach the following three lessons:

- **Awareness of the definition of words describing the many different kinds of feelings people have**. The English language contains several hundred words to describe feelings. This in itself reflects how important emotions are. Describing a feeling in the non-verbal language of facial expressions and gestures is an important step in being able to convey it in words. When children learn to verbalise feelings, they will feel less need to 'act out' such feelings as anger and frustration. Being able to talk things over instead of shouting, shoving and hitting is a major goal of the growing child.
- **Learning the meaning of facial expressions and bodily postures**. By learning to watch for these, family members will become more sensitive to each individual's particular mode of displaying feelings. Sympathetic communication then becomes easier between parent and child and among siblings; respect for individual differences is encouraged as well.
- **Learning to accept negative feelings**. People, especially children, often feel guilty about having negative feelings. Small children need to learn that merely wanting something bad to happen does not make it actually happen. Through these exercises, children can learn that feeling anger and other

negative emotions is normal and nothing to be ashamed of. Bad feelings need not be translated into bad behaviour; they can be expressed in words and resolved accordingly. If a channel is provided for the expression of these feelings, powerful emotions are released through words without causing damage. Otherwise they may stay bottled up inside to suddenly explode in violence with serious harm to oneself and others. This is just as true for parents as for children.

Game One

It has been said that fish swim, birds fly, and human beings feel. All over the world, people have the same kinds of feelings – happiness, sadness, surprise. Below is a list of many different kinds of emotions or feelings that you have probably felt yourself at one time or another. There are several ways that we can tell when someone feels a particular emotion: by listening to their words and by watching their faces and body language (such as posture and gestures). The purpose of this first game is to see how many feelings you can guess just from seeing facial expressions and body language. Most families will play the game without keeping score, but if you wish to score, points are indicated below for each game.

1) Copy out each feeling in the list below on separate slips of paper or small cards. If you are playing the game with small children, you may want to use only those emotions which can be readily identified and leave those with more subtle distinctions for a later time. Go through the list, making sure everyone knows the meaning of all the words. If necessary, older children can check the dictionary and write the meaning on the back of the slip. Discussing the differences between related emotions, such as sad and wistful, helps to refine vocabulary. Each family member should then practise making faces and gestures to express the various feelings in front of a mirror.

2) Place the slips of paper into a bag or box and mix them up. One at a time, each family member picks out a slip without telling the others what it is. He or she says, 'Right now I am feeling this' and uses face, posture and hands to express it. The other family members try to look for clues to distinguish this feeling, each waiting for his or her turn to guess. Every time someone guesses the feeling correctly, the player gets two points and the guesser gets one point.

List of Feelings

Right now I am feeling:

Afraid	Guilty
Angry	Happy
Annoyed	Indifferent
Anxious	Jealous
Appreciative	Lonely
Awed	Loving
Betrayed	Panicky
Bored	Peaceful
Contented	Proud
Critical	Sad
Delighted	Silly
Depressed	Shy
Disappointed	Surprised
Disgusted	Tense
Ecstatic	Terrified
Embarrassed	Wistful
Frustrated	Worried

Game Two

Using the same list, try to guess the feeling only through facial expressions. Do you find this much harder? When the feeling is guessed correctly, both player and guesser receive two points.

Game Three

Using the same list, try to express the feeling by using words and tone of voice only, keeping the face and body neutral. Each person describes a common situation where you would expect to have that emotion. For example, the player who has drawn the word 'contentment' sighs, 'After a big dinner of my favourite foods, I feel soooo satisfied'. If no one guesses correctly after one round, describe the feeling in another way for one more round.

Be aware that special circumstances affect the feeling even when the event is the same. For example, 'I spilled orange juice all over my shirt just as I was leaving for school' would be an appropriate situation for feeling annoyance, but 'I spilled orange juice all over my shirt in front of the whole class' would produce embarrassment. Correct guesses score five points for the describer and four points for the guesser.

Game Four

In this game, the family divides up into two-person teams. If necessary, a third person can be added to a team so everyone can play. Each team should sit where they can pay complete attention to each other without distractions. Each player takes two minutes (or slightly longer) to describe in words, facial expressions and body language how he or she felt in three different situations: happy, afraid, and surprised. The incidents described should be real ones, whether they happened long ago or recently. Each partner should listen carefully not only to what the speaker is saying, but how it is being said. The roles of speaker and listener are then reversed.

The teams reassemble and, going around the group, each listener retells his or her partner's three incidents, noting how facial expression, gestures, and posture were helpful in understanding what the partner felt. After the three stories are finished without interruptions, the original teller may courteously correct inaccuracies if necessary. The person who re-told the incidents with the closest duplication is considered outstanding, but the real winner is the entire family whose members now know a great deal more about each other than before.

5

Family Consultation

Consultation lies at the heart of the successful family; it is an effective mechanism for adjusting to the more egalitarian family structure consistent with the times we live in. Consultation can remove the alienation often found between husbands and wives, parents and children by serving as a bridge to take a family from a tension-filled battleground to a neutral place where peace may prevail.

Fig. 1. illustrates the difference between conflicting and consulting families. Your family can demonstrate for itself what we mean by wasteful energy and useful energy by enacting what is happening in the illustration. First, get a rope or clothes line. Then, divide the family members into pairs and get each pair to pull the opposite ends of the rope (pull gently against small children). Two things can result from such a tug of war: either the energy is equalised and wasted within the rope, resulting in a stalemate, with no movement to either side, or else one person wins and the loser has depleted his or her valuable energies with no benefit. Sibling against sibling, parents against children, husband against wife – the negative results from each confrontation are all the same.

Now use the rope in an entirely different way: tie one end to something heavy and, standing closely together, have all family members grasp the rope at the other end.

The Conflicting Family

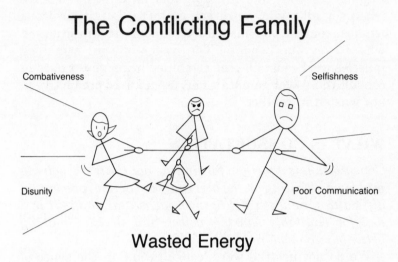

Combativeness

Selfishness

Disunity

Poor Communication

Wasted Energy

The Consulting Family

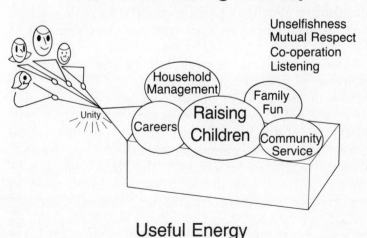

Unselfishness
Mutual Respect
Co-operation
Listening

Household Management

Family Fun

Unity

Careers

Raising Children

Community Service

Useful Energy

Pulling together, notice how much strength you have when you all tug in one direction. Instead of the previous win/lose contest, you have now created a win/win situation where everyone benefits. The power of your combined muscles works just like the combined brain power used in consultation – your mental energies are used productively, not wasted in conflict.

WHAT IS CONSULTATION

Consultation is a method for finding out the truth, solving problems, deciding on the best course of action, preventing difficulties, and generating new ideas and plans. It is a tool for equitably sharing power and decision-making between two or more people.

We do not use the word 'consultation' in the sense of receiving a one-sided expert opinion, as in a medical or legal consultation, but with the original Latin meaning of *conselere*, to take counsel together, the exchanging of opinions and ideas between two or more people. This kind of consultation involves the pooling of minds and goes far beyond other forms of solving problems and settling disputes, such as giving and receiving advice, negotiation or bargaining. Solutions reached through successful consultation benefit all participants and leave no residual hurt feelings. Once you learn and use the techniques of this instrument, you will want to use it as often as possible, at home, in the workplace, or any other setting where small group interaction is feasible.[38]

Some of the more elementary principles of consultation are now rapidly spreading under various names, such as 'conflict resolution', which was little known before the 1960s,[39] 'participatory management', the 'no-lose' method, 'alternative dispute resolution', 'the team approach to problem-solving' and so on. They are being used in corporate management, in labour relations, in legal mediation and many other situations where people must work together with a common purpose and in the spirit of democratic participation. Conflict resolution is now being taught in some schools as part of a Peace Studies curriculum.

Although somewhat similar, consultation as we use it goes far beyond these processes, by whatever name they are known, because it has a much broader scope and application. It requires not only training in specific skills, but important changes in the attitudes and behaviour of the participants. When practised correctly, the group experiences concord and cordially merges individual differences into a single purpose. Consultation creates unity, an energy-releasing and beneficial force. Once well-established within a group, unity can be built upon unity, in an ever-expanding process from a solid core. The group goes from strength to strength, its considerable energies mobilised to attack the issues and problems, not each other.

Based on the free, candid, selfless exchanges of views, needs, and preferences among the participants, consultation allows the group to serve the best interests of everyone in it. This pooling of brain power produces what is called *positive synergy*: not only are two heads better than one, but the combination is much more than the sum of two.

Many advantages await the family that perseveres in mastering the attitudes, skills, and steps of consultation. Ultimately, by using it the way it was intended, parents and children learn how to:

- think logically
- become more articulate
- listen to others carefully and look below the surface to notice feelings and emotions
- think creatively, with mental mobility to see the same things in other contexts and with other possibilities
- go beyond stereotyped solutions
- search for and find the truth (not just the facts) and thereby learn to deal with reality

- link decisions with ethics, morality and fundamental principles, not just short-term gains
- seek the higher common good and deal with long-term consequences
- reduce the ego and avoid taking one's self too seriously
- be courteous when both talking and listening
- refrain from interrupting or 'shooting down' the ideas of others
- be candid and frank in a loving atmosphere
- stand up for one's own belief, yet allow others to believe differently
- respect others and develop a greater sense of justice
- visualise the logical consequences of decisions and events
- uphold the equality of the sexes by putting it into practice
- feel part of a team, completely accepted rather than alienated
- understand that ultimately the good of others best benefits oneself
- struggle against a problem, rather than other family members
- take on challenging problems with a positive attitude that anticipates good results
- experience the greater family love, closeness and co-operation which develops when decision-making is shared

THE STEPS OF CONSULTATION

The following steps convey a general idea of what happens in consultation; each step will be treated in much more detail later on in the chapter. Although the subjects and issues under consultation will vary, the procedure is the same:

1) At the outset, specify clearly the object of the consultation.

2) What are the relevant facts? Who, what, where, when, why and how?
3) What are the ethical, moral, social, and practical considerations to be taken into account?
4) What are the possible solutions, strategies, and plans, and the costs in time, money, energy, and emotion associated with them?
5) Examine each and select the best one, with unanimous agreement if possible.
6) Carry out the decision unitedly. No one should withhold his or her support once the decision has been made. Re-evaluate and modify it if necessary.

ATTITUDES AND SKILLS NECESSARY FOR CONSULTATION

While the steps to consultation are not complicated, the most difficult part of learning to consult is transforming personal attitudes and acquiring the necessary skills. Both involve replacing old habits with new ones. At first glance it may look simple, but truly respecting the opinions of others, subduing selfishness, being willing to speak up, having patience, and listening attentively calls for everyone's best efforts. You will soon find, however, that the results are worth it; you will notice the reduction of tensions and an increase in good-will within the family when you put these skills and attitudes to work. Your family will find itself using them constantly in a variety of situations.

Mutual respect and fellowship

The most fundamental attitude to cultivate is a high regard for fellow participants. Each individual must respect every other person, regardless of age, gender, rank, or any other consideration. This is really the secret. When genuine respect is received from the others, each person will feel comfortable in revealing his or her ideas, confident that no one in the group will ever ridicule or condemn them. Even if a suggestion is not finally adopted as a solution or plan, the one who offered it still retains dignity and a sense of worth if given a respectful and courteous hearing.

Often the least educated or youngest person will have a surprisingly astute grasp of issues and may even have greater insight concerning the topic than older or more educated members of the family. Through friendly encouragement, all must feel capable of contributing; this fellowship unlocks and releases the creative powers within each person to allow wonderful ideas to surface.

This loving attitude should eventually spill over to the general atmosphere of the household outside consultation sessions; at no time should any family member backbite and say deriding things about another. Learning the importance of courtesy, tolerance, acceptance, and amity is crucial. Any rudeness or belittling criticism will surely stifle the easy flow of ideas; it will create disunity, hurt feelings, and might render the effort completely sterile.

Unselfishness

For consultation to succeed, it must be free of ulterior motives and selfishness. Selfish motives are barriers to consultation's essential task of sincerely searching for the truth and attaining the best decision or solution. Each person should think, 'What is good for the whole group?' and not just, 'What's in it for me?' In consultation there are no coalitions, lobbying, taking sides, or preferring one's own way to the detriment of others.

With maturity – something that comes not with age but by learning – we understand that our own best interests lie not in looking out for ourselves first and foremost, but in creating justice and unity. We eventually learn a fundamental truth: the well-being of any single person is dependent on the well-being of the whole family.

Willingness to speak up

Thoughts, opinions and feelings must be expressed in consultation without shyness. Each person has not only the right but the responsibility to express his or her views freely and openly, without fear of displeasing or alienating others.

Here is an example of why we need to hear everyone's differing views. Imagine that four members of a committee were seated round a square table upon which a large box had been placed. Each person could only see the side of the box facing him or her and naturally assumed that the whole box was the same colour. As the committee consulted, however, one person spoke about 'this red box'. Another said, 'But it's not red, it's blue'. When the third member spoke of seeing a green box and the fourth saw only a white one, each reporting from his or her point of view, the real truth was discovered – the box had a different colour on each side. This was information the group had to have to make its decision. If even one person had failed to speak up to report a different opinion, the full facts would not have become known.

The minds, cultural backgrounds, experience, and feelings of the participants form the source from which ideas and decisions arise.[40] To deprive the group of even one person's unique perspective of the issue would be to lessen its ability to discover the truth or find the best solution. Humility is an excellent quality, but it does not mean fear and insecurity any more than it means pride in false modesty. Ideas should be shared with kindliness and goodwill without insisting or forcing them on anyone.

Patience

Patience is the sustaining pillar of consultation. It should not be confused:

... with inaction or being passive. Instead, it involves grace under stress – composure while deciding what action, if any, is appropriate. It means not being deluded by quick and easy solutions. Patience involves calm endurance and perseverance while waiting for results. It implies retaining self-control and perspective; persistence and diligence; and, above all, not succumbing to complaining and anger no matter what frustrations are encountered.[41]

Listening

We can listen for several things at the same time. When someone is talking about a concern or problem, listen carefully to discover the real needs, feelings and the spirit of what is meant. Feelings are important and the spirit of what is meant. Feelings are important because the person who has them is important; they are facts to be considered in the decision-making process. There are times when consultation must first address feelings: 'Why do I feel this way? What can I (or the family) do to change the way I feel?' This can start the process of changing negative feelings to the rational thinking that leads to problem-solving and positive actions.

When something is presented and the meaning is unclear, the listeners should ask for clarification and probe patiently until understanding is reached. All the information must be brought out if the decision is to be a good one. Often there are sub-issues that will only emerge when people listen intently and show they care.

We must harness our natural tendency to interrupt. The Tlingit Tribe of south-eastern Alaska and northern British Columbia have a dignified and effective method for preventing interruption during a consultative session. A beautifully carved 'talking stick' is held by the person who is speaking; as long as he or she holds the stick, no one else may speak.

Listening does not imply automatically accepting what

is said, but it does mean paying attention and keeping an open mind. To weigh the value of an idea in your own mind, you must hear all its advantages and disadvantages described.

Speaking effectively

We should not speak simply for the joy of hearing our own voices! Instead, we should think our ideas through, organise our thoughts, and then present them concisely, without rambling or introducing unnecessary information, no matter how interesting. If an idea has merit, the others will want to know more about it and further elaboration is then in order. In speaking, respect the time of others: you may want to add to what someone else has said, but you never want simply to repeat it.

Ideally we should try to strike a balance in consultation so that no single person dominates the proceedings and everyone feels completely free to speak his or her mind without indulging in lengthy monologues that test the others' patience.

Controlling egotism

Our selfish side sees everything exclusively from the 'I, me, my and mine' perspective. We must harness this tendency, avoiding the use of those first person singular pronouns whenever possible. We can still show humility, even when giving our own opinion. Instead of saying, 'I think it must be done this way', it is better to say, 'Perhaps we may want to look at it this way', or 'How about this approach?'

In consulting, try not to offend, and guard against being offended. The former requires sensitivity, the latter, forbearance and forgiveness.

Each participant should avoid becoming attached to his or her own ideas or preferences. Remember that *once expressed, the idea no longer belongs to an individual, but becomes the property of the group*, which means that the contributor can then look at the idea just as objectively as the other members. This leaves the group free to accept or reject the idea without fear of hurting the feelings of the one who suggested it. If the idea is a good one, it will stand up to scrutiny; if not, its lack of merit will soon become apparent. In either case, the idea brings neither glory nor blame to the one who first suggested it. *All members of the family should fully understand that rejection of an idea is not a rejection of its originator.* When people do not feel they 'own' their suggestions, the consultation process speeds up considerably because useless time and energy is not consumed in the egotistical defence of poor ideas and the group can move on to other matters.

When an idea is freely released to the group, there is an absence of tension; open discussion can then bring forth the best collective thinking so that the suggestion becomes a springboard to newer, better ideas. Clarifying insights emerge as various perceptions illuminate it and the reality of the situation or idea is more and more rigorously defined. Based on the group's enhanced understanding, the truth of the matter becomes more apparent, and the best decision can now be discovered. Imagine several searchlights in a vast circle probing the night sky for an airplane – when all the light beams converge, the airplane is brightly illuminated from all sides and clearly seen.

There will, of course, be differences of opinion, but in properly conducted consultation, *differing opinions* may clash, but the *opinion-givers* need never clash! We can sit back and let the ideas fend for themselves in the battle arena of decision-making and the search for truth, while we enjoy working together in a harmonious atmosphere. To keep egotism under control in consultation, always remember: *what* is right is far more important than *who* is right.

Creativity

When generating solutions and ideas, liberate the mind
to be creative – sometimes even to the point of being
wildly impractical. The opposite of thinking in fixed,
conventional ways is to use 'mental mobility', which
means to loosen-up and spark the imagination to think of
new things or to see familiar things in new ways. There
is an old saying among creative people: when you hear
the sound of hoofbeats, don't just think of horses – think
also of zebras! The wider the range and the greater the
number of alternative solutions generated by the group,
the greater the probability that one or more will fulfil its
needs. Apart from their value in injecting light-hearted
humour, wild suggestions often lead to good ones.

In the preceding sections, we have examined some
basic attitudes and skills fundamental to consultation.
The rest of this chapter is devoted specifically to family
consultation, whether the family includes one parent or
two, grandparents, other extended family members or
friends.

CONSULTATION AND EQUALITY
IN THE FAMILY

'A man's home is *his* castle' is no longer true – the
statement is as obsolete as the castle. As the twentieth
century comes to an end, there are fewer and fewer
families where the husband is the exclusive head of the
household, the final authority and the sole provider. In
the modern home, husband and wife are co-heads, both
contributing to every aspect of their household's operation.
Rising rates of family dissolution indicate, in part, that
couples are having trouble breaking through old traditions
and finding a way to make decisions that accommodates
not only the new equality of men and women, but the
emerging respect for the rights of children.

The transition from a patriarchal family to one in which governance is equitably shared is difficult, but necessary. One person making decisions for others without consulting them is a form of dictatorship – it matters little whether the setting is the home, a business, or a nation. True, such authoritarianism is efficient and gets things done quickly, but in the long run the benefits of such a system are not worth the cost in resentment, lack of willing co-operation, and rebelliousness.

Traditionally, the father not only told his children what to do, he had to show his superiority by punishing those who resisted. However, the democratic revolution in many countries has now meant a change in all relationships, including those within the family – whether recognised by the parents or not. When a child is punished, he thinks, 'If you have the right to punish me, then I have the right to punish you'. Watching and listening, he discovers just what will bother his parents the most and proceeds to do it. Many family conflicts involve this energy-wasting retaliatory warfare.[42]

One obvious drawback with using autocratic parental power with its usually accompanying verbal or physical abuse, is that it ceases to work as the children reach adolescence, when they do what they please. There is no way then that parents can stop them doing things behind their backs. The cartoon figure of the spluttering father pompously issuing orders is ludicrous to a teenager. Physically grown up, teenagers are too big to spank and they can outwit their parents to find ways to avoid other punishments.[43]

It is much more constructive to have a different kind of interaction with children from the very beginning, one that will be effective during adolescence and beyond. This is parental influence and guidance through consultation, where parents and children interact not as combatants, but as a team willing to listen to each others' ideas in order to find reasonable solutions to problems together.

Children will give more respect and credence to a parent who does not feel that he or she knows all the answers, but will value the opinions of others. They do not respect a parent who tries to hurl thunderbolts at them like some remote Olympian deity. When parents give advice without wielding power, it allows children to listen without resistance and encourages them to share feelings and ideas with those they trust. Authoritarianism, with its reliance on unquestioning obedience, stifles the very traits which people will need in the coming decades – initiative, creativity, flexibility, innovation – traits which are well-practised in a family using consultation.

Bringing the children into the consultation process has many benefits. Dr Elaine Blechman, a clinical psychologist at the Albert Einstein Medical College, is convinced that children learn their basic problem-solving skills in the family. In her research she has found that there is:

> a relationship between how well children do in their social and academic life and how effectively their families work together to resolve conflicts. In some families, the research showed, a dispute is handled by all members speaking out, exploring the problem jointly, and finally, finding a solution that everyone more or less likes.
>
> But in other families, one person – generally a parent – would immediately impose his idea on everyone else, often within the first 10 seconds of discussion, leaving everyone else dissatisfied.
>
> The children of the families with open discussion were far more likely than the children from the other families to be well-adjusted socially and to do well at school.[44]

Earl Schaefer and Marianna Edgerton, in their research at the University of North Carolina, found evidence to confirm this.

Parents who subscribe to traditional beliefs, including the ideas that it is of paramount importance to teach children to obey whoever is in authority and that children learn best when they just listen to what they are told, seem to impair their children's cognitive growth.

In a study of more than 100 children and their parents, it was found that those parents who subscribed to such beliefs had children who were distractable and uncreative, expressed little intellectual curiosity and did poorly on tests of basic intellectual skills, when compared wtih children of parents who were more modern in their outlook, believing, for example, that children had a right to ask questions and to express their own views.[45]

Participatory governance has a price. It takes time, patience and skill. But not only does consultation produce better, more equitable decisions, it instils a feeling of self-worth and belonging among the consulting family members. It eliminates the impersonal nature of autocratic decisions and best of all, it fosters a sense of family loyalty, a powerful motive for good behaviour.

How the steps to family consultation work

A consultation session does not have to be an elaborate and formal affair, and it can take place between a husband and wife, a parent and child, two siblings, a grandparent and grandchild, or the entire family. The only essential requisite is that in all instances the attitudes, skills, and basic steps to consultation be followed.

For group consultation, a facilitator or chairperson is generally elected in secret ballot by the group, but you may decide simply to have older children and parents take turns. The facilitator's role is to set the tone of courtesy, direct the flow of discussion and sum up the various contributions made. He or she also describes the consensus as it emerges, identifies a trial conclusion, determines when full consensus has been reached and states the decision.[46] Everyone has a chance to speak and no one monopolises the discussion or intimidates others, including the facilitator.

It is desirable to meet in a comfortable place and sit in a circle, where everyone can see and hear everyone else. The circle itself is a symbol of mutual respect and responsibility, in contrast to an authoritarian arrangement where one person stands and faces a seated audience. The psychological setting is just as important. There must be an atmosphere of caring, mutual support, and conviction that something good will emerge from the effort. Before starting to consult, your family may want to take a few quiet moments to focus your thoughts on the unity that you want to achieve. In a poetic sense, the family must try to feel as unified as the waves of one sea, the drops of one river, the stars of one heaven, the trees of one orchard.[47]

It's a good idea for the family to practise its newly learned attitudes and skills by trying them out on topics that are purely for fun before tackling serious problems or plans. (See the exercises and checklist at the end of this chapter.)

The following explanatory steps to family consultation are guidelines; as you gain experience, you will undoubtedly want to modify these steps to suit your own family.

Step 1: Clarifying what needs to be decided, planned or resolved. Often defining the issue is the most critical task and sometimes a solution will arise from this step alone. Be sure that everyone understands the meanings of relevant words or concepts, especially younger children. Is the stated problem the real one or is there a more basic issue which needs to be addressed? When dealing with a conflict, take time to hear all sides and make sure everyone involved understands the others' viewpoints.

Step 2: Exploring all the facts relating to the situation, problem or project. You may want to use the journalist's 'who, what, where, when, why, and how' to organise the facts. Depending on the subject, this may mean deciphering feelings and emotions in a conflict between siblings or it may mean a trip to the library for some exciting detective work to find current information on a family project. The ethical or moral considerations of a situation, if any, should also be taken into account. When the ethical ramifications of a subject are part of a practical decision-making process, parents can easily share their values and show how to apply them in everyday situations. This is often more palatable to children than abstract discussions.

Step 3: Generating ideas for plans or solutions in the light of all the relevant circumstances. This part is sometimes called 'brainstorming', or bringing out ideas, a technique long known to corporations for developing new products. As the participants start to think about everything they have heard, ideas begin to form. Suggestions are brought forth but none is evaluated at this time, all are listened to without criticism or prejudice.

The imaginations of the consultors should be set free to explore possibilities; this freedom to express ideas without fear of being cut off or resisted is necessary to encourage the flow of creativity. To encourage the children, parents should sometimes hold back and allow them to produce their own solutions. If you wish, you can take notes of all ideas, requests, and suggestions to be examined later. Children may like to use a blackboard if you have one.

Step 4: Putting together the best decision. Next, the ideas are brought forward in order, to be improved upon, simplified or amplified, taken apart and re-assembled with other ideas. As the group's combined mental energies are concentrated on a possible decision, sometimes one idea inspires a member of the family to think of a way to make it work better, followed by an even better idea from someone else.

What makes consultation such an exciting process is the working together of several minds which can produce dynamic new ideas for planning or solutions to problems. Without a frank and loving exchange of views in the stimulating, accepting atmosphere of consultation, these new ideas might never have come to light. Consultation is like a basketball game where the players do not jealously hang on to the ball, but pass it along to whoever can take the best shot at the basket; it matters little whose idea is finally adopted because everyone has 'handled the ball' at some point and contributed to bringing about the decision.

You may want to write down the plan or solution in its final form so that it can be referred to later; preferably all agreements and plans should be detailed to avoid misunderstandings. School-age children can be enlisted in these clerical duties, with some unpatronising help from their parents when necessary.

When the issue has been well defined and when many suggestions are generated, there may be several 'right' solutions, but usually one outstanding decision emerges that works best for all and to which everyone can readily agree. However, if this does not happen, keep on generating ideas or postpone making the decision until more facts are known and everyone has had a chance to think about it. Patience may be rewarded by a later consultation which brings out the best decision. If the decision must be made immediately and there is no unanimity, then the majority rules, with the full support of the minority.

Step 5: Carrying out the decision with unity. This point is most important: each person's wholehearted acceptance and support of the decision is essential once it is made. This is where the attitude of unselfishness really shines out. *The rightness or wrongness of any* *particular decision is of far less importance than the unity of the group.* A faulty decision can be corrected, but disunity is fragmentation and can degenerate into petty hostility – nothing good can come from it.

For some decisions, it is wise to have a trial period with re-evaluation later to determine what improvements can be made or whether the family needs to keep thinking until they find a better idea. It is possible that those who were not in favour of the original decision, but went along with it for the sake of unity, were right after all. In this case, the family should try another solution, but no member should ever have an 'I told you so' attitude. Every effort is made to avoid polarisation and divisiveness.

With unity comes flexibility: when something does not work, the family can immediately try something else because no one is stubbornly committed to a bad decision. Unencumbered, the family can quickly turn about and decide to go forward with a decision in a totally different direction. When your family has experienced this valuable adaptability through consultation, the wisdom of unity will prove itself many times over.

PRACTICAL TIPS FOR FAMILY CONSULTATION

There are a number of points that should be kept in mind in family consultation:

1) It is a good idea for the couple to get into the habit of consulting early on in their relationship so that they can practise and refine the skill over the years. When the children arrive, they can be smoothly initiated into the process. Parents should start including children in consultation at an early age and increase their involvement as they develop greater capabilities, asking for their views on simple things and encouraging them to give their reasons. When very young the children will have a limited involvement, but as they get older, they

should participate in consultation more and more, particularly in matters which affect them directly. By the time the children reach adolescence, they should be experts in mutual problem-solving and planning with their parents and other members of the family.

2) Not every topic can be a subject for consultation between parents and children. Some types of decisions have to be made by parents alone. The parents, with an equal voice in their own consultation, are the final authority in the family.

In language they can understand, children should be told that parents must retain authority over safety and health issues because they have greater knowledge and experience. Knowledge and experience combine to produce wisdom; it is wisdom along with loving concern which enables parents to protect their children from harm. Children should be aware that parents take their responsibilities seriously because they are legally as well as morally obliged to look after their children's health and safety.

Parents can say to their children, 'All of us in the family want the same thing: for you to grow up to be the best person you can become. We can help you do that since we have survived in this world a long time; in all these many years we have learned a lot about keeping healthy and safe. We want to do a good job of getting you through these years until you grow up, too.' Children can also be told that parents have to teach them the difference between right and wrong, so that they will grow up to be mature individuals with decent, caring characters – and so that they can keep themselves out of trouble with playmates, school and the law.

In these three areas – morality, health, and safety – the children are under the care and guidance of their parents until they are well on their way to becoming adults. Obedience in these areas is reasonable and definitely expected. For young children, such issues as bedtimes, nutrition, health care, where to play and so on are not subjects for consultation. But those things which fall into the realm of preferences can be consulted upon and resolved, even with small children. For example, a child's desire to be noisy during play may conflict with the parents' need for quiet. This is a place where consultation is appropriate and each person can be accommodated to reach a solution that satisfies everyone. A situation in which consultation is not appropriate would be in the case of preventing harm: 'I need to have you home before dark so I won't worry about you', reflects a legitimate safety concern which takes precedence over the child's need to play with a friend, a need which can be met during daylight hours.

Consultation is not just giving and receiving advice. It is much more dynamic than that – it is finding new solutions together. In deciding what subjects the children can consult about, you may want to consider the following: when made with the full support of the group, decisions are usually thought out better, have a greater chance of enforcement and success, do not generate hurt feelings, and enhance the unity that makes the home a pleasant place to live.

3) To make consultation work, there must be genuine courtesy and respect for the opinions of others – even the views of a two-year-old child should be treated with respect and sincerely considered in the deliberation. You may be astonished at the insights of small people who have not yet learned to think in conventional ways. It helps to remember that *children are every bit as intelligent as adults in terms of natural ability*. Research shows that basic intelligence remains consistent throughout life. The difference is that adults have the advantage of many years of schooling and the experience of growing up. While still requiring respectful behaviour from children, we should guide them without patronising or insulting them. Let them understand that you sincerely consider them to be just as intelligent as yourself, although definitely still under your care and direction until they

grow up and can function independently. You can remind them that they will, in due time, become loving, caring and wise parents in their turn.

While the parents are the only ones who can decide certain categories of issues, every effort should be made to create unanimity and agreement with the children by including them in as many decisions as is feasible.

4) Participation in consultation should be as unselfish as possible. Even if every choice does not always coincide with one's personal wishes, knowing that others will enjoy or benefit from something makes an occasional sacrifice worthwhile. The children should be taught what the parents have long since learned: the difference between selfishness and genuine self-interest, between short-term and long-term benefits.

If they seem unhappy with a decision, you can tell them that another way of running the family would be for the parents to make *all* their children's decisions. Would they prefer to be ordered about without being asked for their opinion, as in former times? The alternative to unified decision-making is not to anyone's advantage.

5) Consultation should not be confused with 'negotiation'. Negotiation is adversarial: it involves 'horse-trading' and 'bargaining'; negotiators aim to further their own interests at the expense of their opponents. By contrast, there are no opposing sides in consultation. Often several solutions emerge which everyone can enthusiastically endorse with no need for a compromise. It is worth the extra effort, tact, sensitivity and the willingness to see things from someone else's point of view to make sure that no one feels like a loser, that all emerge from the consultation as winners.

6) The principles of consultation work well even with just two people. As we said earlier, most consultations will be between pairings of siblings, husband and wife, parent and child on a one to one basis, rather than by the whole family together. For example, when a

problem concerns just one child, the other children do not need to hear about it. Consultation with the large group does not mean confession, which would be too demeaning. To prevent embarrassment, a problem can be talked over with one parent or both, or even a sibling or two, instead of the whole family. But the principle of receiving the thoughts and wisdom of others remains the same. It is better to consult on as many difficulties as possible to take advantage of collective wisdom.

7) Consultation sessions in which the whole family is present may be enjoyable, but they should not be overdone. There is no need to consult on everything or to go on consulting until everyone is too tired to continue. Fifteen to thirty minutes is usually long enough for a session, but the duration may be whatever the family wishes.

A rule of thumb for qualifying an item for consultation by the whole family is that it must be of concern to other members, it requires drawing from the family resources and it can benefit from the input of everyone's ideas. A sheet of paper can be posted in a convenient place for parents and children to list subjects they would like to consult about at the next session. The list may be a means of remembering subjects or even a way to bring up a topic anonymously.

8) No discussion should be an occasion for disguising backbiting, slander, tattling, 'busybody behaviour' – consciously or unconsciously – in the garb of consultation. Legitimate grievances can be handled in a way that will prevent embarrassment and preserve everyone's self-esteem. Sometimes a problem might actually lie with a family member, but consultation should never be a legalistic trial, where someone ends up 'guilty'. The discussion must be issue-oriented, not personality-centred. In such instances, the family must be careful to avoid all discussions that could harm the reputation of the person involved in the deliberation.

9) The family consultation session should not be a

sombre, taxing occasion – quite the reverse. It is a time for sharing, airing views, harmonising, communicating, and making exciting plans. The parents should make the sessions fun, with plenty of joking and laughter so that everyone will look forward to them with anticipation. Refreshments may be a welcome treat.

10) When the family begins to master the necessary attitudes and skills, consultation procedures will be internalised and become automatic. Just as in learning to walk or drive a car, the earliest attempts are hardest, with each step laboriously thought out and executed. But before long your family will be moving along smoothly, picking up speed and, eventually, efficiently surging ahead. As you become experts in defining issues and gathering facts, ideas will be brought out, examined, improved and agreed upon almost unconsciously. In arriving at these decisions, the formal, separate steps to consultation will probably be used only rarely, but the components of mutual respect, attentive listening, the search for truth, weighing ethical consequences, and the selfless dedication to finding equally beneficial solutions always remain integral to the whole process.

11) The frequency of sessions is up to you. Many families like to schedule a consultation every week so that issues and decisions don't pile up unresolved. Not every consultation session involving the whole family has to have a set purpose or predetermined decision to make. You can meet just to chat, brainstorm, and simply enjoy an intellectual exchange.

THE ADVANTAGES OF LEARNING AND USING CONSULTATION

The attitudes and skills necessary for developing expertise in consultation have many applications outside the family. Current trends indicate that the principles of consultation will be used more and more to conduct the business of society and to release creative talents. These principles are already increasingly used in many settings, from neighbourhood mediation centres to international relations. Undoubtedly in future years your children will be grateful for far-sighted parents who invested the time and energy to teach it to them when very young. But the advantages of using consultation are not just for the distant future, its benefits can be felt every day.

As we said at the beginning of this book, a successful family is one that can create loving unity between husband and wife, parents and children, so releasing their full potential. Consultation is the key. Through sharing ideas, healthily airing differences, and diffusing frictions and problems before they grow, the successful family will enjoy a home-life of love, respect and equality. 'Family consultation employing full and frank discussion, and animated by awareness of the need for moderation and balance, can be the panacea for domestic conflict.'[48]

CONSULTATION EXERCISES

By now, you must be excited about consultation. Why wait any longer to give it a try? By all means, go ahead and start using your marvellous all-purpose tool. We suggest that you begin with imaginary issues that you will enjoy discussing. Starting with the thorny problems of real life would be like trying to swim in the Olympics when you've just learned to float. You can have fun while learning the process and then after a few practice sessions you will feel ready to put consultation to regular use. You may want to keep the checklist which follows the exercises on hand to refresh your memory.

Be particularly sensitive to your children and their efforts to learn effective consultation. Although you can decide things much better and faster than they can, patiently give them the time to learn to do it, and rejoice in their accomplishments.

Just to help you get started, here are a few topics for

the exercises. You will be able to think of many more yourselves.

1) **Respect for the opinions and preferences of others**. Each of us has personal preferences and favourite things which need no justification – we simply like them without having to explain why. In this exercise we will learn something about the variety and individuality of personal choices in the family. Taking one statement at a time, go round the circle and get each family member to give an answer. Then if you wish, each family member can then make up a similar question for the rest to answer.

> My favourite colour is . . .
> My favourite sport or hobby is . . .
> The most fun I ever had with the family was . . .
> The most fun I ever had alone was . . .
> My favourite food is . . .
> My favourite time of day is . . .
> My favourite animal is . . .
> My favourite music is . . .
> If I had a free hour to do whatever I wanted, I'd . . .
> I always wanted to learn to . . .

2) **Imagination and creative thinking**. Imagine that one morning you woke up and found that you could fly. Where would each of you go? Now imagine that everyone in the family can soar in the sky. Consulting together, think of many different places that the whole family would enjoy flying to see. List them. Now find the one that everybody likes. It could be anywhere in the world. If at first you don't come to an agreement, keep dreaming up new places, even imaginary ones, until you find just the right one.

3) **Caring and social sensitivity**. A new family has moved in next door and they are strangers to your town. They have children just about the same age as the ones in your family. Make a simple plan for each of the following:

- What can you do to make them feel welcome in your neighbourhood?
- How can you help them settle in at school?
- What interesting things can you show them in your town?

4) **Moral and ethical values**. Here are two situations that involve moral and ethical considerations:

- Your friend asks you to tell the teacher that he's sick and you know that he just wants to skip school that day. He says that if you don't lie for him, he won't be your friend any more. What do you do? Can you help him in any way?
- What would happen if, for one hour, no one in the whole world told the truth? What effect would it have on doctors, newspapers, parents, children, banks, grocery stores, teachers, fire departments, trains? Any other effects?

5) **Problem-solving**. Elizabeth and Ann are twin sisters in the family down the street. They have to share a very small room and argue all the time about who should keep it clean and orderly. They have come to your family for help and have decided in advance to take your advice. What will you tell them? Remember the attitudes, skills and steps to consultation.

6) **Planning a project**. Your family is going to an isolated house for a vacation. It is so deep in the woods that you won't be able to shop for anything during the entire two weeks that you will be there. The cabin is completely furnished with kitchen utensils, bedding and towels; it has cold running water, but no electricity. Your job is to decide what you need to take for the family as a whole and for each individual member. This problem is similar to the one developed for astronauts, who were asked, 'What will you need on the moon?'

7) **Gathering information**. Think about the hun-

dreds of different kinds of work that adults do. Some people make things, some write, some work with computers, some teach, some grow food, some take care of people or animals, some sell things, some design buildings. What if you blew out the candles on your birthday cake when you were twenty-two years old and got your wish: you suddenly found yourself with all the proper training and education to have whatever job you wanted. In consultation, exchange information about the various occupations that family members choose as their birthday wish, including the parents.

Take a trip to the library, ask the librarian to help you, and read something about these occupations. Find out what kind of training you need, where you have to work, whether you would make enough money to raise a family, and whether there are many positions available. At home, have another consultation to report what you've learned. Do you still choose that profession, or did you find another that you like better?

8) **For very small children**. Teaching a small child how people communicate can be done through an activity that he or she may want to repeat over and over. It helps to have pictures of the animals to point to when describing their 'languages'.

What does the duck say?	Quack, quack
What does the fish say?	(Silently open and close mouth)
What does the lion say?	Roar, roar (loudly)

And so on for lambs, horses, dogs, or any other animal you care to include. The list can be as long as you and your child like, but finish it off with a grand flourish: 'And what do *people* say? Talk, talk, talk'. Then tell the child, 'You're a person, so when you feel good, you can *say* "I feel wonderful", and when you feel bad, instead of being angry and hitting someone, you can say, "I feel terrible". It's good to talk. Poor lion can't talk, he can only scare people by roaring; poor rooster can't talk, he can only say the same thing over and over, cock-a-doodle-doo. Poor fish can't make any sound at all. But people can tell people exactly what they want and feel, even far away on the telephone because we have words for things. Aren't we glad we're people!'

CHECKLIST FOR CONSULTATION

In the family, most consultations are one-to-one and informal. Formal group consultation may be desirable when important decisions which affect the entire family are being considered. This checklist summarises the many things to keep in mind.

Attitudes and Skills

1) Ethics – relate issue to broad principles
2) Mutual respect and fellowship – each is unique, worthy and equal
3) Unselfishness – what is good for the whole family?
4) Willingness to speak up – each opinion is important
5) Patience – self-control and persistence
6) Listening – be attentive, notice feelings, try not to interrupt
7) Speaking effectively – be clear and brief
8) Controlling egotism – once expressed, an idea belongs to the group
9) Creativity – be mentally mobile, think of many alternatives

Steps to Consultation

1) **Identify or define the issue to be consulted upon.** Encourage sharing by family members – describe what the problem seems like to each one. Look for underlying issues.

2) **Gather facts about the issue.** Who, what, why, when, where and how. This may require going to the library or to other sources of information. Facts and feelings are indispensable for productive consultation and discovering the truth. Think about ethical and moral considerations.

3) **Propose as many different solutions as possible.** Do not block, censure or criticise anything. Ask someone to write down all the suggestions. Ask for clarification if necessary. Each person should feel free to modify or suggest further refinements to a particular solution. Let your imagination loose and try to see the issue from as many sides as possible.

4) **Evaluate proposals.** Will it satisfy long-term as well as short-term requirements? Does it satisfy the needs, preferences, and feelings of the people involved? Can a good proposal be made even better? Can the family afford it? Is it too difficult or unrealistic?

5) **Choose the decision, solution or plan that best suits the family.**

6) **Write down what is expected of each family member involved in the decision.** Make time schedules for goal accomplishment and other details to remind people of what they must do.

7) **Put the decision, solution or plan into action in a spirit of unity.** Re-evaluate and modify it if necessary.

8) **Don't be too serious – this should be fun.** If you're not enjoying consultation most of the time, you're doing something wrong. Relax and check your ego is at the door.

6

Drawing Out the Best

The English verb 'to educate' means 'to draw forth' in both its original Germanic and Latin roots. As their children's first teachers, the parents' goal is to draw out the very best that potentially exists in each child. What takes place at home is the foundation of all future learning and achievement: under the tutorship of the parents the children acquire their self-images and the basic fundamentals of good character which enable them to make the finest use of whatever intellectual and social gifts they may have.

True education is only partly dependent on formal learning. A child who is courteous and caring is a clear asset to humanity, even if he is not intellectually gifted, while one who is highly educated but behaves in a boorish or anti-social manner is a menace to himself and to others.[49] Consequently, parents must nurture and educate both the young mind and character, a delicate, time-consuming, and complex operation. In addition to what is written on the impressionable mind, parents must also be concerned with how well the mind is organised, and how it expresses itself. Their responsibility is to serve as loving and wise instructors, pointing out relationships, correcting faulty perceptions, and providing reassurance.

In this chapter, we will discuss the ways in which many problems with children can be prevented by establishing trust, spending time together, developing a wholesome, balanced outlook, enjoying friendship, encouraging independence, exercise and sensory stimulation and, lastly, strengthening character.

ESTABLISHING TRUST

The bedrock of emotional security is laid during an infant's earliest days when its cries are met with loving, patient attention. If there is a consistent pattern to daily life with no prolonged periods of hunger, discomfort or fatigue, the baby can develop a trusting view of the world, able to rely on the fact that food and comfort come along with reassuring regularity. Moreover, unselfish parental love plays just as important a part in a child's growth and development as the physical nourishment parents provide. Without this fundamental stability, a child will be emotionally and even physically handicapped.

As the child grows older, she needs to know that parental love will not be withdrawn, that her parents can be relied upon. If she knows that her parents are permanently on her side, she will also realise that they always have her best interests at heart. Accordingly, when they point out a flaw in her behaviour, she will understand that it must be corrected because the behaviour itself is wrong, not because the parents are unkind or capricious. She will not view their admonition as a rejection or condemnation of her as a worthless person. The following true incident illustrates what we mean.

Two small boys were playfully wrestling next to the plate-glass door of an apartment building. They lost their balance, accidentally fell against the glass door, and shattered it. Neither boy was hurt, but neighbourhood children ran to fetch their parents, who came quickly. One set of parents immediately spanked their son and harshly scolded him. His natural remorse disappeared under the beating of his angry parents and turned into sullen resentment. He was deeply shamed in front of his friends and his feeling of self-worth was damaged.

The parents of the other child reacted completely differently. First they looked to see if their son was hurt and showed concern for his safety. Then they calmly asked what happened and received a truthful explanation. The boy did not have to blame someone else or make up a story since he knew from past experience that his parents would be fair to him; he knew they were on his side. Without anger, the parents quietly said, 'You must feel terrible about this; you certainly didn't intend this to happen, did you? But you weren't careful to look around and see *where* you were wrestling. This carelessness was the real mistake. Next time, think first of anything that might go wrong *before* you do it. Naturally, you'll have to help pay for the damage out of your allowance, since it was half your fault.'

Several valuable lessons were taught. The child was treated with respect. He took responsibility for his action. He was not made to feel ashamed in front of anyone and kept his self-esteem. He could then concentrate on the rational assessment of his mistake and learn from it, without being burdened by a turmoil of emotions. Above all, he learned that he could trust his parents' good intentions to look after his best interests. He was then free to feel sorry for his action and, privately, to resolve to be more careful next time. This incident reinforced a growing belief that helped him throughout his childhood: his parents were not his enemies, but his closest allies.

Building trust between parents and children starts early and continues through the years. It requires parents to make a sincere effort to see things from their child's point of view, not just their own, and to try to understand the child's own reasoning and motivation for acting in a situation. When parents patiently question and receive this information, they can correct his or her faulty thinking. Children who do not have a fundamental trust in the love and concern of their parents will not be able to grow up as well as those who are assured of a dependable, constant flow of love.

SPENDING TIME TOGETHER

Parents should be willing to spend a great deal of time with their child, sharing, talking, listening and just being there. One good reason for doing this is to train the child to speak well and it requires a tremendous amount of patience. It is easy to 'tune out' the endless prattle of children aged one-and-a-half to eight years. Yet if a parent is not reinforcing the talking with an occasional, 'And then what happened?' or 'How did you feel about that?' their unresponsiveness may eventually cause the child's spirited verbal flow to stop, like an unreplenished stream that dries up in the desert.

Over a long period of parental indifference, he or she may lose the chance of becoming a person who can speak and write exceptionally well. The age-mates of a two or three year old child are not capable of interacting in the same way as an adult to patiently teach vocabulary and reasoning skills.

Talking together

Listening intently to our child's sense and nonsense can be an enchanting experience and it is exciting to watch the young mind develop as it acquires the ability to think clearly. A daily, private 'talk-time' during which a child has the undivided attention of one or both parents is indispensable. No career demands, no hobby, no household chore should interrupt this precious time of communication between parent and child. All the cares of the day are set aside for it and many of them are significantly reduced by it.

Anxieties, fears, the puzzling behaviour of other children, questions about the universe and a small child's place in it can be answered in a cordial, non-judgemental atmosphere. When the child is confiding something, the father or mother should not be patronising but emotionally supportive, merely nodding at the self-confession of misbehaviour. When the child himself realises that he has done something wrong, the parents do not need to chastise, but can offer sympathy and encouragement, gently pointing out the way to do it right next time. They can reassure the child that there is always tomorrow, there is always a chance to improve.

When parents give advice without being overbearing and autocratic, this allows children to listen without defensive resistance. Non-confrontational discussions encourage children to open up to their parents and allow feelings of loving trust to develop. Parents are a wise source of advice that children will turn to naturally if they know they will not be harassed or shamed when they reveal their personal problems. They will feel comfortable speaking in a non-adversarial atmosphere. Moral and spiritual values can be shared through answers to their questions in a way that avoids heavy lecturing or saying more than they need to hear at the time. Once you succeed in establishing this mutual appreciation and relaxed loving rapport, you have won half the battle of child-raising because children will be much more likely to take to heart what their parents tell them when they know and trust that you want the best for them.

These talk-times are some of the most delightful experiences of child-raising. Walking hand in hand or sitting side by side, parent and child chat together about the wonders of the great world. Having a caring listener strengthens feelings of self-worth and gives a sense of being both cherished and valued. This will not give children swelled heads, it will give them the self-respect they need to treat others with respect.

Many adult problems begin with the feelings of inadequacy and low self-esteem acquired in childhood; some people remain forever timid, insecure, and unsure of themselves. When children have high self-esteem, it enables them to feel confident about themselves and ready to take on challenges throughout their lives. 'A person's feeling of self-worth forms the core of his or her own personality. . . . High self-esteem is a crucial element in a healthy family. Low self-esteem is sure to be found in a troubled family.'[50]

It takes energy to deal with energetic children. If parents are tired after a long day away at work, a brief transition time between work and home duties can be helpful. A standing hug between two family members that lasts not just for a second, but for a few moments can drain away the tensions of the day, especially when both backs are rubbed at the same time. Lying down as briefly as ten minutes with a child willing to have a quiet talk-time can restore the parents before they start cooking dinner and interacting with the rest of the family.

It is essential for parents to feel rested because meals should be pleasant experiences. The conversation that takes place at family mealtimes is a lively opportunity for sharing good news, jokes, positive thoughts and up-beat discussions. It is not a time for upsetting the digestion and causing tension by relating bad news or discussing problems which should be dealt with at another time. Instead, share pleasant news or anecdotes. Going round the table, each family member can relate the funniest or nicest thing that happened that day. Taught to listen politely without interrupting, each child has a chance to speak to a sympathetic group and develop descriptive and narrative skills.

In some fast-paced societies, the family may not gather to eat together. The microwave oven makes it possible for meals to be cooked 'on-demand' and eaten alone. Try not to let this happen in your home. Sharing meals builds family identity and solidarity.

Everyone in a family has at least some leisure hours, usually in the evenings and at weekends; older children and parents can choose to spend this time either for their own individual pleasure or with each other. By devoting time to being together, the family can prevent many troubles. When family members are indifferent to each other, feelings of loneliness and alienation can set in which may eventually lead to behavioural problems such as alcoholism, drug addiction and immorality. And we are not just referring to the children, either.

Living in a household which is generally tension-free through good consultation and communication is not a sacrifice, but a rewarding experience. This kind of home atmosphere is a magnet that continues to draw people back to it, even after the children are grown. Besides giving emotional support, families teach the socialisation skills needed to interact effectively with other people. In the home, children can test their social sensitivity, verbal and reasoning tools; they can receive feedback and make adjustments. This essential honing process requires a degree of patience and love which few people other than parents and siblings are willing to provide.

Reading and telling stories

Many adults have fond memories of being read to as children. Apart from its value in awakening the imagination and inspiring a love of literature, it creates intimate moments of sharing. Reading that begins before the first birthday and continues for many years instils a love of books almost automatically. Reading time, particularly before the child goes to sleep, is priceless. It puts the child in a state of relaxed security at the end of an extremely challenging day.

To a child every day is a challenging day. There is so much to learn, so much to cope with, so much new information to absorb. A child tries hard to make some sense out of it all. Parents are the ever-present teachers who make understanding it possible. Stories that show how others have successfully overcome problems are helpful. When read and discussed with the parents, these issues can be explained fully in the context of everyday things that happen to the child at home, in the neighbourhood and at school.

Buying books for children should start early: there is something special about having books of one's own, even when a child is fortunate in having a good public library nearby. Taking a gift certificate or book token to a bookshop and making a choice from all the literary riches available is a great adventure. You might look for the books you used to enjoy as a child; you will probably be surprised at how well these stories have stood the test of time.

You can even get your children to write their own true or fictional stories about any subject that interests them. A parent can take down a story that a child dictates, writing or typing it exactly as it is told, repetitions and all. To show your respect for your child's creativity, don't interrupt the flow of words except to make sure that you catch all the words. The story can later be neatly copied into its final form and illustrated. Be sure to make a cover for this treasure with the author's name, title and date. The left sides of the pages can be sewn up with needle and thread to make a booklet. The children will love hearing 'their' books read over and over. This is an excellent way of validating a child's feelings of self-worth.

Children of all ages love listening to a storyteller. When they are very young, all you have to do is lie down next to them and just make something up. They don't care if your stories are not masterpieces; they are mainly interested in hearing your soothing voice and having you around. If what you are saying doesn't hang together, don't worry. For the most part, children use their wonderful sleepy imaginations to fill in the gaps and make sense of your nonsense. Unless you really get nonsensical, then they might gently object, and of course you pay a little more attention to stringing your words together.

Questions and answers

When the story is finished and the children are nearly ready for sleep, take a few minutes for a 'question time' to give them a chance to ask you about God and the big questions of life. These sweet moments are when the love for things of the spirit is aroused, when you tell them about their own eternal natures. They will ask you question after question, so you may want to limit the number ahead of time, because you will enjoy answering as much as they enjoy asking! No matter how tired you are at the end of a long day, you do not want to miss this marvellous opportunity to snuggle up with the little ones and have a story and answer questions. What can we give our children, if not our time? It is the most precious thing we possess and they need it more than anything else.

NURTURING A WHOLESOME OUTLOOK

Fostering a wholesome outlook on life includes introducing your child to the beauty and wonder of nature, to things not manufactured but grown. We are so assaulted with fantasy from over-exposure to television, films and advertising that the line between reality and unreality is alarmingly blurred – we no longer seem to be living life at first hand.

As often as possible, parents should switch off the unreality of the mass media. They can take the children for a walk in the woods, visit the zoo, visit their places of work, or help them plant a garden. Let them see the 'real world' and not just a 'make-believe' one. This allows for direct experience, not vicarious experience filtered through someone else's perceptions.

In the distant past, our ancestors listened to the tribal

storyteller around the campfire. The oral narrative told
of legendary or actual events and imparted the values of
the culture through stories. These days, we have realistic
visual images on television and movies that often depict
role models and convey values that we do not want our
children to have.

Television

Television requires no effort or imagination to watch; the
flickering images capture and hold attention. One dangerous effect of television is that it makes one a passive
spectator rather than a doer. It can become a form of
addiction that robs one of precious time that could be
devoted to active exploration and participation. Children
should have other ways of entertaining and occupying
themselves instead of spending endless hours with the
electronic babysitter. One family we know limited television to one hour a day during the week and only a little
more than that at weekends.

Many television programmes, including some that are
produced specifically for children, promote materialistic
consumption, violence, immorality, self-indulgence and
other warped values. Solutions to problems on television
are usually instant, sometimes violent, and do not
portray the effort needed to cope with life in the real
world. There is a qualitative difference between the
stories we choose to tell or read to our children and the
ones they see on television, which are generally aimed at
attracting as broad an audience as possible. Wise parents
do not want impressionable youngsters to be 'programmed'
by this kind of exploitative medium.

Studies of thousands of children in several countries
over a twenty-year period have shown that the example
of violence on television often leads to more aggressive
behaviour. This aggressiveness results in social ostracism
and loneliness, which brings children back to the television in an escalating cycle of aggression and loneliness,

which sometimes culminates in criminal behaviour in adolescence and adulthood. When children see repeated violence on television, they tend to imitate it. This has been so thoroughly proven by psychological studies that the American Academy of Pediatrics now warns parents about the effects of television violence and urges them to limit and monitor what their children watch.[51]

Some people may say that it is impossible to supervise what a child sees on television or in films. We do not agree. Parents can look over what is available and decide that some things are simply off-limits. When the child complains, you can say, 'I am responsible for how you behave and for what you learn. I am doing my best to be a good parent. If this doesn't please you, that's unfortunate. Actually, you're lucky that someone cares this much about you.' Keep track of what is offered and be firm in your choices of what they may watch. Although you may hear some grumbling, your firmness will be a far better influence for them than indifferent permissiveness. Even if they occasionally see an unsuitable programme at a friend's house, they will still have the guidance of clearly knowing what their parents think is objectionable and what is acceptable.

A wholesome, balanced outlook implies knowing the difference between good and bad influences, and choosing those experiences, television programmes, films and books which will enhance a child's well-being and teach sound values.

ESTABLISHING FRIENDSHIP

Always be willing to serve as a patient, unpatronising friend to your young child. Always a friend, but never a 'buddy' – a small but important distinction. There is equality of status among buddies; they share experiences much more intimately. Being a buddy dilutes the parental role and is not likely to offer much in return. Parents should always be parents first, friends second, and buddies only after the children grow up. Sometimes parents may become so close to their young children that the line of authority is crossed and they become equal chums, finding to their eventual regret that it is hard to re-establish the authority of the parental role. It is understandable that this can happen, and single parents are especially susceptible, but children always need someone in charge of them, no matter how amiable that parent may be.

Friendship implies being comfortable, being able to relax and enjoy common ideas, thoughts and activities together. Love in a family is assumed and axiomatic, but liking one another enough to seek out each other's company is the result of an accepting and affectionate environment. When the parents themselves are fast friends, bonding with the children and between siblings then comes more naturally.

INDEPENDENCE AND FUNDAMENTAL CONCEPTS

To encourage independence, it is important to know when to leave the child alone to explore, to find things out, to play and interact with others. There are times when it is even wise to allow a child to make a few errors as long as the mistakes are not life-threatening or might burn the house down.

Nearly every mistake is the result of not applying certain fundamental concepts. For example, consideration for others is a basic principle, as is kindness, being tactful, not taking something without permission, safety around heights, being careful with sharp objects, watching the path ahead when walking – dozens and dozens of general principles that must, each one, be learned while growing up. These general rules of conduct are based on common sense and are not usually subject to much personal interpretation. Learning to behave rationally and responsibly is what maturing into independence is all about. In a sense, good behaviour is simply connecting the fundamental principles of conduct to the child's daily life.

Children usually learn these fundamental rules by trial and error. 'Watch out!' repeated kindly or angrily again and again eventually teaches a child to look where he or she is going. However, there is an easier way. When a child sees that a mistake has been made, we can explain the underlying logical concept behind it so that the mistake is less likely to be repeated.

For instance, a parent may explain the basic principle of personal property ownership to a child: 'Why did your sister get angry with you? Because you didn't ask if she would mind if you played with her toy. When someone owns something, they have the right to it unless they say you can use it. You must always ask before you take something, that's called asking for permission. This goes for things belonging to others at school, in the neighbourhood – everywhere. That way things won't get lost or taken away where the owner can't find them. No matter how much you want something, you must still ask permission for it.' This type of patient explanation seems obvious, but many parents do not take the time to do it, and then wonder why their child does not stop and think before doing something wrong.

When children understand that there are some basic principles of behaviour that can be applied in most circumstances, they will become more self-reliant and self-directed; they will not need to be 'told what to do' constantly nor will they be without guidance when they are far from their parents. Treat children as if they are intelligent and permit them to investigate things independently as far as safety allows. When the child is a toddler, make it clear which things are harmful and which things are a matter of choice. Later, shopping can be a learning experience for making decisions. The parent might choose a suitable coat, for example, and then allow the child to pick out the colour.

When it comes to food, try not to give too much choice or your children will end up eating peanut butter every day. Food should not become an attention-getting exercise. Give children the same nutritious food the rest of the family eats and let hunger take its course. It helps if children see you enjoying your own food. If a child prepares a part of the meal, this often whets the appetite, even for vegetables. Many families have a 'try everything once' policy of introducing new foods. When a child really detests something, however, don't force the issue; respect his or her preferences and, if not too inconvenient to the rest of the family, substitute something of equal nutritional value. There are probably some strong-tasting foods that you never learned to like either.

Rules are set either by the parents or through family consultation. There should be few rules, but these should be both rational and firmly enforced. Some rules are meant for small children, some are house rules for the whole family. A sensible one is that everyone's where-abouts must be known to someone in the family. This goes for the parents, too!

Starting with the total dependency of the newborn baby to his or her eventual emancipation some eighteen years later, the relaxation of parental control is gradual during this normal process of maturing, while the child's self-discipline and inner direction grows correspondingly. Like two saucers on a balance scale, the parents' side lightens up and empties, as guidance and responsibility are transferred to fill up the growing child's side. The ultimate goal is not to keep the child dependent and clinging, but to raise the most marvellously independent person possible.

PLAYING WITH FRIENDS

Although parents and siblings fill key roles in the process of socialisation, playing with age-mates is needed to develop the sensitivities which make a child socially effective. With other children, a child is exposed to group dynamics, the process of give and take, the inculcation of peer behaviour and a testing ground for all kinds of skills. In this setting, the child is on her own. With great rapidity she has to learn a whole set of social strategies and standards. This is more than just play – it is the serious business of being inducted into a group. Those who are raised in relative isolation from other children tend to be less socially effective as adults and may even suffer from emotional problems.

When the family lives in a remote area or the available age-mates are judged by the parents to be a bad influence, children may not get a chance to play as much as they need. Some parents over-protect their children by being too harsh in their judgement, seeing their own little one as 'an angel among devils'. Yet, sooner or later, they must let their children out into the world. If you provide enough opportunities for your children to interact with others and if you are giving them enough of your own time as well, you can trust them to wade in and do just fine.

STRENGTHENING CHARACTER

Love may be defined as those actions that nurture and benefit another. Of course, children should be comforted, have their legitimate needs attended to, and even entertained in a wise and measured way. But love should not be confused with indulgence. It is desirable to expose children, from an early age, to all sorts of challenges, even difficult ones. This is not cruelty: on the contrary, it is motivated by the highest form of love. Its aim is to develop the strong qualities of character necessary for a successful and happy life. For example, as soon as capable, the children can be enlisted in such household chores as scrubbing floors, vacuuming, and washing dishes. These tasks should be genuinely helpful and not token 'make-work'. This will not only assist the family, but it will give children useful skills as well as enhance their feeling of confidence and self-worth.

Some parents shield their children from hard work or feel that they can do everything better and faster themselves. But what about the child? He or she must do useful work and learn the intricacies involved and the art of perseverance. The reward is the satisfaction felt when one persists, prevails, and gets the job done.

This type of training is a valuable preparation for life ahead. Character building and training will produce useful, competent, contributing members of the human race who are unlikely to have to lean on others. On the contrary, they will be a positive force, a definite asset to themselves and those around them.

Being soft and lazy is a skill-less 'talent' that comes without any effort. Everyone loves to be pampered. It is easy to just coast along, but that's not what life is all about and the children should learn this early. Life is a workshop for the development of great human attributes, in which every individual is to participate fully in building the best civilisation we can. This requires resilient and sturdy people. Children are not born this way. They are shaped in the family, under the care of wise and loving parents.

> While the children are yet in their infancy . . . foster them in the cradle of all excellence, rear them in the embrace of bounty. Give them the advantage of every useful kind of knowledge. Let them share in every new and rare and wondrous craft and art. Bring them up to work and strive, and accustom them to hardship. Teach them to dedicate their lives to matters of great import, and inspire them to undertake studies that will benefit mankind.[52]

Service to the community

If the whole family pursues certain activities which have a noble purpose, children will learn the valuable lesson that life is not only for personal gain, but also for being of service to humanity. Consulting together, parents and children can decide to work as a family to preserve the environment, to help the poor, for world peace, the elimination of racial prejudice, or whatever humanitarian, religious or community service they find most rewarding. To turn inward, to be only concerned with the self is deadly and it brings much unhappiness as well. If the lesson of service is learned early, children will have the satisfaction of a lifetime of helping others, transmitting a humane sense of duty down the generations. If selfishness and self-indulgence is the example set by their parents, they will probably grow up never feeling that tremendous lift of the spirit that comes from working for a good cause.

EXERCISE, SENSORY STIMULATION AND TOYS

Along with food, shelter, love, education and training, children also need opportunities for stimulation and exercise. They should not sit still for long periods of time; this is neither normal nor healthy, because they have muscles to develop, coordinate and strengthen. Too many parents have forgotten their own childhoods and the knowledge that movement is as necessary as breathing. So take your children where they can run and play, and become happily exhausted.

Children also need stimulation to enrich their minds through exposure to all kinds of people, animals, things, sights, and sounds. A mobile of animal shapes placed about a baby's bed is more than a source of amusement, its bright colours and movement are visually stimulating. Researchers have found that even babies less than a month old enjoy looking at bold black and white patterns and simple outlines of human faces.

Gently massaging the hands, chest, limbs, and backs is another way of providing sensory experience for babies and young children; so is the singing of time-honoured lullabies and cradle songs. Providing sensory experiences can be as simple as going to a playground, a shopping centre, the countryside, the zoo, or wherever there is a rich variety of sights, sounds, smells and textures. These trips are not only stimulating, they help contribute to a growing vocabulary and add to the store of happy family memories.

Playing with toys is also a learning experience, particularly when it involves being with another person. Often the best playthings are the least expensive and are made from objects and materials found around the house: measuring cups and spoons, cardboard boxes, pictures cut from magazines and pasted on stiff paper. A piece of masking tape makes a roadway on any open floor; blue cloth makes rivers and oceans; cotton-reels and pipe-cleaners make tiny play people.[53]

Children need toys which stimulate the imagination, rather than those with fixed and limited uses. An old suitcase full of lengths of different coloured and textured fabrics and several dozen extra-large safety pins (with careful lessons on how to use them) provide costumes for as many different characters as your sons and daughters can dream up. A single piece of cloth can become a cape, a turban, a ball gown, a knight's tunic, a cover for a palace couch, a tablecloth, a small teepee, a sari, a sarong, an astronaut's jumpsuit – with these props, your children will make up far more fantastic plots and dialogue than any they might find on television.

Be sure that you do not segregate the toys by gender. Girls need to play with trucks and complicated and constructive toys, while boys need to play with domestic things. *We want to raise whole human beings, not children limited by stereotyped gender roles.* Moreover, parents who take the trouble to teach games like checkers (draughts), backgammon, bridge and chess to their children are rewarded with hours of mutual enjoyment; they have also given their children valuable opportunities to develop their ability to use logic and strategy.

'Children provide a new interpretation of the world around them and, by their presence, they give their parents permission to play and to reinterpret the world they share with their children.'[54] Providing physical and intellectual stimulation through exercising and playing with games and toys is one of the best things about parenting – it rekindles the child in us all.

Drawing out the best in your children brings out the best in you too. What other form of ongoing activity requires as much quick thinking, creative planning, and unselfish strength of character? Keeping a step ahead of rapidly growing children with razor sharp minds is not a task for the faint-hearted. Our own capabilities stretch and deepen while we go through these years with them, especially since we must improvise most of what we are doing; in the late twentieth century, there are few traditions for us to rely on – we are the first to raise children in a computer age.

The question of discipline, in particular, calls for some of our highest qualities of patience, forgiveness and persistence. In the next chapter we will explore ways of making this difficult area of parenting easier and less traumatic for the whole family.

7

Discipline

While no individual should ever be deprived of his or her full rights as a person, order is necessary for any family, group or society to function. As children are inexperienced, it is natural for them to have a lesser rank than adults. This does not imply that they have no rights or are of lesser worth, but it does mean that they must obey the rules of the group, whether at home, at school or in the community.

FAMILY GOVERNANCE

The fundamental laws that govern relationships must be taught early. It is in the family that children first learn about cause and effect; they become aware that, in general, the world is predictably organised along the lines of reward and punishment. People are usually rewarded when they do the right thing; if they do otherwise, they must face the consequences.

Early on, each child should learn that he or she is part of a nuclear family, an extended family, and the larger family of humanity. A child should understand that he or she is a full member of each of these groups and consequently has definite privileges and responsibilities. The purpose of discipline, in its deepest sense, is to assist the child to master these rules of social relationships: to have self-respect as an integral part of the whole, and to learn respect for the rights of others, both inside the family and in the larger community. This responsible, healthy outlook can minimise friction and conflict within the home, and helps the child develop good citizenship.

The authoritarian family

For most of history, children had few rights and were almost entirely subject to their parents' will.[55] Frequently, they were treated as if they were chattel property and the law did not interfere. Parents had the right to beat their children whenever they wished and, in extreme cases, even legally kill them if they were unmanageable.[56] For centuries parents have relied on an authoritarian means of discipline. When there were many children of widely differing ages in the household, there was neither time nor energy to do much more than be authoritarian; backbreaking labour was required on the farm, in the factory, and at home just to feed and clothe the family. Using harsh punishments, they required obedience with 'no questions asked' to keep order. For such parents discipline meant, 'How can I get the children, with strong wills of their own, to do exactly what I want them to? And do it quietly, without much energy expended on my part?' They were looking for expediency, or to put it another way, the greatest amount of docile obedience with the least effort. Children were scolded, shamed, and frequently frightened into good behaviour through tales of 'bogeymen'.

Even if children are not physically beaten, they might still bear permanent emotional scars from the severity of the authoritarian child-raising method when it uses degrading, belittling, and shaming language to control behaviour. Damage may include low self-esteem, a feeling of hopelessness, behavioural problems and hostility towards the parents. In repressive authoritarian families children have no legitimate means of responding. They are not invited to express opinions or listened to when they try to express them. They have little or no influence on their parents' decisions and actions, even though they are profoundly affected by them.

The permissive family

There is another, and in our view equally harmful, child-raising practice in which parents go too far in the opposite direction and become overly permissive. Without attempting to instil any form of consistent discipline, they give in to all their children's whims and self-indulgences. These children dominate, even tyrannise the household, routinely ignoring their parents' wishes and treating them with contemptuous rudeness. In capitulating to their children's escalating demands and ultimatums, parents relinquish their natural right to be respected and deprive their children of the chance to develop consideration for others and mature self-control.

The egalitarian family

These two extremes of discipline in family life involve either tyrannical parents or tyrannical children – clearly both destructive patterns are unacceptable. What we advocate instead is a form of discipline where the needs and rights of both parents and children are taken into account.

The emergence of smaller families in the developed countries has made possible a new form of family discipline which takes children's rights into consideration. The notion of children's rights does not mean that children have the right to disobey their parents, as some may think. It is based on the reasoning that since children are human beings, they should be included under the general umbrella of human rights along with other groups previously thought to be of lesser importance, such as women and ethnic minorities. Instead of being viewed merely as sources of free-labour for their parents, the inescapable by-products of marital relations, or as future care-givers in the parents' old age, children are increasingly viewed as having value in their own right with a natural entitlement to respect, dignity, good physical care and access to education.

The following passage strikes a reasonable balance in modern family relationships:

> The integrity of the family bond must be constantly considered, and the rights of the individual members must not be transgressed. The rights of the son, the father, the mother – none of them must be transgressed, none of them must be arbitrary. Just as the son has certain obligations to his father, the father, likewise, has certain obligations to his son. The mother, the sister and other members of the household have their certain prerogatives.
>
> All these rights and prerogatives must be conserved, yet the unity of the family must be sustained. The injury of one shall be considered the injury of all; the comfort of each, the comfort of all; the honor of one, the honor of all.[57]

The above passage illustrates how power should be shared in an egalitarian family with justice for every member; there is no tyranny on either side, but a shared concern for everyone's rights. All enjoy a mutually caring atmosphere. In summary, here are the three models of family structure:

- Authoritarian family: Autocratic rule of parents over children, as well as husband over wife.
- Permissive family: Autocratic rule of children over parents.
- Egalitarian family: Joint decision-making by parents, incorporating children in the process as soon as they are able. Balance of rights

and respect between parents and children, husband and wife.

We believe the egalitarian model will be the predominant pattern in coming years because it is based on the concept of the oneness of humanity and is best suited to meet the requirements of our age.

RESPECT FOR PARENTS

The parent-child relationship should be one of mutual love and respect flowing in both directions, but this mutuality is qualified by the fact that children owe a fundamental duty of obedience to their parents. This duty is rooted in the practical need for the weak to be cared for by the strong and the ignorant to learn from the wise. It also springs from the principle of reciprocity and the obligation of repaying one's debts. Parents are their children's lifegivers, providers and caretakers, who, with few exceptions, invest much of themselves and their resources in nurturing them. Most parents willingly and generously sacrifice for their children with no tangible or material benefit to themselves. Why, then, do they do it? They do it essentially out of love. Parents are therefore genuinely entitled to their children's respect, deference and obedience.

Let us make the distinction between rebelliousness and disrespect. A degree of rebellion is a natural part of growing up that can even be helpful in bringing about the necessary eventual independence of the child. It need not be a source of antagonism if its value is understood and directed constructively. Recognising that rebelliousness is healthy, parents can view it as a step on the way to adulthood, rather than trying to repress it. This point can be thoroughly explored by all members of the family through consultation.

Respect, on the other hand, can and must be insisted

upon whatever the age of the child, and insolence towards parents should never be allowed. This in no way implies a totalitarian rule because legitimate grievances can always be dealt with through family consultation. If a child is permitted to show impertinence to parents, it is likely that teachers and others in authority will also be treated rudely. It should be explained to children that parental respect is the foundation of respect for others. After all, who is more entitled to the children's respect than the people who care and do more for them than anyone else? This is a logical concept and it is not hard to accept its validity.

Any behaviour or tone of voice that shows discourtesy to the parents must be corrected. Without anger, a parent can say, 'No matter how you feel, you may not speak to me that way. First, I am a person with too much self-respect to tolerate such rudeness from anyone. Second, I am your parent. Please say that again, this time more politely.' By claiming your personal right to courtesy, you are maintaining your authority and self-esteem and, just as important, you are giving your children a valuable role model to follow in their own future relationships with others.[58] They will be more likely to stand up for themselves and refuse to be treated disdainfully by other children or become the butt of merciless teasing. You are teaching them the valuable lesson that you are worthy of respect, just as they are, and just as all people are too.

RESPECT FOR CHILDREN

Some couples have never consulted together to develop a mutually-agreed child-raising strategy. Not surprisingly, haphazard approaches frequently produce unruly, disobedient and disrespectful children. Parents would do well to show respect and consideration for their children by adopting a unified and consistent system for their upbringing which they can both whole-heartedly support, whether they are still married or have been divorced and awarded joint custody. This will prevent the children, with their usually underestimated native intelligence, from playing one parent off against another when it suits them. Additionally, a harmonisation of views will eliminate possible friction and arguments between the parents about discipline.

Patience and informed expectations

The greatest virtue required in raising children is patience. Children are exasperatingly slow in growing up; we want them to hurry, to get through childhood quickly and end their childish behaviour. But we cannot blame them: 'The child must not be oppressed or censured because it is undeveloped; it must be patiently trained.'[59] Consequently, adopting realistic expectations is an important part of developing patience and tolerance. When parents erroneously expect more mature behaviour than a child is capable of achieving, they become frustrated and demanding; the relationship of mutual trust suffers and discipline can break down.

Knowledge about normal child development is extremely useful in setting reasonable expectations. In dealing with one's children it is helpful to know that their behaviour is typical of their age group. For example, most children around six fear the dark, most toddlers prefer to say 'no' rather than 'yes', and so on. Each stage of childhood has a particular developmental goal accompanied by characteristic behaviour and misbehaviour. A great deal of research has been done in this field and there are many excellent books available.[60] This vast subject is beyond the scope of our discussion, but the following list summarises child development goals.[61]

Stage	Goal
Infancy	Developing trust
Toddler	Developing independence
Pre-school age	Developing initiative
School age	Developing industry
Adolescence	Developing self-identity

Every child will go through each developmental stage at his or her own pace, regardless of what the parents or siblings did at that age. Reasonable expectations, tailored to the individual's unique temperament and set of capabilities, are most effective.

Controlling parental anger

There are many occasions when a child, either through wilful misbehaviour or innocent ignorance, will anger a parent. But however irritating their child's behaviour may be, parents must be careful not to lose their tempers and inflict violence, no matter how much they are provoked. It is not permissible to beat even an animal – how much less a small child!

The cruel, old-fashioned approach of slapping, sharp pinching, or spanking has not been shown to be effective in fostering long-lasting good behaviour and can lead to many character disorders and psychological problems. Harsh punishment promotes aggression in children; eventually aggression becomes self-perpetuating as a characteristic way of solving problems. By the time this behaviour comes to the notice of society, it is firmly embedded and not easily changed.[62]

Heaping verbal abuse on a child, whether justified or not, should also be completely avoided. Severely scolding a child, whether alone or in front of others, damages the fragile structure of self-esteem that he or she is gradually building. Instead of being engulfed by an inarticulate anger, you must learn to be calm when talking over undesirable behaviour; *you must make the effort, no matter how difficult it is, to keep your temper under control. Otherwise, how can children be expected to control their own tempers?*

Expressing an emotion can be far more effective when it is under control, conveying what one wants to say in even tones with firm intensity, for example, rather than acting it out with loud shouts and painful blows to the child. Anger can produce a physiological condition that can be harmful to both adults and children, resulting in stress-related physical damage along with emotional tension. Stress and its effects on health will be treated in more detail in a later chapter, but at this point in our discussion we want to emphasise that anger in the home must be avoided as much as possible. Many parents have, over a period of time, stepped up their emotional responses to the point where their verbal outbursts become just bombastic meaningless noise to the child.

Research by psychologist Gerald Patterson points to 'the corrosive role of constant parental irritability, even the familiar sort that causes a parent to snap at a child, in children's learning and intellectual growth'.[63]

Irritability becomes destructive in families where it is the dominant tone rather than when it occurs, say, for a few minutes at the end of a wearying work day.

In a study comparing the families of children who caused trouble at school by fighting, temper tantrums, stealing, vandalism and the like with families of children who do not have such problems, Patterson's research found that the parents of disruptive children were three times more likely to display irritability to their children than were the parents of the other children. He found that when parents learned to use more constructive approaches, their children misbehaved less. 'There is nothing unusual about scowls, frowns and sarcasm,' Patterson said, 'but there is a very strong relationship between the amount of such irritability and a child's aggressiveness at school.' Parents who were especially irritable with their children were typically poor at resolving such conflicts, and seemed to pass on these inabilities to their children.[64]

Anger distorts communication. Faced by a parent who is livid and out of control, a child may be either too frightened to listen or tempted to laugh at the ludicrous spectacle of an adult tied up in knots over the actions of a small person. There are several ways to handle anger. Some parents walk into another room for a moment to regain their self-control, others will mentally count to ten (or whatever number it takes) in order to calm down. Watching a parent struggle to maintain a calm and rational demeanour teaches a child a great deal.

Another important reason not to show anger is to avoid displaying weakness. The child cannot beat you physically, but if he or she possesses the power to infuriate you, you will be emotionally beaten.

DISCIPLINE THAT PREPARES FOR THE FUTURE

At first glance, it might seem to be easier to live with quiet, docile, passive children who always exhibit 'perfect' behaviour, but that is not what you really want. Children who have been shaped this way through harsh punishment, unrelieved strictness, and overbearing discipline may not have a chance to develop initiative, curiosity, flexibility in meeting problems, and creativity. They may even become insecure, incompetent and helpless adults, always looking to others for supervision. On the other hand, children who have been raised in a very permissive household may exhibit curiosity and initiative but lack the essential self-discipline and concern for others which would help them both to fully develop their talents and abilities and to work with others in a co-operative and harmonious way. It takes far more energy to raise well-balanced, assured, competent, self-directed children who learn from their parents how to think, to question, to challenge ideas, to be probing and to be curious. According to current trends, moreover, these very qualities will be needed in the workplace of the near future when the children of today will need jobs.

At present, the developed nations are adjusting to a post-industrial age in which the old factory system is gradually being transformed by computer technology towards automation. The application of the science of robotics will eventually reduce reliance on unskilled manual labour. Society is beginning to turn away from old ways which emphasised obedient, unquestioning conformity on assembly lines and in the bureaucratic hierarchy of corporations. In the future, the working world will require more mental skills than physical labour and this will release individual creativity as never before. Many new fields in technology which will be commonplace in the coming decades are just now being imagined and developed.

Personal initiative is burgeoning, particularly among women, who are establishing new businesses at an unprecedented rate in the United States and Great Britain, partly because they want to have control over their own working hours and conditions while raising children. Already we can see the trends that require working people to meet challenges with flexibility in the commercial and manufacturing world, where entre-preneurship, quality control circles in factories, and participative management in corporations are flourishing.

There is a new method of supervising employees called 'self-management' in which employees are trained in the aims and purposes of the corporation, given basic instruc-tions and allowed to do their allotted tasks without much supervision. For individuals who are well-motivated and self-disciplined, this type of job involvement offers excitement and fulfilment. It is already proving its worth to management in the increased number of innovative ideas contributed by employees, in a new sense of commitment to high quality and in healthy profits.[65]

To be able to respond to new technology and more open-ended supervision in a dynamic work place, children need good reasoning skills as well as a healthy level of self-esteem. They will be handicapped if they have been brought up knowing only blind obedience and subservience. Our present life in the developed countries is far too complex and rapidly changing for parents to impose a comprehensive set of regulations for correct behaviour to be obeyed without thinking. Instead, energies should be devoted to teaching fundamental principles by which they can reason out and successfully deal with each new situation.

How can skills such as reasoning be taught to children? Surprisingly enough, discipline plays a crucial role. Research by psychologist Martin Hoffman, an expert in moral development at New York University, has described three major approaches to discipline: reasoning, assertion of power and withdrawal of love.[66]

With pre-school children, teaching discipline by reasoning means drawing attention to the *effect* caused by their bad behaviour. For example, when a child says something cruel to another child, instead of angrily saying, 'Stop that!' the parent should point out to him that the action has caused unhappiness. The parent can say, 'See, John is crying – we shouldn't say anything that would hurt someone else's feelings. Why don't you go to him, say you're sorry and make him feel better. Next time think about the effect your words can have on someone else.' Parents can teach empathy and consideration for others by explaining that other people also have feelings, just like theirs. Or a parent can say, 'I get worried about your safety when you do that', which is another type of appeal to a sense of concern for others. Helping the younger child understand the consequences of behaviour is an extremely valuable lesson to convey as early as possible.

With an older child, the reasoning approach to discipline involves more sophisticated discussions focusing on the underlying rationale for basic rules of conduct. Parents can also help a child think of alternatives to actions to enhance their child's ability to plan ahead – to avoid, for example, escalating misunderstandings among friends. Learning to reason through possible consequences before they happen will enable children to prevent many problems by themselves.

Information about the past can also help a child to make a rational choice about better behaviour. You may want to describe to the children what the old authoritarian discipline was like, how children used to endure whippings, slaps, being sent to bed without dinner to be hungry all night, standing for hours in a closet, and other cruelties from their parents to force them into good behaviour. Then you can consult with them about ways of instilling the inner discipline which is characteristically found in an egalitarian family. Ask them, 'If we don't want to use the old methods, what should we do instead?' Children will see that it is clearly in their own best interests, as well as in their parents', to be co-operative. They may feel a sense of relief at being born in a more humane era, not like the 'bad old days' when life was often miserable for young people.

Because it is sometimes difficult to get a child to pay attention so that a lesson registers, discipline by reasoning may occasionally be augmented by a more temporarily effective exercise of parental power, such as the loss of privileges.

Dr Hoffman's research, which noted the positive benefits of discipline through reasoning, found that the other two methods of discipline – power and the withdrawal of love – have many disadvantages.

Power alone, without reasoning, can be harmful, the research shows. Using or threatening raw physical force, depriving a child of a possession or privilege or simply giving him a direct order may solve the immediate discipline problem, but may also impart an unintended moral lesson. The children of parents who rely on force or threats, research shows, tend not to console or help another distressed child or even to notice they have caused distress.

Withdrawing love, the other approach to discipline, can have equally negative, though less apparent, effects. Children raised this way, researchers say, show few signs of caring. But, unlike those disciplined through power, these children are also likely to be somewhat passive and withdrawn, according to Hoffman. 'The notion that your parent does not love you is terrifying to a child,' Hoffman said. 'It can leave him so anxious and inhibited that he is afraid to do most anything.'[67]

We should always keep in mind that parents, particularly in the eyes of the very young, are personifications of absolute power. Looking up to see an angry parent looming over is a terrifying experience to a small child. Parents do not have to inflict physical harm to be abusive. Intimidation, sarcasm and cold remoteness can be equally damaging. Also abusive is the neglect of basic needs: not feeding the child when he is hungry, not changing him when he is wet or not comforting him when he is in pain.

If you have been raised by a mother or father who routinely used angry words, shaming or physical punishment, you may fear that you will unconsciously inflict this kind of treatment on your own children. This need not be the case. The very fact that you are mindful of this possibility is in itself a good sign, and if you remain aware in your day-to-day actions, it is by no means inevitable that these behaviour patterns will be repeated for another generation. We should all try to train

ourselves to channel our responses to our children away
from anger and towards positive action.

TRAINING CHILDREN IN
THE SUCCESSFUL FAMILY

Let's turn to the practical, everyday process of raising
children. What about bad habits and misbehaviour? How
do we teach children good qualities and eliminate their
bad ones? How can we train them to *want* to do what they
should? A great challenge facing each individual family,
as well as the larger family of humanity, is to turn away
from the negative forces of oppression, injustice, revenge
and hostility towards the healing, integrating, creative
and motivating energy of love. Discipline in an egalitarian
family operates through both reasoning and a powerful
training tool called positive reinforcement, which can
profoundly influence people through the time-honoured
method of rewarding desirable behaviour.

It is natural to want to repeat behaviour that is
rewarded. The reward, called a positive reinforcer, can be
some desirable thing or event. When we know that doing
or saying something will earn the reward, we are most
likely to persist with that behaviour to receive it. For
example, if a child gets a hug and praise for picking up
toys after playing, he will be more willing to pick them
up again another day because he associates picking up
toys with something pleasant. And if a child discovers
that throwing a tantrum will get him the piece of cake he
wants, he is likely to keep on throwing tantrums
whenever it suits him and might eventually even use it
for getting other things as well. In other words, if
something works, we tend to want to do it again.

We feel good psychologically when our actions gain the
approval of others, particularly people we hold in high
regard, such as parents and peers. If a child does a
kindness for her younger sister, she should immediately

be given appropriate positive reinforcement, for example a remark such as, 'You were thoughtful to go out of your way to bring that book for her; I appreciate it, Carol.' Another example of reinforcing desirable behaviour is when a wife gives her husband an affectionate kiss for preparing her favourite breakfast.

There are many psychological reinforcers including smiles, hugs, looks of approval, and praise. People particularly thrive on verbal reinforcement which can be easily given. Without being overly-generous or insincere, one should look for opportunities to strengthen the habit of good behaviour with an appropriate positive reinforcement. People tend to pay more heed to immediate consequences than those delayed in time, and so reinforcements are most effective when they occur right away.

Instead of concentrating on a child's bad behaviour, watch for chances to catch him or her in the act of doing something good and reward that with praise. This principle was recognised as a key factor in motivating corporate employees in the book, *The One Minute Manager*,[68] which has exerted a very positive influence on American business management policies. But long before psychologists experimentally verified the truth of the effectiveness of positive reinforcement, a man with great wisdom advised:

> Be silent concerning the faults of others ... look always at the good and not at the bad. If a man has ten good qualities and one bad one ... look at the ten and forget the one; and if a man has ten bad qualities and one good one ... look at the one and forget the ten.[69]

Instilling inner discipline means recognising the good in a child and encouraging it to grow. Mild reprimands may be used – as sparingly as possible – which mainly focus on the logical reasons *why* the behaviour is undesirable and not on shaming or labelling the child as 'bad' or 'naughty'. These gentle reprimands should result in a feeling of regret at what happened and a determination not to repeat it; children should not be made to feel disgusted with themselves. Convey to the child that, while control of conduct and competence are expected, the disapproval of a particular action does not mean rejection of the person. Also, make it clear that you love your child, that even in the most wilful lapses of behaviour, forgiveness is possible. Whenever a parent is tempted to give in to the inclination to spank a child, it may help to remember that *the desire to please loving parents is a far stronger motivation than the desire to escape from physical punishment.*

Is it possible to give a child too much praise? Not if it is the right kind. Praise should be specific and descriptive: 'I like the way you didn't give up until the whole garden was weeded', or 'You chose such happy colours for your drawing'. When parents take time to describe a child's thoughtfulness and efforts in such concrete, not general, terms, the child feels loved; his parents have really noticed and appreciated the accomplishment.

It isn't fair to imply to our children through words or actions that we always expect perfect behaviour. Generalised judgemental remarks such as, 'You're Daddy's good little boy', make a child squirm, because he knows that no one can be good all the time and may feel pressured by the fear that any lapse in conduct will result in a withdrawal of love. He knows he has many hostile and jealous feelings; he feels far from perfect. To give judgemental praise can make him feel guilty and ashamed for not living up to it, but to praise a specific effort or accomplishment raises self-esteem. The child can justify his thought, 'Yes, I really did that and Dad liked it'.[70]

We must work on two things at the same time: building up the good qualities the child has acquired and trying to get rid of faults and bad habits. Depending on the nature and seriousness of negative behaviour, the withholding of positive reinforcement can be effective.

The following example demonstrates the strategy. Consider a four-year-old who runs home to share with her mother a word she has just learned from her playmates. She has come to expect praise whenever she adds to her vocabulary. This time she proudly produces a swear-word and confidently awaits her mother's delighted smile. How should the mother respond? In cases like this, all the usual positive reinforcement should be withheld. The parent can quietly say, 'That's not a good word to use. You know so many good words, you don't need that one. Please don't use it again,' and then change the subject.

Withholding approval can also be a means of correcting persistent undesirable behaviour. In those instances, we should intelligently adjust the punishment to fit the 'crime' through consultation. This can be done effectively, in most instances, by temporarily withdrawing appropriate privileges.

Confidence and self-esteem

One of the most valuable things we can do for our children is to help them develop a deep reservoir of self-esteem that will not only allow them to fulfil their potential but carry them through the inevitable stresses of life.

Young people who have assurance and self-reliance believe they have some control over their destinies. Unafraid to try new things, they are optimistic and easily attract the friendship of others. They feel that as long as they make an effort they can achieve success and happiness. Other children who have the same natural intelligence but low self-esteem are less competent, unwilling to volunteer, abandon tasks at the first sign of difficulty, have few social skills to maintain friendships and frequently say, 'I can't'.[71] They think success and happiness come by luck, not effort, and that the world is an unfriendly place. Burdened with self-doubt, they can become helpless and unwilling to try to improve things.

The differences between these two types of children are emotional and motivational.

How can we raise children who will make the best of themselves? By giving our children healthy, as opposed to egotistical, measures of self-confidence, they can feel like winners. We can even create situations in which they are certain to succeed in order to begin the process of building a positive self-image. We can adapt the old saying to a new context: 'No one succeeds like the one who feels successful'.

This point is illustrated in the following true story. A father took his five-year-old son to a bowling alley one afternoon for his very first game. After showing the boy how to hold and throw the ball, the father carefully placed several pins in the right and left gutters. Why? So that no matter where the boy threw the ball, it was guaranteed to hit some pins – success was ensured! You can imagine how much the boy enjoyed his first game. Whenever he bowled the ball, he heard the lovely sound of crashing pins and had points to record. As his proficiency grew, his father gradually trained him in the proper rules and techniques of the sport, but in such a way that the boy always felt competent and sure of himself. The wisdom of building on that initial success was demonstrated years later when the son became a famous international bowling champion.[72]

Success takes many forms. Although not every child will receive the top grades in academic subjects in school, he or she can still be made to feel successful. There are artistic, athletic, mechanical, social, consultative and other skills that can be appreciated so that the child is given a sense of pride in working to develop them. Rewarding someone's worthy achievements is a form of justice as well as the most effective way of enticing any child to further accomplishments. There is an immense power in reward and encouragement for shaping the behaviour of all family members. Husbands and wives can use it in their own relationship, which will continue to deepen and grow as they serve as each other's greatest admirers. The children should also be showered with the same life-giving nourishment of praise.

The difference between an exemplary person and the opposite may only be a matter of the degree to which potential capabilities have been influenced through such factors as learning, exposure to various life events, and interaction with others. The successful family is the one that adopts conditions and practices that help its members keep on growing and changing for the better. Over time, as good qualities are developed and applauded, they tend to become more deeply ingrained; if a child's inappropriate behaviour is ignored and results in no significant reward, it gradually recedes and eventually disappears altogether.

When positive personal qualities and reactions have become second nature, doing the right thing when dealing with people becomes automatic, the first and the most natural reaction. Consider the example of a person who consistently deals kindly with others and who extends a helping hand whenever it is needed. In turn the person who receives the help may praise and thank her, so that her quality of kindness is enhanced through practice and by the reward of appreciation. Both positive and negative qualities are like muscles. The more frequently-used ones become stronger and the rarely-used ones will atrophy.

Seeing through our children's eyes

Discipline in the home should be incorporated into the growing child's character and eventually result in the self-discipline of a mature adult; this is our goal as parents. We, too, must exercise discipline and self-restraint ourselves. Whenever we are tempted to angrily shout at the children or come down on them with harsh punishment, we would do well to think back and remember what it was like to be a small child. Let us not forget the fragile and tender natures of our children:

Most of us know from experience that the hearts of children are by nature very delicate. Their feelings are sensitive, and although we may not be aware of it, their views on those matters which affect themselves are perceptive.

We can compare the delicacy of children's hearts to flower petals, and the sensitivity of their feelings to clear water, while the acuteness of their vision reminds us of a strong microscope: the first will wither and fade away at the first sign of rough handling, the second will be clouded and polluted by the least amount of agitation, while the third will make them keen-sighted and precise.[73]

When we try to look at the world through the eyes of our children, we will become attuned to them. Instead of seeing things from our own impatient perspective, we will be able to work with them from their point of view. In turn we can teach them empathy – the ability to share in the emotional states of another person. Through empathy, children will learn two essential components of good behaviour: to be considerate and to have no wish to harm others. Children want to please their parents, as a general rule, and it is up to us to make it possible for them to do it. When we control our own negative feelings, refrain from being overly critical and practise forbearance as parents, we can help our children control themselves.

As parents, we want to be respected and obeyed, not for egotistical reasons, but because we know that children will best benefit at this stage in life from the boundaries and controls, from the limitations and direction that only we can give them. In this way, we can structure an orderly environment in which they can flourish. *The loving discipline of parents is like the firm banks of a clean, swift-flowing river. Remove those guiding banks and the undirected water turns into a useless swamp.*

8

Siblings

Parental love is of central importance to children from their earliest days. Brothers and sisters compete with each other for all the things that parents can give, including approval, attention and affection. Sibling rivalry can be destructive if it is allowed to get out of hand. Unchecked through parental negligence and passivity, this rivalry may result in years of arguments among the children; its petty jealousies can unravel the fabric of family unity and happiness. Beyond the immediate family, unhealthy rivalry can have lasting negative effects by influencing the children's social behaviour in the neighbourhood and at school. *Even worse, the hostility and constant bickering between siblings can become habits so deeply embedded that their own future marriages and family life will be affected.* In this chapter we will look at how bad feelings among siblings develop and how they can be prevented.

THE UNPREPARED FIRST CHILD

When getting ready for the arrival of a second child, along with thinking about the new baby's clothing, bed and other material details, parents must also consider what the new addition to the family will mean in terms of emotional adjustments. When little or no attention is paid to the psychological preparation of children for the arrival of another child, there is the risk of creating serious problems. This is particularly true for a child who up to that point was the sole object of the parents' love.

From a first child's point of view, the events that surround the coming of a new sibling are disturbing. One day the child wakes up and finds his mother gone. He can't find her anywhere and he becomes frightened. When told she has gone to the hospital, he has no concept of what that might be. Days pass and still his mother fails to return. He is told that he has a new brother or sister and that his mother is fine. But where is she? Doesn't she care about him? Perhaps a grandmother or some stranger has come to take care of him. He doesn't understand the empty feeling he has when his mother is gone for so long. He may experience the fear of abandonment and feel angry and unloved.[74]

Even when his mother finally returns, she is too tired to spend much time with him. There is a commotion in the house and a little baby that makes a lot of noise. Where is the big brother or sister he was waiting to see? Is this tiny, helpless thing supposed to play with him?

It is hard to say what goes on in the older child's head. At first, he may simply be curious. Is the baby going to stay, or will Grandma take it with her when she leaves? Gradually, he begins to figure things out. No, the baby is not going away, it is here to stay. Not only that, some of his own things are given to the baby, like the little blue blanket that he loves. And his parents don't pay as much attention to him as they used to. His mother in particular is now busy with the baby 'all the time'.

These are the conditions that could foster serious problems. The older child resents the loss of his parents' undivided attention; he may begin to dislike the baby, even showing unmasked hostility. Small children cannot disguise their motives and actions. He may do all kinds of things to show anger, such as hitting or pushing the baby, pulling away the blankets, and just being plain nasty. The aggression, motivated by resentment, may take on more subtle forms. For instance, he may pretend that he is really trying to play with the baby, but he may hug it too hard or poke a finger in its eye.

Another possible reaction is what psychologists call 'regression'. The child, observing how everyone is focused on the baby, reverts to babyish behaviour himself in the hope of winning back his parents and their attention. A toilet-trained child may start wetting himself. He may begin to talk and act like a baby. All these are desperate, and not necessarily intentional, attempts of the little one to regain his lost privileges.

Not infrequently the emotional impact of the baby's arrival is so intense that the child actually becomes sick because of the stress. There is plenty of evidence that shows that bodily illness can be directly caused by emotional trauma. He may eat poorly, become irritable, lose weight, sleep badly and run fevers.

SIBLING RIVALRY STARTS

Two factors are largely responsible for jealousy in the first child: sensitivity and self-love. Neither are bad qualities in themselves, but if not handled properly, many years of sibling rivalry can blight a household.

Even when young, children are sensitive, highly observant and alert to situations that affect them. This is healthy and normal, for this sensitivity to relationships is necessary in all their life dealings and should not be seen as a negative quality. Children are usually more intelligent than we think. Sensitivity to slights, unintended though the slight may be, can hurt the delicate feelings of a child. He feels unworthy, left out, an outsider in his own home. He can't be expected to understand changes that have not been explained to him.

In any human being the faculty of love starts with the self and many years of growth are necessary before a child can even begin to consider others before himself. The second child is usually born long before this transition takes place. The older sibling naturally sees everything in terms of his own self-interest and feels threatened by the loss of privileges brought about by the new arrival; he will do everything he can to get them back.

These two normal qualities of sensitivity and self-love easily combine to create sibling rivalry. The older child, being more observant than we give him credit for, becomes jealous. On the other hand, the younger child is not going to take all this passively – as soon as she is able, she will fight back as hard as she can.

SIBLING RIVALRY GROWS

As the rivalry develops, the 'combatants' may adopt the following strategies:

- **Domination**. The older child may attempt to put the competition out of business by trying to dominate in every possible area in order to establish undisputed supremacy over his sibling. This strategy favours the older child for obvious reasons: he has a head start, he is stronger, usually more knowledgeable, and generally gets to take the first crack at whatever there is. To affirm his superiority, he may resort to belittling the younger child, to bullying, using verbal and even physical abuse.

  If this situation is not corrected because the parents are unaware or unconcerned about what is happening there can be damage to both children. It is psychologically destructive to the younger child who may suffer from a poor self-image from the constant berating and hostility, often seriously believing all the disparaging labels and insulting 'put downs' she receives, and seldom getting a fair share of anything when the bossy, older child is around. It is also unhealthy for the older child who might never make the transition from self-love to caring for others. He may remain a self-centred, resentful and jealous person for years or even for life.

- **Distinction**. This tactic is employed when the child does not strive for overall supremacy, but selects one particular way to excel, perhaps in sports or art. Or, instead, the child may seek to distinguish himself in undesirable ways by becoming a truant, a drop-out or a delinquent. The idea is that by so doing he is trying to assert himself, get attention, and 'be somebody'.

- **Giving Up**. Like all battles, sibling rivalry results in gains and losses. One possible outcome is that a sibling may simply give up the struggle altogether. Either the older or the younger child may conclude that since there is no point in keeping on with a losing battle, he or she may as well resign himself to whatever is left over. A sad defeatism is seen in families where rivalry is allowed to run its destructive course and a child completely surrenders to a more ruthless sibling.

PREVENTING SIBLING RIVALRY

Once parents understand what happens in sibling rivalry, they can do many things not only to prevent it, but to provide the means for siblings to become mutually supportive friends throughout their childhoods and beyond.

Let us return to the time of preparing for the forthcoming baby and do it another way. As things are being reorganised in the home to accommodate the new baby, both the parents and the first child must make adjustments to avoid a sudden disruption of the invisible, yet crucial, psychological balance of the family.

Getting ready for the second child

There is a tendency on the part of parents to make elaborate preparations for their first child. Nothing is held back. After its arrival, the first-born is pampered, indulged, waited on, and given all kinds of attention and toys. The baby crib is placed in the parents' bedroom and the child may occasionally even sleep with the parents in their bed. All these things are done with the best of intentions. When in due course another child who will also need love, time, and resources is expected, parents will naturally want to extend their love and care to it in the same way.

Several things can be done in the months before the birth of the second child to reduce the stresses associated with it. The parents should gradually withdraw some of the pampering and dependency that has been showered on the first-born. By doing this well ahead of time, the child will perceive these changes as a natural part of growing up and not related to the forthcoming baby. The new arrival will not then be at her 'expense'.

Now is the time for the older child to get a new 'grown-up' bed and put away her old crib which is, after all, only for babies, not for 'big kids' like her. If the child is to be moved from the parents' bedroom, this should take place several months ahead of the new arrival so that she is comfortable and feels safe in her new surroundings. Sometimes families decide to move to a larger residence and again, this should take place ahead of time. The older child should not feel that things are being taken away from her. A favourite baby blanket or lamp should not be given to the new baby. A child of two or three is not being selfish when she does not want to share, she is just acting her age. Sharing comes later, when she is emotionally secure and able to handle it. Until then she will do all she can to prevent having to give up things that she considers her own 'entitlement'.

The same kind of care should go into the relationship between the parents: as wonderful and important as the birth of a child is, it should not disrupt the bond between the partners. Provisions should be made to allow smooth incorporation of the new gift into the family so that nothing infringes on the legitimate rights of all members. The couple should still have their private times together. The first-born should still receive her ration of emotional and material support. The circle of unity should stretch a little and make room for the new arrival. Nothing should snap, nothing should drastically dislocate the loving family atmosphere.

Preparing the first child for the new arrival

There are a number of steps that can be taken to prepare a healthy emotional environment that will easily incorporate the new arrival.

- **Start talking about the new baby when the pregnancy is certain**. No child over the age of a year and a half is too young to understand at least something of the matter, and at two or two-and-a-half, a child is able to absorb a great deal more than she is able to express in words. Help her out by taking her to visit families where there are babies so she can see what they are like. Allow her to hold a few and tell her that 'her' baby is on its way, even though it will be smaller than any baby she sees. If possible, show her the hospital building where Mother will be going to have the baby. Explain that she will be there for several days, but she will telephone every day to say hello.

- **Make the whole thing a family project**. Tell her that it is just as important for her to have a little sister or brother as it is to you to have another child. Try and get her excited about the fact that she is going to have 'a baby of her own', someone who will soon be her friend for a lifetime, after it grows a little. Show her own baby pictures to her, letting her see what she looked like 'a long time ago', and tell her she also was a noisy baby and cried sometimes, but grew out of it. Have her feel the 'tummy' as it gets bigger and bigger.

Explain, in simple language, about how the baby is developing and how it came from 'seeds' from the mother and father, just like she did.

- **Praise her for being a big child now**. Parents can say, 'See how much love we put into you? That love, plus all the food, made you grow. Now there will be three people to love you instead of two. Your new brother or sister will love you, just like we do. And you are going to love that new baby, too. We're not going to run out of love because there is plenty of it for everybody – it's like air, it expands way up to the sky.'

- **Include the child in the preparation work**. For example, have her help with decorating the baby's room with her own drawings. Ask her opinion on which corner of the room you should put the crib, and have her put some of the baby's things away. Tell her, 'What would we do without you to help us?' Make her feel a valued member of the family. Explain to her that the joy that she brings you had a lot to do with your decision to go ahead and have another child. Give her the credit she deserves and make her feel good being a part of the whole wonderful event.

- **Rehearse with the child over and over again what is going to happen**. You can say, 'In the spring [or whenever] when the weather gets warmer, Grandma will come to visit us. Then Mother is going to the hospital – remember that place we showed you? She'll have our baby there and stay a few days. Then she'll come home with the baby and bring you a nice present. And then you will have another person to love you. And you can be a big help to all of us because you are the big sister. Now you tell us what's going to happen', and the parents can ask the child to repeat the story many times over the weeks. There is not likely to be any unpleasant surprises in a family that prepares an older child in this way.

- **Arrange for the child to spend time with another adult**. As the birth approaches, grandparents become especially priceless. If they are not around, another relative or close friend will do. Someone should be with the child occasionally before the birth so that the two of you can gradually cut back a little on the time that you spend with her. This way, she is not suddenly 'abandoned' when the baby arrives. Perhaps for a couple of days after the birth, a grandmother or someone else can stay with you and slowly ease out of the situation.

The second child comes home

The first few days of the siblings' relationship can determine the pattern of their future together. Establishing positive feelings from the beginning will take sensitivity and energy, but the effort will eventually prove worthwhile. Here are some suggestions:

- **Bring the older child some new toys when you bring the baby home**. You can say the toys are for celebrating the happy occasion and are gifts bought on behalf of the baby. This is the beginning of the great love the baby is going to bring to everyone as he grows up. You just helped the baby buy toys because he couldn't do it himself. This way the older child doesn't feel left out on arrival day. She is more likely to develop loving feelings towards the baby when she associates him with good things happening to herself.

  When the mother arrives home, someone else should take care of the baby while she turns her full attention to the child she has missed so much during her absence. A few hours with the child next to her while the mother rests in bed can remove the anxiety of the separation and begin to normalise the home again.

- **Have the child participate, in her own limited way, in helping to care for the baby and praise her for the help she gives**. 'The baby is so lucky to have a big sister like you who helps bring him toys. See, he's smiling at you.' This type of nurturing is an excellent way of creating affectional bonds between the two of them, a way of initiating the process of loving exchange. You help in the formation of this exchange of affection because the baby obviously cannot. Before long, however, the younger one will be able to return the love and kindness of the elder and the foundations for a close and enduring relationship will have been laid.

- **Make time to have private moments with the first child**. Naturally you will take her on to your lap, rock her, sing to her and, yes, 'baby' her a little too. This assures her that nothing has happened to displace her as a centre of your love. The 'centre' has simply become bigger. There is no need to be subtle about this: you should come right out and tell her, 'We love you as much as we did before the baby came. If anything, we appreciate you more. You're a big help to us. We've been loving you much, much longer and you have piled up more years of love than the new baby by now. But you're helping us to love him, just as we have loved you all this time. We're glad that we have you and we'll always love you.' Variations on this theme should be given on a daily basis for several weeks to firmly dispel any lingering doubts. Occasionally you'll want to talk about it again and in the future, just as preventive medicine.

- **As the children grow, always encourage team-work, co-operation and healthy striving instead of rivalry**. Be alert to signs that the older child may be dominating the younger, or that the younger is becoming too dependent. Make sure that the younger one gets his own way sometimes. The older child should not do all the talking nor should she be permitted to interrupt when the younger one is speaking. Make certain that the younger child gets a turn at being in charge on a regular basis. You may simply say, 'It is his turn now to tell us what he wants to do and we'll do what he says. All right, John, you're the leader for now.' In this way, you will instil self-confidence, allow him to vent any frustrations he feels about being the one at the bottom of the heap, and you also enforce the rule that everyone, irrespective of age and gender, is entitled to standard privileges.

For the siblings' relationship to flourish, parents must strike a difficult balance. On the one hand, they naturally want an older child to feel responsible for a younger one, to look out for his safety and teach him many valuable things. On the other hand, the older child should not become a 'third parent', reprimanding and telling the younger child what to do all the time. If you patiently explain this to both children, you can consult together on the best way to handle this delicate matter.

- **Parents should discourage tattling**, which is frequently a means of getting attention, by simply refusing to listen to backbiting. When they see that you do not respond to it, they will soon stop. Explain that saying bad things about a person is like stealing their good name and, in fact, is just as bad as stealing. Unless a child has been hurt or is in a dangerous situation, they should not 'tell' on each other. Backbiting can poison a family and its effects can last for many years.

- **Children are extremely sensitive to the way their parents treat each other**. Their parents' relationship is a model that shapes their behaviour in childhood and influences future responses to their own spouses as adults. If the mother and father are constantly engaged in a pitched battle, they cannot expect good relations between their children, who are much more likely to imitate actions than empty words. If the adults set a good example of patience and tolerance towards each other, the children will pattern their own interaction after them.

- **Revenge between siblings can spark an unhappy spiral of bad action and reaction**. One child says or does something at which the brother or sister takes offence, becomes angry and one more spiteful act results. This type of feuding can continue *ad infinitum* with acts of revenge piling on top of each other. No one can remember who started it, but everyone is made unhappy by it. If this happens, sit the two children down and tell them about the insidious nature of revenge: When a person does something in retaliation, he or she is just as wrong as the one who committed the original injury. Both actions are equally blameworthy; the only difference is the passage of time.[75] There is nothing to be gained from revenge – ever. It will not take away the harm of the first injury and it will only prolong the bad feelings of disunity.

- **Children should learn to consult** in order to be able to handle disagreement in a civilised manner. They should know how to discuss and resolve their differences among themselves as early as possible. When they understand the principles of respect, accommodation of preferences and feelings, and rational decisions based on facts, they will have less reason to quarrel. If they cannot resolve something on their own, they should go to their parents for family consultation. Open, loving and frank consultation either one-to-one or in the group can ease the tensions of sibling rivalry or even eliminate them.

- **Praise and reward them for solving a disagreement amicably**. Parents can say, 'You two are learning to talk things over well, we're proud of you. The way you both gave in a little to compromise and kept on trying until you found a solution that satisfied everyone was excellent.' Encouraging their good behaviour rather than just paying attention to bad behaviour saves trouble for parents and makes happier children. Anger, bitter arguments and physical blows have no place in our homes and we should not permit them between any family members.

- **Teach your children early on about the uniqueness of each person**. Tell them that just as each of us looks different, so do we all think and act differently. These differences are what make us interesting. Sometimes children see things in terms of 'good guys' and 'bad guys'. Explain that it is not as simple as this: just because one person is good, it does not mean the other must be bad. On the contrary, everyone is good at heart, even if they may still need to be taught right from wrong. Tell a child that as wonderful as she is, she is not the only wonderful person in the world and every child in the family wants the same things: affection, respect, appreciation, sympathy, time with their mother and father, and so on.

- **Parents should intervene whenever necessary**. When an unfriendly situation is brewing between older children, a parent can say to them, 'When you are grown-ups, you two can either become lifelong friends or never speak to each other again – then it will be up to you. Think for a minute. How do you want to remember each other? Do you want good memories or bad ones? It's much better to be friends. You two are closer in blood than anyone, even your parents, because you each have inheritance from both of us.'
  When children become too hotly argumentative, you

can separate them for a while, sending them to different rooms so they will learn that getting along and playing together is more fun than being forced to be alone. They will probably be glad when you call them to come back after ten minutes or so. If they immediately resume their bad behaviour, however, separate them again so they understand that you will not tolerate their inability to resolve their differences in positive ways.

- **Children should learn to apologise to each other when necessary and learn how to patch up a quarrel**. You can suggest that they shake hands or give each other a hug to erase bad feelings. Being able to admit that one is in the wrong is part of growing up. Even though a child might not actually regret doing or saying something, he or she can always be sorry to be the cause of disunity and apologise for it. You may want to emphasise that the child who initiates the reconciliation is not weak, but strong enough to subdue his or her selfishness and excess pride.

Sibling co-operation

Close friendship between siblings cannot be forced, but it can be encouraged as a by-product of the unity and nurturing atmosphere in the household. Let the children know that brothers and sisters can be a great help to each other throughout their childhood, adolescence and long after, understanding and sympathising with difficulties that are unique to their age group. This valuable source of comfort and insight should not be underestimated.

From the earliest days, both mother and father should spend time with each child alone, during talk-times, doing chores, or being together at any time that is suitable, even if only for a few minutes every day. The assurance of a special place in the affections of both parents will dispel many insecurities and anxieties that can affect friendships between siblings. Far from spoiling them with this attention, you will give them the gift of being capable of loving others because they themselves feel deeply loved. This assurance of worth will instil in them a spirit of optimism that will help them in subduing their selfish tendencies.

Finally, we can realise that rivalry need not be destructive: when guided and controlled, a friendly vying with one another for excellence can be healthy and can enhance a sense of pride in family accomplishments. Parents can help children channel their competitive energies towards challenges to achieve excellence, without pushing them too hard. Encourage them to thirst for knowledge, to strive for new discoveries and to aim towards the acquisition of useful skills. In this way, their healthy need for achievement and recognition can be satisfied at the same time as they are training to become the scientists, artists, craftsmen and thinkers of the coming century.

9
Psychological Well-being

The family home is not just a place where a group of people live: it also has a spirit of its own, an ambience where certain conditions must be present to create a general sense of well-being. Psychological health for both children and parents is composed of several factors which will be examined in this chapter. We will begin with truthfulness, consistency, flexibility, the capacity to admit mistakes, and the avoidance of role assignment and labelling in a family. We will then consider the ways in which reverence, prayer and meditation contribute to emotional well-being. Finally, we will discuss how humour and fun add the spice of laughter to the vitality of a healthy family.

TRUTHFULNESS

Truthfulness is the base upon which lasting and successful relationships are built. Not only is it the foundation of all human virtues, we need it as a practical matter to function in everyday life. It is hard to imagine how a family can possibly endure, much less flourish, in a corrosive atmosphere of distrust and deceit.

Unfortunately, truthfulness is sometimes discouraged and even punished within the family. Children may learn early in life that 'telling it like it is' produces unpleasant consequences for them. For instance, a child who admits to his parents that he has just discovered where the candy was hidden and helped himself is likely to receive a spanking or scolding. Next time around, even though his whole face is covered with the evidence of the 'crime', he will insist that he has not touched the stuff. He is only doing what comes naturally – protecting himself against harm. This is how people learn to lie.

What makes lying so easy and tempting is that it provides a 'quick fix', a shortcut that diffuses immediate danger. Truthfulness is often more difficult because it contains an element of risk. Over time, lying may become a dominant feature of one's character. Some people lie only when they feel they have to in order to avoid unfavourable consequences. Others may become so entrapped in the web of lying that, for them, telling the truth is abnormal. They lie even when they do not have to, merely to hone their skill!

Just about any flaw of character can be dealt with, more or less, in the context of the family, except habitual lying and deception. The husband and wife should make an early pledge to be truthful and trustworthy in their relationship. To nurture these indispensable virtues, the couple should never make telling the truth a cause of estrangement and anger between themselves, no matter how justified it may seem.

Children should also never be punished for telling the truth. They should be praised for it. But, at the same time, they should be informed of the undesirability of the behaviour when necessary. A parent can say to the child, 'Tell me what happened and I promise I won't get mad at you. I might not like what you did, and I might not want you to do it again, but we can talk about it without being angry.' Or, 'It took some courage to admit doing that. I'm glad you told me. Let's consult on what to do about it.' Without fear of harsh retribution, a child will more willingly admit to the mishaps and mistakes that have occurred before they are compounded with further errors. The behaviour can then be talked over, underlying principles pointed out and many future problems avoided.

Society at large frequently does its best to discourage truthfulness. Often the justification is that we must be tactful, socially sensitive, not speak ill of others, and so forth. Clearly, there is a fine line between being truthful and being a blabber-mouth. Being truthful does not mean shouting out everything that one knows or thinks through a megaphone. But it does require an uprightness that prevents an individual from lying, irrespective of costs.

It is fascinating to observe the developmental process of lying and truthfulness in children. Early on, they really cannot tell the difference. Gradually, they begin to learn about right and wrong as their parents point out what is truth and what is deception. With great patience and dedication, they must be taught over and over again to link what they say and what they do to a moral code that is in effect at all times, even when no one is looking, even when no one would ever find out.

Morality is not just an empty ideal; without it, there can be no complex civilisation. Without morality, human dealings become impossible, from truthfulness in commercial contracts to honesty in reporting scientific research. We cannot function without truthfulness – there could never be enough law enforcement agencies to cope with policing a society full of habitual liars.

CONSISTENCY

Consistency represents a fundamental harmony and agreement of conduct. It is like a bright sun that burns away the fog of confusion and uncertainty; it brings stability, delineates boundaries, establishes expectations, and provides for the orderly dispensing of reward. It removes capriciousness and unpredictability.

When children are treated inconsistently, they are liable to feel considerable anxiety which may lead to all kinds of physiological and psychological complications.

Never being certain of what is in store for them can be traumatic. Parental inconsistency takes many forms, ranging from mild to severe. Let us examine some of them.

Inconsistent standards of conduct

Consider the case of a child who is trying to make sense of life and its complications. Her parents have made a point of teaching certain moral principles, such as being truthful under all circumstances. Yet the child observes that her parents lie. For example, when the telephone rings and a parent says, 'Tell him I'm not home'. The child wonders what her parents really mean when they say, 'Always tell the truth'. She may conclude that they mean that one should tell the truth only when it is convenient to do so. Or do they mean that one should tell the truth only to one's parents? Maybe it is all right to tell certain kinds of lies, such as 'white lies', or 'unimportant lies', if it keeps people happy. This kind of situation is a seedbed for 'expedient ethics', a type of mentality that says, 'Suit yourself, do what feels right at the moment. Say whatever you can get away with, bend with the wind. There are no absolute standards, just go along with whatever the situation calls for.'

Inconsistency over time

Not only are parents often inconsistent in upholding standards of conduct, their own moods and behaviour may also be unpredictable from one moment to another. Consider the case of the moody individual whose temperament goes up and down like a roller-coaster. The only predictable thing about such a person is his or her unpredictability. The spouse and children, as well as others, are never sure of the current mood and what behaviour to expect. Everything hinges on the conditions of the moment. Discipline may be strict at six o'clock and permissive by seven. This keeps children in a destructive state of suspense that generates anxiety and undermines stability. Some may blame themselves for their parent's actions or even give up relying on the parent's believability and rationality at any time.

Concurrent inconsistency

An example of concurrent inconsistency is seen in the following episode. Let us look again at our earlier example of the four-year-old who runs home to try out a newly-acquired profane word on her parents. The mother and father may react with verbal disapproval but, at the same time, grin from ear to ear. Children may be little, but they are not stupid – they are much more observant and sophisticated than they seem. They pick up subtle and not so subtle cues. The child hears disapproval, but also sees the smiles. The question in her mind becomes, 'What shall I do? Is that really a bad word? If so, then why did they both smile and seem to enjoy what I said?'

FLEXIBILITY

In recommending consistency, we are certainly not advocating uncompromising rigidity in family or social relationships. Rigidity and consistency are two different things. One can be inconsistent, yet rigid. *Rigidity means doggedly holding on to a position irrespective of its merits.* Sometimes a parent will automatically say 'no' to a child's reasonable request without thinking it through. Then he or she refuses to relent, even after the request turned out to be fully legitimate. This is not consistency but rigidity.

It is very important not to be rigid in the way one responds to situations. For example, when a very young child says something untrue, the most appropriate response may simply be gently to re-phrase the whole story into the truth, instead of scolding the child. We should be flexible enough, in both our thoughts and actions, to see each situation for what it is. This type of flexibility and sensitivity is especially important with small children, who often have difficulty in distinguishing fantasy from reality. It takes a long time to succeed in separating the two effectively. What may seem to an adult to be a clear case of a small child caught in a lie may simply be the child's inability to make this distinction. Patiently pointing out fact from fiction in a reasonable tone will guide the child into learning to make those distinctions.

APOLOGISING

There are parents who would never bring themselves to apologise to a child because they fear that their authority will be undermined if they admit to making a mistake. This is unwise for several reasons.[76]

- When children hear a mother or father express feelings of being sorry, they learn to say it, too.
- Knowing that even parents can make mistakes teaches children to be more self-accepting. It reduces the probability of the child becoming an excessive perfectionist by showing that one does not have to hold oneself up to being rigidly perfect all the time.
- If a child never hears apologies, she may think that apologising is a sign of weakness. Parents can maintain their dignity and show that being wrong is not shameful – a sincere apology is an honourable way to admit mistakes.
- When a parent is out of sorts and cranky, this should be admitted to the rest of the family so no one feels guilty about causing the upset. Having a bad day can make any person irritable sometimes and it is easier on everyone else if they know they are not to blame.
- When a parent says, 'I'm sorry I hurt your feelings', it shows a child that the parent really cares how he feels,

and opens the way for a discussion of why people act as they do.

- Parents should not apologise for every little thing, only for specific acts. Apologies are not appropriate when the parent must justly discipline the child for misbehaviour.
- Apologies should be made after anger has subsided and one is sincerely sorry. It then clears the air of troubled feelings and the incident can be laid to rest.

Consistency combined with flexibility and the ability to express regret fosters an adaptable yet stable environment suited to the development of psychological and emotional well-being.

AVOIDING LABELLING AND ROLE ASSIGNMENT

Fairness is as essential to the family as the air it breathes. No one – child or adult – should be assigned a negative role or label. Calling someone a liar, stupid or careless will define that person as such, in his own mind as well as in the minds of those who hear it. Given enough labelling from others, he may become what people call him. Children believe what parents and siblings say; it is not realistic to expect them to realise that a family member 'didn't really mean that'. The damage from thoughtless labelling can be long-lasting, if not permanent.

Research has shown that labels tend to stick permanently in the minds of all who hear them, even in the face of massive evidence documenting the falseness of the label.[77] When a child is teased that he has big ugly ears, he believes it, even though his ears are no larger or uglier than those of anyone else. He may begin to feel self-conscious about his ears and wear hats to cover them. He may be sensitive about them for many years, all because he was given a label as a child.

Role assignment can also be harmful. Just as there is a

division of labour in the family along various lines, so there is role assignment to each member. Intentionally or unintentionally, families ascribe qualities and roles to their members. In a given family, Billy may be designated 'scatter-brained', Carol is the 'angel' who can do no wrong, Daddy is 'grouchy', Mother is the 'soft touch', and so on. Like good actors, the individual members go diligently about the task of becoming what they are labelled. Studies show that mental illness is often the result of negative role assignment in the family.

It is as if the family unconsciously 'decides' which member is going to become alcoholic, which one will be psychotic, which one a school drop-out, and so on. Immature parents may set this destructive process in motion by being physically and verbally abusive and by expecting the worst instead of looking for the good in their children. Every effort must be made to avoid falling into the trap of negative labelling and role assignment. No one should be designated the family loafer, the neurotic, the failure, the stupid one, and so on. Misfits are not born, they are created through injustice, neglect and disfavour.

On the contrary, everyone should be labelled positively. This approach is most effective in nurturing desirable qualities and behaviour. For example, sociable Billy can be honestly told, 'You have a wonderful knack of getting along with people'. By affirming this budding quality, we validate his talent for social sensitivity. Carol can be told, 'With your good mathematical mind, how would you like to help me with the family budget?'

Some people may object to the view that social misfits are the products of role assignment and role assumption. They may point to evidence that implicates genes and brain chemicals as the real culprits. It is true that there is some evidence which implicates genetic factors as well as brain chemicals in various forms of abnormalities. Yet there is no evidence that maladjustment is genetically programmed. By far the largest body of research into human behaviour affirms the axiom that genes predispose, but environment decides. Humans are neither bad nor good; they are only potentially one or the other, or some of both.

Consider, for example, the disease of diabetes, a disorder of glucose metabolism which is well known to be a genetic trait, passed down in families from generation to generation. Yet although an individual has the genetic predisposition to diabetes, the disease need not invariably occur. There are documented cases of identical twins in which one becomes diabetic while the other, although carrying the same inherited gene for it, does not. What is the difference? It lies in such environmental factors as eating, exercise habits, stress management, and exposure to infectious diseases. In the same way, genetic inheritance does not necessarily result in mental disability.

The emotional atmosphere of the home is the most important environmental factor which can determine whether a predisposition to mental illness ever becomes a reality. For this reason, we have emphasised throughout this book the necessity for parents to dedicate themselves to creating a wholesome environment for the education and training of their children.

REVERENCE

We define reverence as a mixture of love, respect and courtesy. Reverence should be shown to oneself, others, the whole of creation, and the Creator. Because reverence is the keystone on which peaceful, courteous and appreciative attitudes are built, it should be implanted in children at the earliest possible age. This is first done by treating *them* reverently.

It is essential that the children learn to revere themselves. Revering oneself is more than self-love and it should not be confused with the type of egotistical love called 'narcissism'. Reverence is founded on the principle that each human life has value. A person with a strong sense of self-reverence is not likely to engage in harmful, degrading and demeaning acts such as drug and alcohol abuse or sexual promiscuity. Further, he or she is far less likely to display cynicism and contempt towards others.

The family plays a critical role in fostering reverence. The mother and father must revere each other for their own sakes as well as to set an example, for they are not only the trainers of their children, they also serve as loving teachers to each other. When parents speak to their children with quiet, courteous voices, children find it natural to respond in the same way and to assume that this is a normal mode of behaviour. Reverence goes hand in hand with the concept of the oneness of humanity since people of every age, gender, racial, religious, ethnic and social background have equal human value and are entitled to courteous and respectful treatment *simply for that reason alone.*

It may be hard sometimes to be reverent towards your children when they troop in from play, covered with mud, shouting and boisterous! Even then when you are hard-pressed to remember their exalted stations as human beings as they stand there, dripping and dirtying the floor, you should try to treat them in such a way that they will not feel ashamed of themselves, but keep their vigorous joy – while they show reverence to *you* by helping to clean up!

PRAYERS

When a husband and wife eat together, the sharing of food enhances the enjoyment of eating. As well as sharing their physical gifts, they can have wonderful conversations and enjoy the humorous things that happen to them. In the same way, there is something special about praying together. It brings added comfort and strength to the union. In all religions, prayer is considered to be the food of the spirit. Without prayer, the soul starves.

The couple may want to allocate a certain block of time, preferably daily, for praying together. There is a special force of unity when prayers are said in a group. Whatever the religion of the partners, praying is helpful to every aspect of marriage, especially when the pair considers having a child. Not only is the decision to have a child reached after much prayer and consultation, prayers become a means of attracting blessings for the formation of the new family. Once conception takes place, then the couple should specifically pray for the unborn child and continue this practice of praying together after its birth and throughout life together as a family.

Even though a baby's mental and physical faculties are undeveloped, its spiritual nature is already fully present.[78] It is incorrect to assume that children do not understand prayers or that they are not ready for them. Certainly, they are not ready for prolonged, sombre sessions. But having prayers together should not be an occasion for rigid rituals and routines. These are the trappings that the children find difficult to tolerate; they are not integral elements of prayer anyway.

Love of prayer should be instilled in children early, as soon as they are able to use words. Teaching children to pray is teaching them to use the most precious of resources to nourish the soul at any time and any place. One way to encourage praying is through listening to them. It is a profoundly touching experience to hear a two-year-old pray, stumbling over some of the words, earnestly communicating with God.

We spend time caring for our physical selves every day. We wash, dress, eat, and exercise. Our spiritual selves need attention too. When we take a moment to turn to a higher power, it lifts our spirits. A brief gathering before the children leave for school, during which they choose and read short excerpts from the writings of their religion and say a few prayers, may only last four or five minutes, but it will energise and sustain them for the day. We are happier when we do this spiritual 'tuning up', forming a habit that serves us well. Instilling the love of prayer in children is giving them a gift they will cherish throughout life.[79]

MEDITATION

Meditation can be a significant way of enhancing an individual's well-being. There is no single correct method of meditation; on the contrary, if it is to yield its full benefits, it should be done in a way that is most comfortable for the individual.

Meditation means taking time out of the day in order to create an interval of quiet serenity, a mental stillness. It is an occasion for self-reconstitution, an opportunity to relax, reduce tension, and feel good. It is a means of sorting things out, promoting mental health, and cleaning the dross of daily life from the mind. It provides a break from routine and a reconnection with one's inner being, an opportunity to get to know oneself better. Meditation is also a key to the development of insight.

A busy physician we know spends one hour every morning in prayer and meditation. He seats himself comfortably, closes his eyes to shut out distractions, and meditates for a time. Then he reads brief passages from the writings of his religion and concentrates deeply on their meanings. In today's hectic life, not many people find the time to spend the first hour of their morning in prayer and meditation. How can this man do it? To him it is a simple matter of priorities. He has concluded that one hour must be set aside for prayer and meditation, and he has found the investment to be well worthwhile.

We know another person who meditates throughout the day, but not by sitting quietly. This woman meditates in brief intervals between other activities. Her morning drive to work takes 20 minutes, and instead of listening to the radio, she simply meditates with her eyes open. Sometimes she meditates when walking from one place to another: the time varies anywhere from a few seconds to some minutes. For her, this procedure fits nicely into a busy schedule. What does she do during meditation? Several different things: she recites certain beautiful phrases or words, she might bring to mind fond memories, or the faces of the people she loves.

In short, meditation is a flexible tool for personal well-being, an activity that everyone may want to consider doing. Even the very young should be encouraged to meditate, without imposing on them the 'best' method. There is no best method, there are many good ones.

LAUGHTER AND HUMOUR

A home without laughter is like a garden without flowers. It is a wonderful thing to be able to laugh – genuine, loud, prolonged, sometimes-to-tears laughter. We are all capable of enjoying this priceless gift, but a sense of humour is something that has to be developed. Some people never invest enough energy into this art and are deprived of it, others sharpen their sense of humour to near perfection.

The best kind of humour is that which does not involve having fun at someone else's expense. Unfortunately, this is the most common and the easiest form, but there are higher levels of laughter that one can attain through practice. Family humour should be free of racial, ethnic and gender degrading overtones and connotations as well as abusive language. There is a very old, very true Eastern saying: 'Teasing and mockery are the sharp scissors that can sever any relationship'.

You may say, 'Well, you just took all the fun out of jokes!' Not so. Our point is that ethnic, sexist and personally degrading jokes are little more than disguised insults. They hardly require any talent. A sense of humour which has only demeaning references to people belongs to someone with an unimaginative and lazy mind. *A good family rule: a joke or remark is funny only if no one is embarrassed or made the butt of it.* Then *everyone* can comfortably laugh, not just the jokester. With a little work, the family can develop a witty system of humour completely free of traditional demeaning comments that inflict injury on others.

We can teach each other to see the incongruities, quirks and foibles of life when we see them ourselves. In addition to its life-affirming power, humour of all types – whimsy, word-play, just plain silliness – is delightful. You don't have to try to be a first-rate professional comedian to make others laugh. Even if your jokes bring groans at first, the chances are that you will improve.

Above all, you should develop a sense of appreciation for your own humour – don't worry whether your jokes will be well-received or not. If you enjoy them, that is what really counts. After all, you are the one who has to hear all your jokes anyway! Don't worry about it. Just follow the rule of keeping your jokes insult-free, tasteful, and non-personal, and the quality will eventually come. The fact that you genuinely enjoy your own humour can be contagious. Others, even when they don't find the joke particularly funny, just by observing you laugh, will join in. We should make sure that humour permeates family life so that the children join in and automatically acquire the love of laughter.

FAMILY FUN

The family home is not just a convenient place to eat and sleep, somewhere to hang one's hat or keep the picture albums – it should be a place where you have fun together in family projects of work, games and consultation. Just being in the company of people who understand us so thoroughly is a pleasure.

Enjoy outdoor recreation together, for instance by going to the parks for picnics. Later, as the children grow, hiking together in the woods or hills, going boating, camping, exploring nature, and travelling are

priceless experiences. Many activities are free. What can
be done is limited only by your own imaginations. For
example, family fun can be as elaborate as the children
writing and producing their own plays, perhaps beginning
with dramatising nursery rhymes, or as simple as the
family singing or dancing together during musical
evenings. Or it might mean each person curling up with
a good book and a favourite snack, everyone reading, yet
cosily being together at the same time.

When our family finds its own resources for recreation,
we not only increase our enjoyment but encourage our
creativity by being active participants rather than
passive recipients. Just sitting together and watching
television is all right if the programme is especially
worthwhile, but parents should ensure that more often
than not, the family can entertain itself. Shared experiences cement family relationships. Having common
memories and experiences are like partially overlapping
existences. It creates closeness, strengthens affection and
engenders good long talks together.

Taking photographs is an excellent way to capture
those experiences and events. The picture albums become
special treasures to be enjoyed over and over again. It
serves as a re-living instrument, particularly when
grown children return for visits with their own families.

The family should not become an island and its
members inward-looking hermits. After all, there is a
larger family out there, the family of humanity, and our
lives would be impoverished if we did not form friendships
with others. At the same time, we should do things as a
family. It is not a case of either/or, it is a case of doing
both.

Enjoying the present is essential. People who always
look exclusively to some ideal time in the future to enjoy
themselves are likely to be the biggest losers. 'I'll be
happy only when . . .' means setting up preconditions
that seldom, if ever, come to pass. *In a sense, there is
really no such thing as the future. The 'future' always*

comes to us in the form of the 'present'. In the family, every day offers special occasions to rejoice in the gift of life and to have wholesome fun together. Be alert to them. Get into the habit of enjoying your family to the full because each day that passes takes with it those opportunities.

While our own children were growing up, it felt like a long, slow process, even though we had a great time raising them. We didn't know then how swiftly the whole period of living together as a family would pass. Suddenly it was all over. They grew up and went off to college far away. If you still have your little ones with you, be grateful and cherish them right now, this moment. Our lives are long, but the time together as a family is short. Savour each day, it will never come again.

10

Family Finance

People in the developed nations belong to a highly materialistic culture. Never before has there been such an abundance of things to wish for and acquire. It is not surprising that finances are often at the heart of many family problems. Let us first look at some underlying concepts which may influence how we feel about material things. These have to do with 'needs' and 'wants'. We will then address some practical financial matters.

WANTS AND NEEDS

Everyone has only a few biological 'needs' that must be met to sustain life: breathing, eating, drinking, resting, keeping body temperatures stable and avoiding physical harm. These are basic requirements that humans have been satisfying for countless years all over the planet. There are also other needs that should be met to permit people to lead happy lives, such as affection, a sense of belonging and achievement.

Biological needs can be satisfied through simple provisions. Hunger drives us to find something to eat, and when we have eaten our fill our hunger ends. The process of fulfilling physical needs works like the thermostat on a furnace. When the temperature drops, the thermostat signals the furnace to switch on and heat the house. When the temperature rises to the desired level, the thermostat tells the furnace to switch off. There is a built-in limit.

In contrast to needs, there are human 'wants'. There is a major difference between the biologically-based needs and the psychologically-rooted wants. Needs are self-limiting, but there is no end to wants: clothes, furniture, appliances, cars, trips, art objects – the list is endless. As children, we have all had the experience of looking at a storeful of toys, mentally spreading our arms and gathering them all in to take home with us. How happy we would be if we just had . . . !

It is this linking of happiness with having things that fuels our materialistic culture. We are swamped by advertising on television and radio, in newspapers and magazines, on posters and billboards. From every direction we are invited to buy, own, enjoy things which will make us better looking, more lovable, witty, and fun to be with – the implication of this unreal assumption is that 'not having' these things makes us feel as though we are bereft, unhappy and missing out on life.

The experts in advertising do their job magnificently well. They can create the desire for the products they sell in a highly efficient and professional manner, manipulating their audience in awesome ways. When consumer goods are presented through the finely crafted art of advertising, one becomes irresistibly attracted to them.

Much of the dissatisfaction that exists in families can be directly traced to behaviour motivated by the desire to 'keep up with the Joneses' – who are themselves caught in the trap of materialism. This type of enslaved mentality starts in the family and is further exacerbated by friends, relatives and the community at large. In some mysterious way material possessions have become synonymous with merit and virtue. If you are prosperous, you are therefore respectable and more worthy. Children will even sometimes feel deprived of affection if they do not receive a desired thing – 'If you loved me you'd get me that' is an underlying negative theme frequently found in the home.

Obviously, we are not saying that families should not enjoy the things of this world, or that they should sit around with long faces eating bread and water. Far from it. But we caution against becoming the captive of material wants and being imprisoned by their perpetual demands. We should refuse to become entrapped in an accelerating spiral of wants and protect our children from a lifetime of unsatisfied materialistic craving. Early on the children should be taught moderation and a proper balance. They should realise that in this material world there are some minimum needs that must be met. They should learn that making and having money is neither an evil nor the absolute standard of virtue.

Television is a major source of creating demands for advertised products. By sitting down with their children and watching television, parents can point out how advertising manipulates us; in this way the children become aware that they do not have to have everything they see as an unthinking response. Parents can explain that there are many choices in the number and kinds of products that are offered for sale in the marketplace. Naturally, each manufacturing company wants customers to buy its own products and this free-for-all competition between companies generally helps the consumer. In theory at least, the system ensures that the best products at the cheapest prices will be selected for purchase most often. But this economic principle is thrown out of kilter by the skilful use of selling techniques. Huge amounts of money are spent on advertising to persuade people to buy things. This is not necessarily bad in itself – the system has provided us with the highest material standard of living in history – but we must, no matter what our age, be careful in what we buy and not be fooled by advertisements.

It is, however, even more essential for parents to

explain that, although some are necessary, material goods are not the most important things in our lives. Certainly we can use and enjoy the material resources of the earth, but having more than we require must not become an all-consuming affair which dominates us. Parents can help their children in adopting valid expectations. There is no reason to jam children's rooms with every imaginable toy or to lavish innumerable articles of clothing on them. It is distinctly short-sighted to drown them in material luxury, even if parents can afford it. Children would be ill-prepared for future adversity if their wants were never denied.

As parents we must tell children, and believe it ourselves, that true happiness is not found in material things, in toys, clothes, or stereo sets. Our sights should be fixed on activities that bring inner contentment to us and will benefit others. To achieve this objective of finding true happiness, the first step is to keep our own wants in check.

Do your children often hear you regretfully sigh that you cannot have that particular thing that you have always wanted? Do they see you make a sub-career out of looking at ads and shopping? Do you visit rummage sales every week-end? In some places these are called 'tag sales', 'jumble sales', 'yard sales', or 'garage sales' and are proliferating everywhere as people try to make room in their houses for other, newer things. Are you a compulsive shopper who cannot walk through a store without buying something? Perhaps, instead, they see that you devote some of your time to non-materialistic activities such as community service. How you choose to spend your time tells your children a great deal about the way you feel and what you consider important.

No matter how many things we have, there will always be people who have more and we can allow ourselves to be poisoned with envy. No matter how little we have, there are many who are far less fortunate than ourselves. We should be grateful at all times because whatever we may have today may become less tomorrow. There is an ageless tale that teaches children the lesson of appreciation: 'I complained bitterly of my poverty because I had no shoes. Then one day I met a man that had no feet . . .'

Eventually, we must confront our wants and see them for what they are – illusory, frustrating, and intrinsically incapable of ever being completely satisfied. It is up to us and our children to realise that we cannot possibly have it all, even if we were trillionaires with no taxes to pay. And even if we could have every last thing on the face of the earth, it would prove a transitory pleasure, for we would then begin to build a rocket ship to look for *more*.

What we can have at this very moment is the real treasure in life, precious and golden: the deep, lasting unity and love in the family that will warm and content us as long as we exist. A home glowing with this enduring fire is rich indeed.

THE FAMILY BUDGET

Having decided that we will not dedicate our lives exclusively to the futile pursuit of material things, we still need to plan our family's finances intelligently. Here are some suggestions for you to consider.

Irrespective of how much or how little money you have, it is an excellent practice to work out a family budget, if you do not already have one. There are some people who manage without establishing any formal budgets for themselves, but it is generally a poor practice to run one's life without a well-thought-out budget, without an accurate knowledge of where the money is going.

Preparing a family budget need not be a difficult job requiring a lot of time and expertise. There are many excellent books on the subject and we particularly recommend *Make Your Paycheck Last* by Harold Moe, which has been widely praised and has gone into several editions.[80] It contains practical suggestions for organising your finances which will go a long way towards protecting your family from financial risks and troubles.

By using a budget, you are in control of where and how your money is spent and you can be freed from constant financial worry when times are normal. Arguments over money can spill over into many other areas of a couple's life and may become a cause for estrangement. With a liberating perspective on the true nature of material things, good consultation and prudent judgement, the family will find that handling their finances can be a means for bringing them closer together.

To paraphrase Mr Micawber's famous statement in Dickens's *David Copperfield* into modern terms: Annual income: twenty thousand. Annual expenditure: nineteen thousand nine hundred and ninety-nine, result happiness. Annual income: twenty thousand. Annual expenditure: twenty thousand and one penny, result misery.

In the successful family, handling the finances well will be the result of frank and loving consultation. For much of a couple's life, there will probably be two incomes. If the wife stays at home for several years to take care of small children, her lack of income should not diminish her right to share in the financial decision-making process. Marriage partners are permanently equal.

In every country in the world, there is a gap between the average amount of wages earned by men and women. In the United States women college graduates earn approximately the same amount of money as men who have less than a high school diploma. For every dollar earned by men, women earn only 68 cents. The gap is closing only at about two cents a year.[81] A similar wage differential exists in the United Kingdom and elsewhere. There are many reasons, but this disparity is partly the result of sex discrimination. A wife's smaller income should not be interpreted as a lesser effort than that of her husband. When both partners work, the stress and fatigue is the same, no matter what numbers are written on the pay-cheque. Unjust sex discrimination is beyond the individual wife's control and we can all hope that it will end soon.

Buying on credit

A great source of financial danger is the ever-increasing practice of buying on credit. This can have devastating consequences for a family that fails to exercise caution or experiences unforeseen difficulties such as redundancy or ill health. It is our view that credit purchases should be kept to the absolute minimum. There may well be justification for buying the family home and car with bank loans; external financing for higher education may also be unavoidable. Beyond that, we have serious reservations about any other credit purchases. In short, as you can see, we are not fond of the prevailing mentality of 'buy now, pay later'. The temporary pleasure gained from easy purchases seldom equals the emotional stresses of a family burdened by large debts. Beyond the irreducible necessities of life lies an infinitude of wants – no matter how rich we are, the only way we will ever have enough money to be contented is to cut down on our greed.

THE CHILDREN'S ROLE

Children of school age have a definite role to play in the matter of family finances. When appropriate they can be included in the discussion and planning of the budget during family consultation, not only to enlist their co-operation and teach them about finances, but to benefit from their valuable insights as well.

When possible, parents may want to give their children an allowance so they can learn how to handle money, as well as to cover the things they need to buy. While the allowance may be only a small amount of money, even a tiny sum for these categories can add up over time. In planning their own budgets, the children might consider at least three areas.

- Expenditures for clothes, books, recreation, and personal effects.
- Savings for future expenses such as college education, travel, and personal emergencies.
- Contributions to charitable or religious organisations. By giving to worthy causes, the child is forming permanent bonds of care with others, as well as materially contributing to the common good.

We do not think children should be paid allowances for helping with household chores. These are two separate entities and should not be connected. No one pays parents for their work around the house for the family; they do it out of love and a sense of duty – and so should children. Otherwise, what would happen if the parents became poor and had no money for these payments? Would the children then stop helping?

Money should not be over-valued. By severing the cash connection, helping with household chores is ennobled to the level of service and this takes it out of the category of a commercial transaction; it will also de-emphasise materialism. Children in the late twentieth century experience enough materialism in their culture, they do not need more of it at home. Your children will do well in the world if they have ambition and training, but they will do even better if you have taught them to enjoy, *for its own sake*, the pride of accomplishment in a job well done.

UNEMPLOYMENT AND POVERTY

It has been correctly said that twentieth-century man is a scientific and technological giant, but a moral and spiritual dwarf. Worldwide, hundreds of billions of dollars, rubles and other currencies are spent on weapons of annihilation and death, while only token attention is paid to human problems. Families are being rapidly uprooted from their traditional farms by large-scale mechanised farming; industrial workers are swept aside by automation; skilled workers are made jobless by new and more efficient technologies. We do not criticise science and technology – that is where the future of humanity lies. What we object to is the imbalance of our present order and its lack of adequate care for the individual and the family.

If permanent world peace were to be established, those governments which now allocate massive shares of their gross national product to war would be able to redirect that allocation to address the human needs of their citizens, and channel extra resources to relieve and retrain the poor. Few things can be as devastating to the human spirit as poverty, unemployment and homelessness which subject the family to tremendous strain, its very existence placed at risk. In some cases the traditional family structure falls apart. If the husband is the sole bread-winner and loses his job, he feels powerless and disenfranchised; he may even flee in disgrace, abandoning the family home. His wife and children may become wards of the government, their independence and dignity destroyed. In families where both parents are trained and work, such disasters may be cushioned if at least one salary continues. This is another reason why there should be equality of men and women in all areas of life, with women participating in income-producing work.

In addition to the financial hardship that results from unemployment, obsolescence, and displacement, these misfortunes deal a severe blow to the man or woman's sense of self-worth. Often the individual experiences misplaced guilt along with serious depression, and even self-hatred. The psychological trauma can be even more debilitating than the material losses. During such times the family needs to pull together more than ever and come to the aid of the vulnerable member, giving him or her critically-needed reassurance and encouragement. With this loving support the hard times, the tests and trials of life, become easier to bear and the family may well emerge stronger and closer than ever before.

11

Love in Action

We all need to hear the words 'I love you', but it is even more essential to see them in action. When they are experienced as loving deeds willingly given by family members, we can believe them and know that the professed love is genuine. Loving exchanges can take place within the following relationships that exist concurrently in a family:

- The husband and wife interact as a couple, if both are present in the home.
- The couple or single parent interact with all the children in the parental role.
- Each parent interacts individually with each child one-to-one.
- Each child interacts with every other sibling one-to-one.
- Other relatives such as grandparents living in the same house interact with the nuclear family as a whole and with each individual member.

In a unified home there are many kinds of things members of the family can do for each other that make love a living reality. In this chapter we discuss some fundamental components for successful family relationships: mutual reassurance and approval, verbal nurturing, affectionate physical contact and caring consideration. In the final section we deal with the work of maintaining the household, an area in which love in action can most clearly be expressed.

ASSURANCE, APPROVAL AND VERBAL NURTURING

Even as adults, the child within us is always looking for reassurance and approval. Our age does not really make much difference when it comes to this need, which is based on the desire to please, to feel loved and to excel. Not doing well generally attracts disapproval, criticism and even punishment from others, from ourselves, or from both.

In daily life sooner or later everyone does something foolish or says something that simply turns out to be wrong. For example, on a Sunday drive in the country, the husband might say, 'I'm sure we'll find a restaurant in the next fifteen minutes'. Later, when the children are nearly crying from hunger with no sign of a place to eat, the wife might be tempted to say sarcastically, 'Listen, Mr Know-it-all, I timed us. It's been an hour since you said a restaurant was only fifteen minutes away. You know, you always guess wrong. You don't have a good sense of timing about things. Remember the other day when you were certain that the supermarket would be open and it was closed . . .'

This is not only being critical, but ruthless. No one likes to be proved wrong, incompetent or stupid. The husband is bound to resent the person who made him feel ashamed and the relationship suffers. We should try to avoid overstating our position in dealing with people. If we must make a point, we should make it as gently and lovingly as possible. Instead of making the person feel inadequate and worse than they already do, the best way to deal with these cases is to be kind to the one at fault.

Despite outward appearances of self-confidence, people are often unsure of themselves and the quality of their effort; they depend on feedback and validation from others, particularly those they love and value. We all need assurance and approval, and we need them often. Life is full of uncertainty which generates considerable anxiety, and people will do almost anything to ease the burden of anxious feelings, sometimes at great cost to themselves – even to obtain only temporary relief through alcohol, other drugs or over-eating.

Many individuals never acquire a healthy and effective means of dealing with anxieties, worries, and problems because they think they will soon go away; they believe that life should ordinarily be smooth and free of difficulties. The truth is, problems and challenges are the everyday stuff of life. We should realise that we must face up to challenges and problems all along, not just occasionally, and we must concentrate on finding ways of helping those we love as well as ourselves.

It is natural to want to feel that what we are doing is excellent, passable, or at least adequate. We feel reassured if someone we love approves of our actions, since what we do represents what we are. When the sources of anxiety are specific people, as is often the case, then these people are in the best position to eliminate the anxiety. For example, a child may feel anxious about her parent's opinion of her. She is doing her best, as far as she can tell, but she doesn't know whether her best is good enough to please her parents. It is important that she be told, for only her parents can eliminate that particular anxiety. Similarly, an admired older brother or sister is in a good position to assure worthiness and relieve feelings of inadequacy for a younger child.

Family members live together in very close proximity, constantly exposed to one another's scrutiny. There is no way of insulating oneself from close attention in the intimate setting of the family home. Any pairing of family members, whether two siblings, the husband and wife, or a parent and child, can deal with this enforced intimacy in two possible ways.

The first strategy is to attempt to maintain psychological privacy and protection by building ever-greater barriers in order to maintain an emotional distance from each other. By not expecting love and approval, a person feels less disappointment and hurt when it fails to come. But building a wall is unwise because then the interaction of the two individuals can deteriorate into a defensive war of attrition, in which each combatant tries to seize the upper ground and torment the other into subjugation, so as to win at least a grudging recognition of worth.

In nearly all human interactions, there is a constant comparison and evaluation going on which is motivated by the desire to be better than others. An insidious by-product of this potent desire is that one says or does things to make another person look bad. This 'ascending by oppression' operates on the assumption that if we do not want to be dominated, then we must ourselves dominate either through words or actions. 'One-upmanship' becomes so habitual that it is acted out almost unconsciously. Put downs, belittling, sarcastic and cutting remarks can cause a potentially courteous relationship to degenerate into rudeness and alienation.

Husbands and wives can waste years of their married life in emotional distancing and futile attempts at dominating each other. What started out as a love relationship can turn into a running battle through constant criticism and self-centredness. This distinctly unloving way of communicating can have tragic reper-cussions when the children learn from their parents and use verbal or even physical abuse among themselves.

There is a second, more positive, strategy for the interaction of two family members. When they both become a reassuring source of genuine approval for each other, there is a balanced equality and reciprocity instead of a struggle for ascendancy and dominance. In this strategy, the husband and wife, brothers and sisters all realise that they are not in competition against each other, but are on the same side in a life-long team. This attitude encourages a reciprocal upward spiral of warmth and affection that increases with each exchange. We should not be afraid to show our approval and affection. It does not diminish us to say good things to a spouse, sibling or child – on the contrary, it enhances our bond to give affirmation to each other.

One aspect of showing approval, which we call 'verbal nurturing', involves family members giving one another generous but genuine amounts of praise, of a constructive nature rather than that which merely gratifies the ego. Verbal nurturing draws individuals closer together by demonstrating acceptance, assurance and love. As an instrument for positive reinforcement, it brings good qualities to the fore.

In developing and strengthening our own good qualities, we all need help from the most significant people in our lives. The positive interaction in a loving family stands in stark contrast to that of the outside world, where we usually receive prompt responses from others whenever we do something wrong. Ordinarily the school principal or the supervisor do not call us in for doing well, since doing well is expected. We are only summoned for rebuke. This makes it all the more important that we recognise and praise each other's good qualities and actions at home.

There is no need for husbands and wives to fall into a rut, taking each other for granted and letting the early fire of courtship become a pile of cold ashes – each partner waiting for the other to take the first step towards showing appreciation. Anniversaries come along too seldom to be the only time for exchanging loving words; verbal nurturing should occur daily. Be affectionate, give one another praise for specific acts as well as saying 'I love you' and 'I think you're wonderful' often. When love is supplemented with kindly words and actions, it becomes like oxygen-bearing air, preventing the death of the relationship through suffocation. The unifying power of love begins with the mother and father and expands to include the children. In a family where there is clearly an abundance of assurance, approval and love between the couple, their attitudes and behaviour are likely to influence the children, who will then go on to support and encourage each other. Such a family will flourish, develop and evolve through giving each other self-confidence and emotional security.

AFFECTION AND PHYSICAL CONTACT

There are many things that go into the making of happy human beings. Our need for intimacy means that not only do we want to know that we are loved, we want it proved by physical contact. When the children arrive, there should be plenty of physical contact: cuddling for infants and small children, walking down the street hand in hand, slipping an arm about the shoulders of older children, engaging in regular 'rough-housing' sessions, and giving backrubs. Hello and good-bye hugs and kisses are a much-loved, customary routine in many families.

In some cultures, affectionate physical contact within the family is discouraged, while in others this form of emotional bonding is widely practised. If one or both of the parents come from families that felt embarrassed about affectionate contact, special efforts should be made to overcome these inhibitions. Irrespective of cultural norms and practices, everyone needs a generous amount of this type of intimacy, beginning at birth and continuing throughout life.

Developmental psychologists working with small children have found that bodily contact is necessary for healthy physical as well as emotional development. Without it, babies can even fail to grow at a normal pace. One reason for having pets such as dogs and cats has to do with the satisfaction of this emotional need to touch. Freed from the fear of violating cultural standards, people can relate affectionately to their pets. They can stroke them, hug them, talk to them and interact with

them in a loving way.[82] These animals are live, warm
and willing sources of comfort, but they are not substi-
tutes for human beings and never can be.

In our view, physical contact expressing affection is
essential for the emotional health of family members of
all ages, from cradling the newborn in our arms to gently
patting the hand of an elderly relative. This non-verbal
expression of love assures us of our valued place in the
family and reduces the daily accumulation of stress and
tension. Children will not have to look elsewhere for
affection, either prematurely or inappropriately, if they
receive plenty of it at home.

CONSIDERATION AND CARE

Husbands and wives should actively seek ways to be of
service to one another. Naturally every marriage has its
own particular circumstances, but the overriding concern
should be to discover those things that the other
appreciates. Each one should ask, 'How can I best care
for my spouse and do those things he/she values?'

The wife may ask herself, 'What will please him?
Maybe this weekend I'll take the time to make him the
home-made soup he loves so much.' The husband may
say, 'She's had such a hard day at work; maybe I
can take the children out this evening and give her a
chance to be alone for a couple of hours.' Or, 'I like
wearing a moustache, but she doesn't like it. Well, I'll
shave it off. I care for her.' She may think to herself, 'He
likes my hair long even though it's old-fashioned and I
think I look silly that way. But he is the most important
person in my life so I'll keep my hair long, just the way he
likes it.'

These may seem like trivial things, but these little
actions, when done willingly and frequently, make for
contentment in marriage. When a great many small
items of satisfaction are added together, they can out-
weigh several large items of dissatisfaction. In the day-

to-day dealings of a husband and wife, there are not many chances to do 'big things' for each other, but there are opportunities to do small, pleasing kindnesses, like fountains constantly giving and being refilled. This type of love-in-action is a way of cementing the relationship to keep it safe from the inevitable periodic shocks that can tear less unified marriages apart.

Care and consideration in the family should not be confused with the often shallow practice in certain cultures of exchanging gifts on every imaginable occasion. This form of 'caring' may even produce the opposite effect: it may encourage individuals to feel hurt because, rightly or wrongly, they believe that they were not given the gift they deserved, that the gift was only a token to discharge an obligation, that it was less expensive than the one they gave, and so on. The financial drain can be substantial and, rich or poor, the gift givers and receivers seldom feel satisfied.

We know a family with older children that has stopped buying gifts entirely. Instead, they give things they make themselves, such as a drawing of a favourite place, a brief poem or quotation which someone has copied in calligraphy and framed, or other things that have no monetary value. Even birthday and holiday greeting cards are home-made, as funny or sentimental as the sender wishes. Removing the pressure to 'out-give' each other has been an enriching experience for the entire family. Caring and consideration should be an integral part of everyday life; family love should not be expressed only in material exchanges on special occasions.

In the successful family, everyone is concerned with each other's welfare without making it an all-consuming chore. There is a feeling, a certainty, that one is loved and cared for, that one's legitimate preferences and personal eccentricities are accommodated, that home is truly home, that being with one's family is the most cherished experience.

HOUSEHOLD WORK

In addition to maintaining emotional well-being in the home, another essential aspect of love-in-action is the performance of the day-to-day household tasks which are necessary to sustain the physical well-being of the family through nourishing meals and clean surroundings. Unfortunately doing work is not something that comes as naturally to people as breathing. Everybody likes to play, everybody likes a 'free ride'. Work is generally shunned, unless there is some good reason for doing it.

People are usually best motivated to work by linking it to some sort of reward. Work performed for others outside the home is rewarded by money; unpaid work within the home is rewarded by expressions of appreciation and recognition of its worth by the family. The best reward for work of any kind is the deep satisfaction a person feels at having done something useful; the belief that any work performed in the spirit of service to others is a form of worship, is a high moral principle which can also be a strong motivator.[83]

Even though this concept was expressed in the mediaeval Latin phrase *'Laborare est Orare'* which means 'to work is to pray', the prevailing mentality in the past was exactly the opposite. Work was the duty of the lower classes: the slaves and peasants. The gentlemanly thing to do was to avoid it. Today, in nearly every country in the world, the cherished ideal of the leisured class has vanished. Aristocratic titles may remain, but they are likely to belong to people who have careers and hold jobs. No longer are the wealthy called the 'idle rich' these days because they are, more often than not, hard-working executives and professionals. Here again, we can see the result of the oneness of humanity concept: no one is exalted above another – all should contribute.

Once a family subscribes to the notion that work in the spirit of service to others ranks with worship, everything changes. In this kind of home, people stop trying to take advantage of others to do the least amount of work; they begin to pitch in and help because they feel better about themselves when they share responsibilities with the others. Productivity increases while idleness, time-marking, and free-loading disappear. Everyone stands to gain from such a mentality. In this healthy, co-operative family atmosphere, each member guards vigilantly against anyone carrying a disproportionate share of the work. At the same time no one, young or old, is deprived of the opportunity to contribute significantly to the maintenance of the household.

When it comes to work, children are not exempted. While still very young they should learn that doing useful work is part of being a worthy person. When children are not asked to do anything, parents convey a silent message that they do not consider them to be capable; children may feel valueless because no one expects them to do valuable work. Actively recruited to work in accordance with their maturing capabilities, however, children come to take work seriously and consider it an integral part of their existence, taking pride in being useful members of the team. Sociologist George Vaillant has written that the most important forerunner of mental health in adulthood is the willingness to work in childhood.[84] A thriving family does not create conditions that foster laziness, encouraging spoiled and pampered children to become like sponges, always taking in and never giving out.

When the children are very young, it is easier for the parents to do the work than to ask the little ones to do it. But taking the easy way out in this matter is shortsighted. It is well worth the effort and time to teach a child about useful work at the earliest age possible. Not only does it build good character, it prepares a helpful member of the family for many years to come.

To teach a child to enjoy work, parents must first show by their own example that they believe in helping others. Do you complain and groan when faced with adult tasks?

Or do you attack them with enthusiasm? Do you procrastinate or even 'run out on the job' when it is time to do something? Your own attitude towards work will be copied by your spouse and children. The way we deal with work affects the atmosphere surrounding it; when we use praise and encouragement with each other, instead of scolding and harsh words, we are all far more likely to work cheerfully at our tasks.

What can very young children do? Start with small things. For instance, ask a child to hold your keys while you are shutting the door. Of course, you do not really need someone to hold your keys, you can just put them in your pocket. But you want the child to feel the pride of being helpful to you and to enjoy receiving the hearty thanks you will give. Later, ask the child to fetch things for you. Remember that children are in constant motion and love to move about. So we capitalise on this and direct it to useful activity, making sure our request falls within their capacity to perform it.

With their short attention spans and inability to stay with a task for long, young children should be given assignments they can finish quickly, simple chores that will earn them immediate praise and satisfaction, and which they can learn to do well in only a few attempts. When taught to do simple tasks at three, four, or five, they will be enthusiastic. Even a child of six can dust, fold the laundry, wash vegetables and fruits, sweep with a broom, set the table and do many other things as well. They will feel more capable if they know they will not be criticised for getting a task wrong the first, second or even third time. You can then systematically teach them further skills so they will soon feel able to tackle more complex duties with confidence. Children should never be shamed when they have done something poorly, but gently asked to do it again. You can say encouragingly, 'That wasn't easy, but you'll learn it in time. I'm glad to have such a good willing helper around here – let's do it once more now and see what happens.' Even though the initial performances will be less than perfect, if we keep willingness high through positive reinforcement and the tasks attainable, improvement will come in time.

Chores

As long as people live in a household there will be 'maintenance' chores that no amount of gadgetry and time-saving tools will ever completely eliminate. They are seldom matters of life and death but they accumulate and never go away. In every home someone still has to do the housework. In the past, women have always been in charge of certain domestic matters such as cooking, laundry, cleaning, sewing, bathing children, putting them to bed, telling them bed-time stories, singing them to sleep – all known as 'women's work'.

Suddenly, there is change. Yet the woman who now works outside the home in a responsible and stressful job is still expected to do all 'her' household chores as usual. And the woman who interrupts or even sacrifices her career to undertake the valuable but exhausting task of caring for very young children is constantly distracted by the endless demands of running the household without help from anyone. She did not lose her salary and career advancement just to stay home and clean the house, but to act as a first teacher to her child during those precious early years when so much emotional and intellectual development takes place. In the interest of fairness, the situation calls for adjustments. All maintenance chores must be assessed and redistributed among the family members.

Both husband and wife must look on marriage as an equal partnership based on the principle of fairness. The labour, the losses and gains are split right down the middle. Nothing less than an equitable arrangement makes for a successful and happy family. There are no genetically determined, gender-specific abilities when it comes to doing household chores. Women do not have a 'cooking gene' nor do men have a gene for repairing the family appliances. It is all in the culture, tradition, and the old standard way. If a woman is mechanically inclined, why shouldn't she be the 'grease monkey' of the family? If a man loves to cook, why shouldn't he? Most people are not affluent enough to hire servants, therefore the husband and wife, as well as other members of the household, must do their full share of the work with little regard to the predetermined roles.

This is one area where women usually have much more expertise than men and sometimes it may be tempting to play the role of 'the authority'. Even though she may be completely unaware of it, a wife can sabotage many future years of sharing work with her husband by making belittling remarks or, worse, saying, 'Here let me do that'. It may not be easy for a woman to give up sovereignty in domestic matters, but it is much better to have the household managed by 'co-presidents' when the children are young and then through family consultation when they are older. Positive reinforcement and affectionate appreciation of all efforts is necessary to bring husbands and children into full participation with housework.

It is helpful to develop a chore list. What follows is a basic checklist of chores found in a typical household in the developed countries, but its general categories can be applied to the households of any culture. When allocating responsibilities, the frequency of the chore (daily, weekly or as needed) and how long each chore takes to complete should be taken into account.

- Food preparation
    - Planning meals
    - Shopping
    - Cooking
    - Setting and clearing the table
    - Washing dishes

- Cleaning
    Vacuuming or sweeping
    Washing floors and bathrooms
    Dusting and putting things away
    Washing windows, vacuuming furniture and cleaning curtains
    Washing the car
    Cleaning the stove, refrigerator, cupboards and closets
- Laundry
    Sorting, washing, drying, folding, ironing and putting away
- Exterior and interior house and car maintenance
    Painting
    Gardening
    Repairing small appliances
    Car repair

The above list is just a start; every family has its own routines and schedules for these tasks. As much as possible, personal preferences should be taken into consideration when assigning chores. Particularly onerous jobs should be rotated regularly so that no one is burdened with an unpleasant chore for too long. Family consultation is the way to ensure that agreement is reached fairly. Specific chores should be given to all family members, young or old; even those with limited abilities can be responsible for something that will help the common weal.

Each one should clearly understand his or her tasks and be taught to do them well. In a setting where there is confusion and no one is really sure what to do, maintenance chores either go unattended or are loaded primarily on to one family member. The immediate result is that justice and fairness are violated and the entire foundation of the family is undermined by transforming it from the egalitarian, supportive, participatory system it should be to an exploitive, oppressive, unjust institution.

The best way for children to become useful, contributing individuals is through the 'hands-on technique' rather than by watching their mother and father do things. By actually cooking, children develop an appreciation of what it takes to put an edible meal on the table. By sorting and washing, they learn where clean clothes come from. They may then have a realistic and appropriate picture of life as a workshop, a serious yet enjoyable undertaking that requires useful contributions from everyone.

The chore list should be occasionally revised, not too frequently to cause confusion, but frequently enough to allow for the rotation of tasks. There are few chores that only one person can do. In deciding who should do what, the fact that the mother cooks the best, for instance, should not be the sole determinant of her assignment. It is often desirable to assign a particular chore to someone who is not proficient at it, so as to afford them an opportunity to master the task or lose an aversion to it. Ideally everyone should take their turn at all household duties to learn skills useful for a lifetime.

As much as possible, a two-person team approach to chores should be adopted. Doing things together not only increases the proficiency of younger children, but tasks are more enjoyable and finish much faster when done by a pair of workers. It increases the time spent in each other's company and allows for the sharing of the fruits of common labour. For instance, there is no reason why the husband should prepare a meal by himself while the wife cleans the house. The two of them can carry out both tasks much more companionably together.

A parent and child can have many delightful talk-times doing useful things together in the kitchen or elsewhere in the house. One family we know solved the problem of tidying up the children's rooms. A parent comes in every night before the child goes to bed. Chatting and picking up things together, the two of them tidy the room and strengthen their affection at the same time. Work time is quality parenting time, too.

Certain common household chores should be done by the entire family as a project: organising the basement or the attic, gardening, spring-cleaning and a host of other such activities. This strategy reduces the drudgery and loneliness of doing the unpleasant yet necessary work. Playing music or singing speeds the time along and a game or some other reward might help to celebrate when the chores are over.

These days no one should be expected to work full-time at a job outside the house and then be completely responsible for everything at home, not even single parents. Through consultation, the family can put its considerable combined brain power to work to improve efficiency and reduce the number and extent of chores considered necessary. For example, a family may want to do elaborate cooking only at weekends and be contented with simple but wholesome meals during the week. Or everyone might have enough clothes to be able to get by if the laundry is done only every two weeks instead of weekly. When curtains and furniture are vacuumed to remove every trace of dust and the floors are scrubbed to a shine, the house will stay clean much longer. Always remember: your home belongs to *you* – the standards and requirements of other people should not over-influence your decisions.

Children who are part of the pick-up crew will have less trouble remembering to put their things away. The basic principle of unity is felt here. It can be a happy time when the parents and children work together to clean and beautify their home together. When everyone does housework at the same time and then relaxes together afterwards, undercurrents of anger and resentment at being taken advantage of do not have a chance to develop. *A basic philosophy of 'work at the same time, play at the same time' makes the whole business more fun for everyone.*

Many men have not been raised to do housework and it may be difficult for them to do it at first. Old stereotypes

die hard: a man may even feel that he is compromising
his manliness. In our view, however, it is far more manly
for a husband to want to share responsibilities than to
shirk them, to be fair rather than to take advantage of
someone. Even more important, a husband will find that
living with a happy, relaxed wife is preferable to one who
is constantly overburdened and angry. It is always to
one's own advantage to ensure the contentment of one's
partner.

In the interests of justice, we must rethink the whole
process of creating a home. Wives who have careers are
not just temporarily helping out with 'his' finances, nor
are husbands just helping out with 'her' housework
whenever she needs assistance. It is a fact of our time
that in many households there are now two bread-
winners and two household managers. Ours is the first
generation to experience this fundamental change and
the adjustments are not easy. But, frankly, we think it is
a better way of life, and one which has many advantages.
The husband has someone to share the burden of
financially supporting a family and the wife no longer
feels deprived of the chance to use her abilities in the
larger world.

Love in action is love that lasts and earns its keep.
With consultation and a commitment to fairness, couples
who learn to work together experience less tension and
become closer in their partnership. When the children
are included in sharing responsibilities, love grows even
deeper as mutual contentment surrounds the well-cared-
for home.

12

Problem-Solving

Families without problems do not exist in the real world
and they never will. There are simply too many difficulties accompanying each childhood developmental phase
from infancy to late adolescence. At the same time,
parents themselves are also coping with several stages in
their own lives, as they usually pass from late youth,
when their first child is born, to middle age by the time
their youngest child leaves home.[85] When these normal
challenges are augmented by the increased stresses of
the present time, it becomes clear that every family
needs to acquire positive ways of problem-solving.

Sometimes the source of a problem lies within the
family itself, quarrelsome parents, for example, and
sometimes it comes from outside, such as moving to a
new city or even to a new country. In this chapter we will
first look at reducing problems which can be avoided,
optimising personal attitudes towards unavoidable problems, controlling stress and relating to reality in healthy
ways. In the final sections we will examine several
specific approaches to problem-solving.

REDUCING AVOIDABLE PROBLEMS

Naturally the best way to handle problems is to prevent
them occurring in the first place. Whenever possible, the
successful family should have consultation on future

events so as to anticipate any potential difficulty. For example, if you know in advance that a new person will be joining the household – perhaps an infant, step-sibling, step-parent or grandparent – the family members can consult to explore all the ways to make the transition easier, both from their own and the new person's perspective. The necessary adjustments in physical arrangements, the emotional and psychological elements to be accommodated – all these things can be examined ahead of time. Also, annual, semi-annual and monthly plans can be consulted upon with goals set, information gathered and skills learned in advance to head off many problems.

You may want to have some 'what if . . .' consultations, in which you look at a problem that another family has, perhaps one you have read about in a newspaper, and see what kind of solutions your family can generate. 'What if' consultations should involve problems which are not too remote, and which present a real spur to creative solutions. A few practice runs of this type will increase the group's confidence in being able to cope with real troubles when they arise.

UNAVOIDABLE PROBLEMS AND PERSONAL GROWTH

No matter how conscientiously we plan ahead, there will still be times when problems arise. When that happens, our attitude and immediate reaction to the very existence of the problem can be a crucial factor in summoning up the energy and clarity of mind to solve it.

Ask yourself some questions. Do you look on a problem as punishment, blaming yourself for it even if you didn't cause it? Do you see yourself as unlucky, as if a cloud were always hanging over you? Do you feel paralysed by the thought of coping with the problem, feeling that the effort required is just too much? This negative outlook practically guarantees failure at the outset.

There is another, more positive way to look at troubles when they come to us. First, we should cease to waste energy on guilt or self-pity. Rather than viewing the problem as 'just one more rotten thing to deal with' we should look upon it as potentially valuable. Although troubles and misfortunes are difficult to go through at the time, in retrospect we often recognise them as learning experiences and opportunities for growth.

If we believe that a major purpose of our existence is to acquire and practise the positive human virtues, then clearly it is not the problem itself but how we handle it that really matters. Life is a school where we learn to develop our higher qualities, such as compassion, kindness, generosity and patience – they really are what define us. We have these virtues only to the extent that we have taken lessons from our good and bad experiences. When we have to deal with a difficult person or situation, we can view it both as necessary to our growth and as a means of realising where we are in our personal development. If never given a test of strength, how can we recognise and overcome our weaknesses? With no situations requiring us to be patient, how can we ever learn or understand patience? Without having to care for others, how would we ever develop compassion?

Taking a test and rising to the challenge represents advancing to the next level of proficiency. If people are unaware of this profound process of drawing wisdom from tests and only see difficulties as punishments or 'bad luck', they lose valuable opportunities for growth as well as a psychologically healthier outlook on life. Each of us is continually tested in our own personal way, and although we may never advance to the point where we will honestly welcome such tests, we can recognise their usefulness and be much more accepting of them. This acceptance by itself can reduce the anxiety that freezes us into inaction; it enables us to gather the energy to meet adversities and overcome them.

STRESS

There is considerable medical evidence to show that the mind and body are inseparably connected, each influencing and affecting the other.[86] When we are under extreme stress, our hearts speed up. Adrenalin, sugar, fats and cholesterol pour into the blood stream; respiration becomes fast and irregular; blood is directed away from the stomach and intestines to the brain and muscles; the stomach secretes more acid and sweating is increased. At the same time, the immune system slows down. This is the body's way of mobilising its resources to meet both real and imagined dangers or threats. Dr Hans Selye of Canada and others have shown that under stress, the interconnected system of the mind and body prime the heart and muscles for action, either to fight or to run away – hence, the name 'fight-fright-flight response'.[87] We can also feel stressed from exceptionally happy events.

Everyone experiences stress at times. When it comes in small, infrequent doses it does no harm.[88] In fact, we need some stress to stimulate us, to make our lives interesting, to learn to deal with our environment more effectively, and to prod us to greater achievement. However, when the stress response occurs too strongly, consistently and without relief over a period of time, the body can be adversely affected. A major trigger of harmful stress is negative emotion. Feelings of hostility and anger should be avoided as much as possible because they contribute to a detrimental level of stress. So it is not only virtuous to control anger and irritability, it is actually good for your health! We noted earlier that constant irritability around children resulted in their increased fighting and misbehaviour; here we point out that parents should avoid anger for the sake of their own mental and physical well-being.

What makes a situation or job stressful? Different individuals have different susceptibilities to stress. Two people can have identical training, intelligence and job responsibilities and yet react quite differently. One will see the work as highly pressurised, another will see it as undemanding and even rewarding. As beauty is in the eye of the beholder, stress is in the mind of each one of us.

Controlling stress

How can we reduce stress? Social support from family and friends, physical exercise and a strong constitution all help. Psychologist Suzanne O. Kobasa, in her extensive studies of the subject, has defined three positive tendencies that combine to produce a psychological 'hardiness', which helps to reduce the perception – and thus the existence – of stress:[89]

- **Commitment to self, work, family and other values**. For example, not being committed to the value of good parenting can make being patient with children a strain.
- **A sense of personal control over one's life**. Its opposite is feeling helpless and not the master of one's circumstances. A family can greatly reduce its stress by feeling in control through the use of consultation for planning and conflict resolution. Family members can also relieve tension through active deeds of caring and concern.
- **The ability to see change as a challenge or opportunity instead of as a threat**. When a family is flexible and competent in dealing with change, its children will be less fearful in the face of situations calling for courage and adaptation.

Many people think of stress as principally affecting corporate executives who live in fast-paced cities. Actually, because executives have more self-supervision in their work, they are less likely to suffer from stress than their secretaries, or others who have jobs with little security, status or control.[90] Likewise, although urban life is commonly seen as stressful, those who live in the country are as susceptible to stress as city dwellers.[91]

Current research indicates that no one is inevitably condemned to react negatively in a potentially stressful situation.

> Merely adopting a positive attitude toward problems or difficulties may prevent the tilt in body chemistry that harms immunity ... if you create a way of dealing with the event mentally, it decreases your chance of being negatively affected.
>
> [Events should] be categorised according to a person's perception of them: good or bad, controllable or uncontrollable, predictable or unpredictable, intense or mild.[92]

It is not the problem, the job, the place and so on which is fully responsible for stress. Each one of us chiefly determines whether something will be stressful to us or not through our own mind set or personal attitude. For instance, if we don't train ourselves out of it, we can spend our whole lives being critical of everything and everybody. It is possible to avoid this by developing mental faculties that allow us to accept the situations and encounters with people that come our way and transform them into constructive and enjoyable experiences. Truly, the world is a mirror of ourselves. If we look for the good in people and situations we will find it.

Aside from developing psychological hardiness and changing our attitudes, what else can we do to guard against stress? We can become aware of the heavy 'mental suitcases' that we all carry around with us. Whether we are conscious of them or not, each of us has worries which load us down like excess baggage. Most troubling are the unexamined free-floating anxieties that keep us in a perpetual state of tension. It helps greatly to identify the contents of each of your mental suitcases and then drop as many as possible. Even those you can't jettison completely can be opened up and the load lightened with rational assessment and a positive attitude. When emptying our suitcases, we should ask ourselves: how much do we allow ourselves to be bothered or stressed by trivial things? To what extent are we dependent on other people and material things to make us happy? We should learn to rejoice in insignificant things – to be happy here and now instead of making detailed pre-conditions for a time when we will *finally* permit ourselves to relax and be happy – a far-off day that may never come. Each time you set a piece of luggage down, you will feel physically and emotionally relieved; your whole system will then be able to recover and unwind.

As a defence against stress, the parents should infuse themselves, each other and their children with regular doses of realistic optimism, enthusiasm, and appreciation of life. Attitudes are contagious: an enthusiastic and friendly person makes others feel good too. Four thousand years ago, an Egyptian vizier named Ptahhotep understood that life is borne more easily with a smile when he said, 'Be cheerful while you are alive'. Science today is in effect telling us, 'Be cheerful and live longer'.

PERCEPTION AND REALITY

Central to effective problem-solving is the way we deal with 'reality' and 'facts'. We should be aware that even 'facts' are, in most cases, only approximations. After all, both fact and fiction are perceived solely through the mind. And the human mind is anything but an unemotional, objective computer. Perception is a mental function which involves gathering information and assigning meaning to it, necessarily a subjective and personal process. Even the seemingly objective business of fact collection can be selective and subjective according to individual biases. What are the implications of this? Is there no objective reality 'out there' that two or more people can agree on? Perhaps one of the most definite points of agreement must be that 'reality' is illusive, imprecise, deceptive and relative. In jest, we may say that half of the time we misperceive things and the other half we misunderstand them!

The perceptions of two human beings are never identical, although they may be extremely similar. A useful comparison is the way our eyes work together. The right eye sees an object from one angle, the left eye from a slightly different angle. Each eye sends visual signals to the brain, which merges the two different images into the three-dimensional picture that we perceive. In the same way that the brain reconciles the two slightly different images, the perceptions of each person merge with those of others into a generally held version of reality. Although people's perceptions are never completely alike, they are usually close enough for practical purposes. This similarity in perception constitutes what people define as 'objective reality', or what is 'actually out there'. If it were not for this facility of reconciliation, of give-and-take, of adjustment of differences – within the minds of individuals as well as among people – there would be no basis for agreement and no objective reality.

Psychologically, every person is unique; even twins who are genetically identical have different experiences from one another. All these differences in experience combine to make up the perceptual individuality of each person. This uniqueness of perception is neither bad nor good – it simply exists and we must accommodate it. Therefore, you have to deal with all other people, including spouse and children, with the clear understanding that:

- Your own perceptions belong to you alone.
- Others may not see things from your point of view.
- Generally speaking, the perceptions of other people are just as valid as your own and should be respected.

If there are a great many common elements in the
perception of a group of people, there is harmony and
togetherness. When there are few common perceptual
elements, there is disagreement, possible alienation and
even confrontation, unless real efforts are made to see
things from others' points of view. The way one sees the
world not only depends on what is really 'out there', but
also on how the mind perceives and interprets it. The
person then chooses his or her reaction based on that
interpretation.

At the heart of most interpersonal problems is the
simple fact that two people are not seeing a particular
issue in the same way: both people assume that their
view is not only correct, but shared by the other. When
they discover a disagreement, each is surprised that
anyone could possibly see the situation in another way.
Sometimes the conflict is resolved successfully. At other
times, even though the issue may be trivial, the disagreement can develop into a row.

The important lesson to learn from this discussion is
that, on any given issue, neither your views nor mine
necessarily represent the absolute reality and truth. We
can be both equally wrong, equally right, or somewhere
in between. By remaining flexible, accommodating,
tolerant and appreciative of other people's points of view,
we can short-circuit the whole process of fruitless
argument and conflict.

Regulating perception

Since an essential aspect of problem-solving is the
perception of things, events and people, the individual
should be aware that it is actually possible to learn to
regulate perception. We can think of perception as
operating like a radar apparatus with a revolving beam
that scans the field and reports its findings. It can detect
all kinds of objects and can be adjusted to focus its search
in the short, intermediate or long-distance ranges.

An individual's perception scanner can be directed to focus on any one of the three fields: the external or long-distance field which represents paying attention to the 'outside world'; the intersect or intermediate range field, which represents the overlap of the person's inner awareness and the outside world; and the internal, short range field which represents the person's inner awareness alone. When people are awake their perception scanners, like beams of radar, search the various fields and detect items of interest.

For instance, as you focus your attention on a lovely sunset you may fail to notice other things around you, even forgetting your severe headache. It seems to go away while you are absorbed in viewing the beautiful scene because your perceptual scanner is focused on something in the external field, not on yourself. In other situations critical for our well-being, the perceptual scanner should be set on the intersect field. For instance, crossing a busy road we must pay close attention to oncoming vehicles and adjust our movements so as to avoid them safely. Focusing on the intersect field is our way of dealing with matters of the outside world that can directly affect us – things which usually require some sort of active response. An example of focusing the scanner on our internal field – thoughts and memories – is when we reactivate a pleasant memory from the distant past by bringing it to the centre of our awareness and spend a few moments reliving it deep in reverie.

Sometimes an individual makes no conscious effort to direct the perceptual scanner to any specific item or to any particular field. The scanner then goes on auto-pilot and just wanders around until something attracts its fancy. Irrespective of whether something is consciously chosen or randomly picked up, however, the 'item' becomes the main business of the mind's 'awareness zone'. Once in the forefront of consciousness, it is examined, understood and classified. The mind processes and disposes of it in order to clear the field for the next piece of business.

Our complex perceptual mechanism is dependent on the physical integrity of the brain as well as on our experience. If we experience an emotionally powerful situation, our perception of the actual events can be affected. If something interferes with the normal functioning of the brain, our perceptions can also become distorted. For example, alcohol consumption alters the chemical environment of the brain and results in perceptual distortions. Some of these effects are transient while others may be long-lasting. Well-known temporary effects are varying levels of intoxicated behaviour. The long-lasting consequences for the brain are not so well known – they may involve irreversible damage or even loss of brain tissue.[93]

We all develop a uniquely individual private mechanism for perception at the heart of our frame of reference. This determines our outlook on life, the dominant field of our attention, the type of items selected for treatment in the limited field of awareness, the length of time and amount of energy invested in each item and the way each is dealt with and catalogued.

Provided that the perceptual mechanism is not seriously incapacitated through disease or injury to the brain, an individual can correct and improve perception in various ways. First, a person's scanner reflects the condition of his or her frame of reference; one that is most useful is firmly-grounded in human spiritual and ethical values, knowledge and the acquisition of useful skills; respect towards all people; and reverence for other living things. The incorporation of all the above into one's daily actions and attitudes is critically important to the quality and success of life. Therefore, if any of the above ingredients are absent in our frame of reference, this will influence the scanner and we will want to take steps to correct the situation. Working on perfecting our scanner is a lifetime job.

The second way to improve perception is to divide the attention of the scanner equitably among the external, intersect and internal fields. All three domains are important to the individual and must receive their fair share of notice and evaluation. For instance, it is not healthy over the long run for one's consciousness to remain exclusively fixated in the internal field – people labelled 'schizoid' focus their scanners primarily on their inner-selves. Frequently, this condition is an early warning sign that full-blown mental breakdown is just around the corner. Similarly, a scanner set to focus only on the external field is likely to create other problems by not allowing the mind to organise itself and attend to a person's contemplative needs.

When consciousness is basically confined to the inter-sect field, there may also be problems because an individual may be viewing everything in the universe only as it pertains to him; his perceptual mechanism is locked-in on only those things of direct interest or relevance to himself. Everything else is nothing more than a passing distraction from his obsessive self-preoccupation. Examples of this are everywhere. We can all think of someone we have met who seemed personable enough at first but after a while revealed an annoying personality quirk. Every time you say something about yourself or someone else, he brushes aside those state-ments as quickly as possible and starts talking about himself. You might say, 'I just visited the most beautiful little town last weekend', and he immediately interrupts by saying, 'Speaking of beautiful little towns, you should have seen the one I visited last summer . . .' Then he goes on to tell you all about it. Obviously, we are all guilty of this type of behaviour sometimes. After all, everyone has an ego. Yet, most people are mature enough to strike a balance in conversations. Some even develop the capacity of listening to things that bore them to death out of sheer courtesy to others.

The inability to step out of oneself, to abandon the ego

temporarily and to become absorbed in the views or anecdotes of others represents perceptual defectiveness. We should become aware of what happens when our scanners are stuck in the intersect field and take conscious steps to correct it.

The third way to improve the quality of the perceptual scanner is to deliberately select positive things for the awareness zone whenever possible. Somehow, the natural tendency of the scanner is to home in on negatives. This is understandable and has a certain degree of survivalistic value, because the negative items are the ones that are likely to hurt us if they go unnoticed. For example, it is clearly unwise and possibly fatal to continue to enjoy the beautiful scenery of your safari (a positive item in the external field) while ignoring a hungry lion which is looking at you with interest (a negative item in the external field). But it is equally inappropriate to choose to pay attention to a row of rubbish bins when you are strolling down a street instead of noticing the birds singing and the blossoms in the trees.

Make a conscious effort to avoid unnecessary negative items as much as possible. This positive bias is not the same as burying your head in the sand (or in the clouds) and ignoring genuine concerns. Deliberately developing a positive perceptive mechanism will release your mind to be far more creative and constructive, rather than to dwell on the negative things in life. A healthy frame of reference almost automatically shuns those negative thoughts that can needlessly depress and inhibit you.

Lastly, there are times when the best thing the scanner can do is avoid bringing anything at all into the awareness zone, and actively expel any perceptions or ideas that manage to sneak in. This is important to rest the mind. It doesn't have to be long – a few seconds or a few minutes at a time are often sufficient. Freeing your conscious mind for short periods from the usual bombardment of thoughts and perceptions gives it a useful respite. At first you may have difficulty but with practice you can achieve it. Simply close your eyes, expel any thought that intrudes, and enter a state of mental stillness for a moment. Gradually you can learn to sustain this form of meditation for several minutes.

It is worth the effort to improve the quality of our scanners, to organise, enrich and fine-tune them, because after all we live largely in our minds. This being so, many perceived problems are merely the creations of our minds and can profitably be dismantled.

APPROACHES TO PROBLEM-SOLVING

Consultation can be used to solve nearly any type of problem, but in some circumstances you may want to use another approach. In the remaining sections of this chapter we will discuss several different ways of addressing problems. The nature of the difficulty itself and the personalities of the individuals involved will influence the appropriate choice.

The confrontational approach

Confrontation tends to be over-used in our society as a way of dealing with conflict. We recommend that family members use other approaches which hold much greater promise of peaceful settlement.

Confrontation has its genesis in a combative mentality. There are people who have a habit of looking for trouble unnecessarily; whenever they find something with the slightest potential for becoming a problem, they quickly see to it that it becomes one. By relentlessly ferreting out misunderstandings in the hope of resolving them, they think they will improve their personal relationships. Focusing on points of contention rather than areas of agreement in interpersonal conflicts, they may say, 'Let's isolate the issue and sharply define it. Where do we disagree, what are our opposing positions?' They justify this approach by reasoning that it eliminates ambiguity and pinpoints the problem. But by provoking possessiveness and egotism in people, additional, more serious trouble is created which forces the parties to adopt adversarial positions and defend them to the bitter end. Once the stubborn wills and egos begin to fight, one side must inevitably lose. People cannot withstand bruised egos, much less broken ones and all battles leave lasting scars.

When dealing with someone who wants to use the confrontational approach to solve a problem, we can calmly come to a more productive conclusion in the following ways:

- Avoid belligerent attitudes and polarised positions – polarisation destroys the harmony essential to a family.
- Avoid digging in and holding on to positions in the psychological trenches of argument which are as dangerous as those in wartime.
- Avoid jumping to conclusions too hastily or adopting a position for or against something or someone, if it is not necessary – and never without careful reflection.
- Instead of looking for items of disagreement, look for common ground and, with a positive approach, search for things to agree upon as a foundation for further concord.
- As far as possible, never cast the other person into the role of an adversary and keep cordial communication lines open.

The non-confrontational approach

In most instances, it is more effective and desirable to approach a problem in a non-confrontational way which often prevents small problems from escalating into larger, potentially explosive situations. This involves a diffusing or dispersing strategy, which is the opposite of the focusing, confrontational solution. This approach is not head on, but sideways, at an angle from which all parties can view the situation together. The difference between confrontation and non-confrontation is perhaps best illustrated by an example.

Let's say you have reason to believe that your twelve-year-old has started experimenting with alcohol, drugs, and cigarettes. One response that springs to mind is to lock the child in a room with you and tell him that you hate boozers, drug abusers and smokers and you are going to beat the living daylights out of him. Furthermore, you shout, if that does not make him drop the filthy habits immediately, you are going to throw him out on his ear and never have anything more to do with him!

This is a situation where a confrontational approach is clearly wrong; the problem would be better handled by approaching it in a non-adversarial way. Invite the youngster to sit down and talk, taking care, both for his sake and your own, not to create a hostile atmosphere. Tone down the rhetoric and don't assume a threatening posture. He should feel confident that you don't intend to shame or berate him, and that you are going to address the issue rationally. Without jumping to any conclusions about his behaviour or motivations, give him some factual information about alcohol, drugs and cigarettes. Assure him that you want him to make well-informed decisions in all facets of life and, as his parent, it is your privilege and duty to share with him what you know, just as you share your love and possessions.

Let him know that he will always have your help and support in warding off any dependencies which could affect the quality of his life, and tell him that you are not against his having fun: what you are against is anything that might hurt him. No matter how much you love him, you must not misinform or lie to him, for this would be to underestimate his intelligence. Besides, dishonesty and deception are hardly the ingredients of a trusting relationship. If you exaggerate by claiming that *everyone* who uses these substances ends up on skid row, their brains withered away and their lungs destroyed, he is less likely to believe anything else you may say.

Instead, without referring to him personally, tell him that these chemicals are potent compounds which have been around for a long time and which various people in different societies have used for centuries. They have certain benefits for the user. Alcohol, for instance, might quickly relax a person and give him a feeling of euphoria, but there is a price to pay for the pleasant effects. The chemical works on the brain to create the temporary delusion of well-being. As soon as the drug wears off, however, he might find himself in an even lower emotional state from which he will have to work his way up. He might be forced to use even greater amounts of alcohol more and more often to buy shorter and shorter periods of pleasure or even relief. The same is true for other chemical dependencies which can and often do ultimately become the central controlling focus of the dependent's life. Tissues in the brain and liver can be permanently damaged, even resulting, in some cases, in death.

Tell him that there are healthier ways of relaxing and feeling good than using chemical substances – for example, sports, music, the arts, camping and exploring the beauties of nature, meditating and praying. Pointing out other enjoyable choices is very important – simply saying 'don't do that' is not enough. Ask the child what wholesome things he likes to do and explore ways of making it possible for him to do them.

As this example indicates, the non-confrontational approach requires more patience, understanding and faith in the eventual emergence of the best solution than the confrontational method. It is a process that demands a great deal from the person who adopts it: a considerable degree of detachment; the imagination and compassion to put oneself in another person's place; the self-control not to deliver an ultimatum or indulge in angry recriminations; the initiative to inform oneself as to the real facts regarding an issue. As in consultation, the parties work as a team; in the long run, the outcome is generally much more satisfactory to all the participants than a more dictatorial approach.

Seeking professional help

In facing problems it is important not to panic or lose one's composure because this increases the likelihood of saying or doing something rash which would only compound the difficulty. Part of retaining a calm and rational perspective is to ask oneself whether the problem is sufficiently urgent to take any immediate action at all. Some predicaments simply go away of their own accord. Napoleon was once asked how he managed to deal with all the problems brought to him from the various points of his vast empire. He replied, 'For three weeks I do nothing. By that time most of them have taken care of themselves and then I do something about the rest.'

Sometimes, however, we have a problem which we cannot ignore. There are times when, after trying very hard, we simply cannot effectively deal with a problem either alone or even with the help of family consultation. In these situations, it is appropriate to look for professional help. This does not mean that we should not make the attempt to solve our problems ourselves or that we should automatically turn to others for every little difficulty. But in certain cases, arranging to see a psychotherapist, a marriage guidance counsellor or family therapist, for example, can be the most effective, responsible and decisive way of tackling a problem. We must not make the mistake of assuming that meeting with such professionals involves handing our problems over to them to solve for us. On the contrary, we must still do most of the work ourselves. All any trained counsellor can do is enlarge our perspective with informed and experienced guidance and advice, and equip us with certain techniques to enable us to resolve our difficulties ourselves.

There is a wisdom in knowing when to solve things by yourself and when to go for help. Whether in marital problems or difficulties with your children, be aware that assistance is available and there is no shame in asking for it.

The spiritual approach

Human beings have the freedom to make choices – a finite and conditional freedom to be sure, but we are not limited by the iron will of inborn instincts which require that we do things only in specified ways. The price for this precious gift of freedom is the responsibility of having to make our own decisions. Humans will always need to look after their own survival, well-being, and destiny; they are left to figure it out for themselves and to take the good or bad consequences resulting from their own conscious choices. For this reason the rational mind is both extremely developed and highly important to people – we rely on our gift of the intellect, and we are proud of it.

Even so, there are instances when a rational approach to a problem is ineffective or has made its full contribution without resolving the difficulty. Sometimes the best solution may emerge when we set rational measures to one side, adopt a prayerful approach and seek help from a higher power, the Source of spiritual guidance. Psychiatrists, psychologists, and other mental health professionals are increasingly recognising the importance of prayer in dealing with personal problems.[94] It develops an individual's capacity to deal with anxiety, frustration and stress. Furthermore, it enhances life's enjoyment and makes for a happier existence. In the earlier section on controlling stress, we discussed the intimate relationship between the mind and body and how mental states can affect one's physical health. There is also a connection between the spiritual nature of a person and the mind, which influences emotions and moods, as well as a connection to the body, which influences stressful tensions.

Prayer takes us beyond the troubles of our material existence and transcends rationality. The feelings of serenity that prayer can provide us with are rewards in themselves. Yet the change in feeling and attitude, the lift in spirits that we experience from turning, even momentarily, towards a higher power has other, more tangible benefits. By some inexplicable means, we find ourselves with a more positive outlook after praying, even a sense of elation, and in this altered mood we can find new strengths and energies. We can cope with our problems much more calmly and effectively when we are feeling this way. Why is this? Because being happy increases our ability to concentrate and gives us emotional strength. When we are sad, we are weakened, depressed and our minds do not function as well.

When we think about our problems, there is one central fact which is true about each of them – they are all related to this world of material existence. The spiritual reality, however, only brings us good feelings. This does not mean that we should not deal with this world of physical reality, but it does mean that our spirits can soar and be free in the spiritual realm whenever we turn to it. Recognition of this basic truth enables us to avoid looking for all of our comfort and consolation in the things of this world. Even so, solutions to the problems of day-to-day life can be found by turning our faces to that spiritual source which enables our minds to work much more clearly. Strengthened in spirit and determination, we can then do our best in solving difficulties. Our mental well-being is positively influenced by developing and using our spiritual side on a regular basis.

The spiritual approach is also beneficial during those rare times when the only possible way open to us is to endure the problem, to persevere and eventually outlast it. When this happens, one should flow with the 'current' of events when it is obvious that attempts to swim upstream are useless. There should be a touch of acceptance, understanding and detachment that serves to moderate the effect of negative events. In these unusual instances, 'letting go' is necessary and healthy if we are desperately trying to manage situations that are actually beyond our control. Recognising the existence of a power higher than ourselves is then actually the most rational thing to do.

However, for most problems, we need not simply endure them. We need not become 'drifters', taking what comes our way in a fatalistic manner. Indeed, we are suggesting exactly the opposite. Knowing how to minimise the harm from adversity is an invaluable quality of being an 'actor' rather than simply a 'reactor'. Most people never develop this ability of being an active force for creating situations and events. People are usually passive reactors, like a bundle of reflexes which are triggered automatically. It is a challenge to us to develop this capability to act.

The spiritual approach to solving problems is not a delusional system of rationalisation. It does not mean losing contact with reality and withdrawing into a world of fantasy, nor is it a way of superficially covering up traumas and unpleasant events. Firmly anchored to a spiritual frame of reference, it is a perfectly healthy, realistic strategy for solving problems which can be used alone or in addition to other methods. It is an approach which uses the individual's inner strength, both mental and spiritual, to minimise the hurt. In a sense, it works like a microscope in reverse – it takes what appears to be an immense problem and reduces it to microscopic size. This reassures us that no problem is as deadly as it at first seems to be and that there is always relief in prayer when we know how to find it.

We can also benefit from the spiritual and psychological support of family members and friends. Caring for others and being cared for is part of being a human being. No individual can expect to lead a full healthy life without the establishment of affectionate and spiritual bonds

with other people. At times of distress, we should feel free
to draw strength from those we love. The positive
spiritual energy of family and friends can be tapped in
problem-solution. We can ask for prayers and emotional
support without spelling out all the details of the
problem to them.

Life is full of potentially devastating events which
threaten to defeat us. Our mental hospitals are full of
those people who have cracked under unbearable stress
and many others are barely hanging on. Some individuals
give up struggling entirely and commit suicide, some
develop various forms of mental illness and others abuse
alcohol or drugs. Most people, however, find inner
resources to come through it all in relatively good shape.

What makes the difference between being overwhelmed
or surmounting life's difficulties? It is a combination of
many things: possessing a healthy perspective which
views troubles as learning experiences, acquiring the
knowledge and skills to deal with problems and having
the spiritual strength and courage to rise to the challenge
of adversity itself. Indeed, it is often adversity that
rallies the human spirit, brings out the best of human
qualities, and unites us with others.

13

Growing into a Larger World

As children grow towards adulthood, their attention turns to the larger world. This chapter deals with issues that relate to life beyond the intimacy of the family home: raising unprejudiced children, planning for a career and the important subject of adolescence. The twenty-first century is approaching quickly and we can already see the outline of the dynamic societies in which our children will spend most of their lives. As far as possible, we want to prepare our children to feel comfortable and competent in the exciting time to come.

RAISING UNPREJUDICED CHILDREN

Gender, racial, religious, national and ethnic prejudices have no place at this time in history and we do not want our children to be burdened with them. As the diverse peoples of the earth draw closer together through international trade, the exchange of scientific information, the arts and travel, the trend towards a global civilisation and a more international consciousness will only increase with the passing years. Therefore to raise children to believe that their own culture, race, religion and nation are somehow superior to those of others is to handicap them severely in their future professional and social relationships with people from different backgrounds.

Attitudes towards other groups are learned primarily

in the home, usually through an unconscious process. Transmitting prejudice in the family is easy and insidious. A facial expression, a joke, a shrug, a casual remark and the infectious disease is spread. As parents, we must struggle to eradicate the prejudices that we were brought up with and be especially vigilant not to pass them on to our children.

Gender prejudice

The way family members treat each other has a great influence on whether the children will grow up believing in the equality of men and women. Does the father listen to the mother with respect? Are the major decisions of the family made jointly? Does the mother refuse to be spoken to rudely by anyone in the family?

Are the daughters challenged intellectually and encouraged to plan for their careers with the same seriousness as the sons? The vast majority of women in the coming decades will work for most of their lives, and girls should be given the same attention and financial help with their education as their brothers so that they may have access to the same levels of occupational achievement.[95] Being a mother is a very wonderful experience, but girls should be taught that motherhood is no longer a lifelong profession and that they can also achieve in the larger world. While it is true that the girls will probably rear children, so will most of the boys. Parenting is becoming a shared responsibility that requires the best in all of us. Both girls and boys should learn to do every kind of household task, from sewing to car repairs.

If sons are not trained to believe in gender equality, they may have a difficult time with women supervisors at work, as well as finding and keeping a wife who will be permanently happy in a subservient role. If daughters are not made to feel equally capable of achieving to the best of their abilities, they may remain arrested in their development and the larger world will be deprived of their unique contribution.

Racial prejudice

One of the best ways to ensure that your children grow up without the handicap of racial prejudice is for the family to form genuine friendships with people of other races and enjoy socialising with them. If children often see people of many racial backgrounds in their own home, they will have the precious gift of knowing from first-hand experience that humanity is in reality one and that racial prejudice is wrong. Government laws can prescribe racial equality, but until the family sofa and dining table are integrated, racial unity will not become a reality.

If there are no races different from your own in the town or village where you live, be sure to have picture books or illustrated magazines around so that the children become accustomed to seeing people who look different from themselves, whether they are from Asia, Africa, Europe, Australia, the Pacific Islands or the Americas. When you travel to a larger city, you may be able to visit the neighbourhoods of other races.

The following facts about the physical variations of the family of humanity may be helpful for both children and adults:

Racial characteristics are mainly the result of physical adaptations made over many thousands of years to various intensities of sunlight, temperature and humidity. Now that much of humanity has migrated away from ancient homelands, these once expedient differences are no more than a reminder of the various climates where our ancestors once lived.[96] For example, the purpose of the nose is to moisten and warm incoming air before it reaches the lungs. In a climate where the air is already warm and humid, noses tend to broaden and flatten, whereas in cold or dry climates, noses tend to be much larger and narrower.

Skin colours evolved according to climate to ensure the best rate of absorption of ultraviolet light, important in producing vitamin D. Colour-bearing melanin granules in the skin are numerous or few depending on the prevailing intensity of sunlight in ancient ancestral areas. Dark-skinned people have more melanin granules to prevent an overdose of vitamin D, while people living where the sun is less intense have fewer melanin granules and lighter skin in order to absorb more vitamin D. When exposed to the sun a great deal, as on a beach in summer, light skins will temporarily develop a tan to prevent too much absorption of ultraviolet light. The epicanthic eye fold characteristic of northern Asians provides more facial skin surface to absorb vitamin D.

The eye colours of blue, grey and green have developed, many anthropologists believe, as an aid to better vision in the mists and fogs of northern Europe. Generally speaking, in very hot climates the hair is extremely curly to facilitate the evaporation of perspiration. Straight or wavy hair, found in colder climates, can grow straight downwards to warm the neck. Longer arms and legs along with shorter trunks ensure that heat is dispersed over a wider skin area. Longer trunks with shorter arms and legs conserve body heat. The tall, long-limbed people living far south on the River Nile in East Africa and the broadly built Eskimos in the far north demonstrate the wisdom of these adaptations.

All these physical variations make humanity resemble a multicoloured flower garden, each blossom adding its own distinct beauty. It would be a dull world if everyone in it looked just like everyone else. The range of basic intelligence has been found to be the same among all peoples, whatever their present level of material development. When education and economic opportunity are more equally available world-wide, the material means of civilisation will become more justly distributed. We will then see the full release of the intellectual and creative potential of all of the peoples of the world.

Religious prejudice

The freedom to choose and practise one's religion is a fundamental human right that must be safeguarded – this includes respecting the right not to believe in religion, as well. To learn about the spiritual beliefs of others, parents may want to take their children to various religious services. Worshipping with others, it is easy to understand that a common thread runs through every religion, linking all of humanity in a spiritual bond. When children learn this, they will see that religious prejudice is illogical, since the people of all religions worship the same Creator of the universe.

The Golden Rule is found in the scriptures of all major religions and expresses one universal truth:[97]

Hinduism:
'This is the sum of duty: do naught to others which if done to thee would cause thee pain.' *The Mahabharata*

Buddhism:
'Hurt not others with that which pains yourself.' *Udana-Varqa*

Judaism:
'What is hateful to you, do not to your fellow men. That is the entire Law, all the rest is commentary.' *The Talmud*

Zoroastrianism:
'That nature only is good when it shall not do unto another whatever is not good for its own self.' *Dadistan-i-Dinik*

Christianity:
'All things whatsoever ye would that men should do to you, do ye even so to them: for this is the law and the prophets.' *The Gospel of Matthew*

Islam:
'No one of you is a believer until he desires for his brother that which he desires for himself.' *Hadith*

Bahá'í Faith:
'He should not wish for others that which he doth not wish for himself, nor promise that which he doth not fulfil.' *Gleanings*

National and cultural prejudice

There is nothing wrong with fostering our children's love for their own culture and nationality – they ought to have a sense of their own identity and be proud of it. But we should also impart to them an awareness of the world at large so they do not think that their own culture is 'the only right way'.

At present, some nations have a more advanced material culture than others, This may lead people to think that having access to technology and science implies greater worth. Nothing could be further from the truth. Materialism can prevent the appreciation of the intrinsic value of each human being. Also, one nation has never held the 'most advanced' status for very long. What we must do is respect and value all societies in the world. Human cultural diversity is a richness to be appreciated and enjoyed.

History is the story of the widening of loyalties, from the hunting band, the clan, the tribe, the village, the city-state to our present societies organised around the concept of loyalty to a nation. Each time loyalties widened, a sense of unity had to be established for a greater number of people. These transitions were difficult, but every time humanity made them it achieved a more advanced social and material civilisation. Children brought up with a sense of history which includes this idea of evolving progress towards higher levels of unity will have a greater understanding of the world and will be better equipped to live in it.

The next logical progression of this process, we believe, is towards a federation of all nations in a world community. In such a federation, each nation would continue to govern its own people and be autonomous within its own borders, but would co-operate with other nations at the global level on issues that concern them all. This system is becoming increasingly necessary in view of the common need for stabilising relations among nations, for caring for the planet's natural environment, and because of the growing importance of world trade to every national economy. Indeed many experts in international trade believe that separate domestic economies are giving way to a larger entity; today, in a real sense, the global economy is the only economy.[98]

It is essential that parents work to remove every trace of prejudice against other cultures and nations so that our children will be well-prepared for the changes that lie ahead. In becoming more international in our thinking, we need not give up any of our natural love for our own country. We have no problem being fond of our neighbourhood, our town, region and nation all at the same time. To these, we can simply add one more level of loyalty: a sense of world citizenship.

CAREER PLANNING, EDUCATION AND SELF-DEVELOPMENT

Looking to the future, parents need to ensure that their children receive the education and training appropriate to their intellectual capabilities and interests in order to acquire a useful trade or profession, one which will give them the material means to support themselves and their own future families.

While it is true that individuals are born with different capacities, effort determines how much is accomplished. We all know individuals of limited ability, even people who are incapacitated in some way, who have none the less achieved extraordinary things. No one is without something worthy of development. Parents should carefully watch for their children's natural abilities and interests, even when they are very young. When a special interest or talent is found, it should be encouraged through praise and training. All children deserve to have their unique capabilities recognised and developed to enrich their own lives and those of others.[99]

Often parents neglect this facet of child-rearing and make negative judgements about their children based on limited observations. For instance, we may be dismayed because one child is not talking much or another one shows no interest in reading. If a medical evaluation reveals that the child is physically normal, we should not conclude that the child lacks intelligence – this would merely reflect the misguided view of our society. Children who start talking and reading earlier than usual are considered intelligent, those who do not are seen as backward. Intelligence tests are heavily biased in favour of those who are proficient in reading and mathematics.

There is no question that verbal and mathematical abilities are important tools, yet there are other kinds of ability which should not be overlooked. A recent study has proposed the existence of at least five additional fundamental areas of intelligence: musical, spatial, bodily-kinesthetic, self-knowledge, and others-knowledge.[100] For instance, a child with outstanding bodily-kinesthetic aptitude is an excellent candidate for becoming a great athlete or ballet dancer. The one with exceptional spatial ability may become a first-rate painter or designer. Those who have astute insight into human behaviour have the abilities of 'self-knowledge' or 'others-knowledge'; they may become attorneys, psychologists or poets.

It takes care, wisdom and sometimes even professional skill to locate a child's talents and inclinations. Exposure to a wide variety of experiences through hobbies, travel, science and mathematics projects, the arts, crafts and interaction with people in social organisations will usually draw them out. Devotion to a particular field is frequently kindled by a childhood experience, as the biographies of many famous people show.

Parents may overlook a child's gift for a variety of reasons. It may not match their own interests, or they may have trouble visualising their daughters in certain professions, or they may expect uniformity among their children, not realising that each one of them is unique. Not only do children have differing talents, each equally valid, but the very fact that an older sibling is flourishing in a certain area can actually serve as a psychological inhibitor. A younger child may decide, perhaps unconsciously, to shun that particular activity in order to assert his or her own personality.

As new technology is developed, specialisation in the workforce grows along with it. Whenever possible children should see people at work in factories, offices, hospitals, farms, universities, commercial establishments – as wide a number of occupations as possible. Keeping abreast of developments in the job market will give family members some idea of the kinds of employment available in the decades ahead. Visits to libraries or bookstores to leaf through the books, periodicals, and trade journals of the various occupations are a good way to encourage a child to think of his or her future. Something may catch the eye and engage the interest enough to want to research further into a particular field.

The trade or profession eventually chosen should be the one most congenial to the young person's interests, that matches their natural talent and ability, and that also provides a decent living. In addition, it is to be hoped that the chosen occupation contributes something useful to society.

The same quest for self-development is also worth considering for the parents. Mid-life career changes are common these days and ambitions need not be abandoned because the mother or father is no longer young. Adult education is available in many localities. With the sharing of financial, parental and household responsibilities at home, advancement or retraining in an occupation may be possible for the adult members of the family, too.

In our view, the key to the discovery and development of the vast untapped talent among the children of the world is publicly financed education. Through the training that public education provides, merit becomes the criterion for success and differences in family backgrounds are irrelevant. Here again, response to the growing concept of the oneness of humanity is beginning to remove the barriers of social class, and racial and gender prejudice in the workplace. We now often see people in professions previously closed to them by law or custom. With this in mind, parents should encourage their children's aptitudes and strengths and, through consultation, help them set reasonable goals to attain the highest possible level of achievement.

ADOLESCENCE

The time when children are between the ages of twelve and eighteen is often thought to be a family's most difficult period. Growing towards adulthood, children sometimes battle every step of the way with their parents. Some young people even run away to escape the unbearable tension in their homes. Adolescence may not be perfectly smooth for either parent or child, but it need not be a terrible time. In spite of all the bad publicity, many parents are surprised to find it the most fascinating and rewarding time of all in raising children. This is possible if trust and communication have been built up through the years. If these are firmly established, parents can actively help their children through adolescence, instead of being perceived as the cause of their difficulties.

In a successful family, consultation provides a safety valve which allows parents and children to keep the lines of communication open. In this way, when adolescence approaches, the mechanism for mutually respectful exchanges already exists. Continue to set aside a regular time each day for talking together. This is now more necessary than ever, as the young person tries to make sense of a bewildering new stage in life. Let these talks be a haven, a time to confide experiences and mistakes and learn from them. By now, he or she has probably developed a sense of right and wrong – no need for long heavy parental lectures. Instead, sharing feelings and concerns with a parent helps the young person clarify in his or her own mind how ethical and intellectual principles might be applied to life.

During this time, the parents' first priority is non-critical, non-judgemental listening; they should make the adolescent feel welcome to talk to them whenever and as often as needed. They must also respect a son's or daughter's right to privacy and make sure he or she has time alone in which to explore a newly-emerging identity.

Young people are trying hard to complete the construction of their frame of reference and to form their own way of looking at the world as a member of the rising generation. It will naturally be different in some ways from yours, and you should not only expect but appreciate these differences. If you take the trouble to listen to the music your adolescent likes, go to current films, read some of his or her favourite books and share your uncritical yet thoughtful insights, you will find that you will grow closer together as you see things from a new point of view. You will also keep in touch with a world that has moved on considerably since you were young. One of the benefits of raising children is the access it gives you to the perspective of the generation after your own.

During these quickly passing years, you are polishing the final rough edges from the character and personality of your child. The values and morality that you have instilled with such patience are tested severely in the chaotic marketplace of ideas that your child deals with every day in school. Not everyone would agree with the view that parents should teach children their values. Some might ask, 'What about allowing children to make up their own minds about moral values? Shouldn't parents refrain from imposing their own views in the interest of individual freedom?' While this sounds reasonable, there is a problem with it:

> Children do not wait until they are older, wiser, and more mature to develop a set of values and goal orientations. If the parents leave a vacuum in the value-goal area, the void will soon be filled by other adult models, peers, or influences via mass media. An investigation at Stanford [University] of families with children who were drug users compared to families with children who were non-drug users is enlightening. Parents of drug users often took the position early in the lives of their children that they would not impose values but would let each child be free to 'do his own thing' . . .
>
> As the children grew older, they adopted behaviours and practices with which the parents did not agree and which led to a disrupted relationship. The drug-using children were more conforming to the values of their peer group and less creative than were the non-drug-using childen who had initially been exposed to strong traditional values through their parents.[101]

We believe that people have a basic human right to choose whatever value system they want after they have grown up and left home. Until that time, however, children are under the care, protection and guidance of their parents and should be expected to conduct themselves accordingly. It would be a great disservice to our children if we failed to convey to them the hard-won insights, values and understanding which we have acquired over the years.

Establishing an identity

If parents have given children enough love and a good self-image throughout their childhood, they should have sufficient self-confidence to handle themselves well in a peer group. They should be able to make their own choices independently, instead of anxiously following others due to low self-esteem and feelings of inadequacy. Sometimes adolescents copy the fashions, opinions and preferences of their age-mates with an almost slavish deference. Parents should be alert to how their children feel about themselves and be ready to offer encouragement and praise to boost their self-assurance – they should be especially sensitive to the natural insecurity of teenagers and avoid being over-critical.

Nearly all adolescents go through a period of separating themselves from their parents' view of the world and turn to their peers for approval. This is actually a necessary, but temporary, step on the way to the mature formation of their own world-view. To a teenager trying to forge an independent identity, parents can sometimes do nothing right: speech patterns, taste in clothing, ideas – nearly everything is rejected. The youngster rolls his eyes upwards and says to a parent, 'Oh, how can you wear/think/say/do *that*?' Younger siblings, as part of the general home scene, also come in for their share of criticism. Normally, this only goes on until the young person forms his or her own way of thinking things out, after which parents usually come back into favour. To paraphrase Mark Twain, by the time young people reach seventeen or eighteen, they are astonished to find out how much smarter their parents have become in the last few years!

Parents should not expect their children to be carbon copies of themselves. Each new generation has its own way of looking at things and not all new ideas are bad. In any case, the more quickly an adolescent assembles a personal way of thinking based on ethics, morality and solid values, the easier it will be for everybody. Parents who have for many years encouraged both independent thinking and good values have already made this transition to maturity far smoother for their child.

Parents can put serious obstacles in the way of this normal maturation process, however. Sometimes immature mothers or fathers may not want to confront the fact that they are old enough to be the parents of grown children, and try to deny this ageing by imposing a prolonged childhood on them. Parental indifference can also be a barrier to growing up; in extreme cases, teenagers who find themselves engulfed in drugs, alcohol and immorality are really neglected or alienated children looking for the love and assurance from others that they never received from their parents – it is a long, fruitless search. Other parents, who never trained their children to be self-reliant and make decisions, continue to lack confidence in their children's self-control; they then try to keep them on an excessively tight rein. A protracted battle of wills can ensue with everyone losing.

Young people may take on unsavoury adult behaviour – consciously or unconsciously – simply to show their parents that they are growing up. Parents may then react by being even more repressive, treating their youngsters like small children in order to retain control over them. However, if parents have shown their young people respect throughout their childhood, and increased both their privileges and responsibilities as they grew older, they will not feel the need to 'prove' their new-found maturity in negative ways. For example, if you already interact with them with the same dignity and courtesy you give to other adults, they do not have to go to great lengths to receive this treatment. You freely give it to them without being forced. You are proud and happy that they are growing up – and they know it. With sincerity, ask for their advice about personal problems sometimes. Not only will they feel flattered, you will probably get some good advice.

Parents who wisely and reasonably use consultation to

decide such potentially contentious issues as using the family car and hours of expected arrival, rather than arbitrarily 'laying down the law', save a lot of wear and tear. Some issues are not subject to consultation but most can be, with the result that a mutually acceptable solution is found that makes both parents and adolescent 'winners'. The trusting knowledge that parents have the young person's own best interests at heart fully bears fruit now.

A larger world exists beyond the adolescent's school with its intense peer pressures. Parents can foster a broader outlook by encouraging their children to participate in activities away from school, perhaps through humanitarian or religious organisations, hobbies, sports or trips. Teenagers should have a sense of being a strong person in their own right, able to meet new people and feel successful in a variety of social situations. It is good for them to know that their school friends are not the centre of the universe and that their own identities are not solely dependent on pleasing them.

In a previous section, we recommended taking youngsters to interesting work places as a way of learning about future careers. There is another good reason for this: by introducing your son and daughter to the exciting reality of the working world, you will create an enthusiasm for growing up. The young person will then correctly see adolescence as merely a temporary phase. Often younger children look forward to their teenage years as the high point in their lives and think of adulthood as a dreary time; everything seems so dismal after the age of 22. When they actually reach adolescence they may say, 'I thought this was supposed to be the happiest time of my life and I'm miserable – nothing ahead of me but adulthood, which is bound to be worse than this'.

This immature thinking is fostered by various influences, including the advertising industry which shows happy young people, as in soft drink commercials, and pathetic old people needing arthritis remedies. Movies and television generally depict youth as the peak experience. Such false concepts should be refuted by parents who are themselves enthusiastically adult and continuing to grow spiritually, intellectually, emotionally, as well as keeping physically fit. If you show your children that adulthood is, in fact, the most rewarding period and that you are happy with your life, they are less likely to turn to drugs, alcohol and immorality as hedonistic answers to the cynical question, 'Is this all there is?'

Setting limits

There will be many, many times when your child will want to do something which you refuse to permit. Sooner or later, you will hear the old argument, 'But all my friends do this . . .' Your response might be, 'Those friends do not belong to our family. You do. It would be far easier just to give in to you. We love you and we'd love to please you. It takes a lot of effort to say no to what you want. But we're older, we can see further than you and we're responsible for bringing you up as well as we can. So far we think we've done a good job, judging by how well you're turning out! Trust our judgement just a few years longer; then you'll be on your own. I'd be surprised if you still want to do everything your friends do then.'

Your children will test your firmness and standards over and over again. Be strong. You will feel as if you are doing the impossible to try to instil good values and good sense in a world that seems upside down. Sometimes you feel as if you are swimming up Niagara Falls, the pressures are so great. But persevere. Use every ounce of your strength and pray for more. Your children will eventually respect and appreciate your dedication to their well-being. Though they will probably not admit it at the time, the security in knowing that someone cares so much about them means a great deal.

Setting limits helps adolescents save face in front of their friends. When under pressure to conform, it is far easier to be able to complain, 'My parents are so strict, they won't let me do this', than to endure the disapproval of others by admitting, 'I don't really want to'. Young people whose parents are unconcerned and overly-permissive suffer from feelings of insecurity as well as from the problems arising from misbehaviour itself; they may feel hurt that no one really cares enough to set limits for them.

Schoolwork

As adolescents enter their later school years, studying becomes both harder and more necessary. Should parents keep after their children to study? It is much better to use consultation to define educational and career goals jointly. A long-range perspective and rewards for good study habits are effective motivators. Assist the student to set up the best conditions possible for doing homework. New or old, a good lamp and a well-supplied desk will give a sense of importance to schoolwork. Help them become wise planners and managers of time. Watch for studiousness and praise it, making sure that the habit of completing work successfully is established early on.

If they falter, an embarrassing reprimand is more harmful than the faltering itself; feelings of failure and being a disappointment are very destructive. You can say instead, 'No one can do better than their best; just make sure that you've given it. What do you think? Was this your best?'

Many young women and men of only average ability have excelled because they had a strong desire to succeed. Self-motivation is the key: pushing someone too hard for high marks can be counter-productive. A good balance is to encourage young people to set their own pace in line with their talents and career goals, not the parents' wishful expectations.

Talking about sex and chastity

Long before adolescence, you will no doubt have discussed with your children the way new human beings come into the world. The subject of sex probably comes up naturally and fairly often during talk-times. Healthy sexual attitudes, which will be a blessing throughout their lives, are rooted in the reverence for human life begun in a spiritual home. We have written an extensive discussion on sex and chastity which you may want to use as a basis for consultation with children aged ten or eleven and older. It is found in Appendix 1 at the end of this book.

The topic of sexuality is too important to be ignored. Children will learn about it sooner or later; the question is, who will teach them and at what age? Many schools have incorporated sex education into their curricula, with the endorsement of some parents and to the dismay of others. If neither schools nor parents do the educating, however, children end up learning about sex from their peers, through trial and error, or possibly even from unqualified and none too well-meaning adults. The consequences of this neglect can be tragic.

We believe that children's first teachers – the parents – should also be the first to educate them in this subject. More than the graphic description of a physical event, sex education deals with many subjects that befuddle a child if left unanswered. Some if not most parents are embarrassed to talk about sex; they are particularly worried about revealing anything of a very personal nature. You may want to state in a gentle but dignified way that you will be happy to answer any and all general questions, but you never discuss your private life.

Over the years, the dialogue between parent and child should continue, with information given on anatomy, physiology, health, ethics and morality as they relate to sex. If children are taught these subjects at home, the additional instruction they receive at school can only supplement the strong foundation of facts and values they already have.

Adolescents at risk

During the last several decades rapid social, economic and technological changes in the developed nations have been accompanied by increased alienation and social dislocation of many young people; some of them are even at risk of failing to grow into productive, mentally healthy, responsible adults. A research study in the United States conducted by business leaders indicates that at least 15 per cent of all American teenagers between the ages of sixteen and nineteen have already experienced 'disconnection' from society as a result of drug abuse, delinquency, pregnancy, unemployment and dropping out of school. Reported drug and alcohol use among teenagers has increased sixty-fold since 1960 and suicide statistics are up more than 150 per cent since 1950. The report stated that these findings 'are all signs of alienation and disconnection. All suggest that family, community, school and other agencies of socialisation and integration are not working as they once were.'[102] American statistics may be more extreme, but similar trends are to be found in many other countries.

Freedom in the political sense is a precious right to cherish and uphold. Excessive personal and social freedom in the sense of wantonly doing whatever one pleases, without any restraints or long-term concerns, can be disastrous. Some parents, as disorientated as their children by the change and chaos of modern life, distance themselves from their teenagers and retreat into a frightened silence about what is right and wrong. We believe that this silence is very dangerous to each child and to all of society as well. We have emphasised throughout this book that parents must overcome their own deficiencies to respond to their children's profound need to receive guidance. They must abolish that tragic silence which abandons children to listless drifting and calamitous disconnection.

Even if you make mistakes in your deep longing to do

the right thing for your children, they will perceive your love shining through to them like a beacon in a very dark night. Hold them to your hearts, love them, keep reaching out to them and endure. These years will pass and if the children turn out well, it will not be a matter of luck.

THE TRANSITION TO ADULTHOOD

It is not just our imagination – raising children *has* become more difficult since we were young. In former days, children were expected to obey their parents without being given reasons as to why they must. do things. We now think that the old 'spank first and explain later' technique is cruel and, more than that, ineffective in raising children to become the self-motivated, self-disciplined, independent-thinking adults that we want them to be in an increasingly complex, innovative and changing society. We have higher expectations for our children than in former times, as well as greater demands of ourselves as parents. We know that we need every ounce of our ingenuity, informed intelligence, and strength of character to get them through the final stage of their childhood and make the transition into adulthood.

Although we have high aspirations for them, we must be careful that our ambitions and dreams do not outrun reality. If we had hoped for a scholar or star athlete and they have not attained it, we can convey a sense of disappointment in them in subtle ways. Sensing our dissatisfaction, they may draw away from us, not knowing that it is we who are wrong in expecting them to compensate for our own shortcomings by succeeding in ways that we could not.[103]

At some point, perhaps when the adolescent is somewhere around seventeen, we should stand back, square our shoulders, take a deep breath, and recognise that *no person is infinitely perfectible*. No matter how good the parents are, no matter how hard they try – by nagging, putting on severe pressure, or even by praise and encouragement – no son or daughter is ever going to be perfect. Our young adults should be loved, cherished, and enjoyed *as is*, as a complete package of virtues and faults, strengths and weaknesses, just as we want them to love us, imperfect as *we* are. Of course we can continue to guide and share our views with them, but there eventually comes a time when we must relinquish our infinite expectations and be pleased with all the many good things our son or daughter already has.

Harvest time

The final years that the children still live at home are the swiftest passing years of all. The tall young man or woman strides about the house with all the enthusiasm and optimism of youth. For parents, it is a harvest time when the fruit of all their labours stands vibrantly before them, filling the home with great plans, hopes and ambitions.

At a certain age, people seem to cease being children in the eyes of others, and are considered to be adults. In reality, there is no fixed boundary between childhood and adulthood; this division is basically external to the individual. Growing up means a total transition from a dependent, helpless, resourceless recipient to a competent, resourceful contributor. It is only in this sense that there is a distinction between childhood and adulthood – it is not just a question of how old one is. Even when maturity is reached, childhood does not disappear, nor should it. Inside every adult there is a child longing to express itself through many characteristics which should be retained, such as exuberance, a sense of wonder, playfulness, innocence and spontaneity.

In the final years the young man or woman is home before going away for further education or a job, genuine friendships with parents can develop in ways that were not possible previously. Opinions can be challenged and tested; the parents can enjoy sparring with the wit and knowledge of the new adult. While the young man or woman eagerly looks ahead, the parents cherish these final months of being together.

Epilogue

In the past, the time between the marriage of a couple's youngest child and the onset of their old age and death was only a few years. Today, with a smaller number of children to raise and a longer lifespan, it is a surprise for many 'empty nest' parents in their early forties to realise that they may have nearly half their lives still ahead of them!

As we approach the twenty-first century, we need to redefine the concept of old age and change our thinking about it. Not only our attitudes, but our plans about ageing should be examined. Advances in medicine, sanitation, nutrition and other fields have meant a dramatic increase in life expectancy, especially in the last few generations. Three thousand years ago, the average human life span was eighteen years. By 1850, it had risen to forty; by 1900, to forty-eight. Today, in the developed countries, we can expect to live at least into our mid-seventies and perhaps into our eighties.[104] In fact, half of all the people on earth who ever lived past the age of sixty-five are alive at this moment.[105]

Old age was once thought to begin at fifty; now people in their eighties are running marathon races and climbing mountains. And the end of the increase in life expectancy is not yet in sight as the advances in health care continue. More and more people are living beyond the century mark. At present there are 32,000 Americans who are one hundred years old or over, 300 per cent more than in 1960.[106] By the end of the next century, an average lifespan may be one hundred years, or perhaps even longer.

We do not yet know how long human bodies can remain functioning in good order, but we are learning more and more about the brain. Dr Marion Diamond, of the University of California at Berkeley, states that the brain does not appear to deteriorate as it grows old; its neurons could last 150 to 200 years if bodies could remain healthy that long. The number of brain nerve cells remains constant after a person reaches one or two years of age and, just as exercise is good for muscles, so the brain relies on regular stimulation to keep strong and healthy – without it, the cells wither.[107] In the same way that infants need a stimulating environment to develop the power of their brains, older people need mental challenges, as well.

In traditional societies, younger people revered the old for their wisdom and reserved for them a place of great honour. In the western world of the present, old age is often seen differently. An eroding belief in the certainty of eternal life may contribute to the current emphasis on the desirability of youth, or a perception that the knowledge and experience gained from an earlier era is old-fashioned, even obsolete, in a time of rapid technological and social change. Whatever the reason, many people have a negative attitude to old age. Some become almost frantic about it.

Many people anticipate old age from the financial point of view by saving money and enrolling in pension plans. Other than that, people have a tendency to put growing old out of their minds and just drift into it. Here again, however, the most constructive way of dealing with the situation is to prepare for it in advance. Even if you are now only in your late twenties or early thirties, you have reached a vantage point from which you can begin to see beyond your youth. This is the time to get your physical well-being in order, if you have not done so already. Regular exercise, a well balanced diet, healthy stress management, good dental care – these are things that you probably know all about and plan to do 'some day'. That day is here. It is necessary to establish desirable habits while the resilience of youth is still with you. In other words, you have to invest in your body from now on because the credit of youth will eventually run out.

Sometimes parents concentrate so much on their children's health that they ignore their own. They become sedentary and do not take the time to exercise. Forty years from now, your children will be grateful if you have kept yourselves active and fit so that neither you nor they need be overly concerned for your health.

Good health is essential, but it is like the background scenery of a stage play. The important thing is what you do with your healthy body rather than becoming obsessed with every detail about it. Many decades before old age arrives, develop several hobbies that you really enjoy. You may want to take classes and begin serious study in a field which has always interested you or develop new skills in a sport. Some of these activities should involve other people. For example, as wonderful as reading is, it should not become your only hobby, nor should gardening, because they are both essentially solitary pursuits. Try to achieve a balanced life that involves both individual and group activities.

As leisure time expands when the children have gone, it gives a sense of fulfilment to do things with a high purpose: for example, to make efforts to abolish illiteracy, racial or religious prejudice in your town; to work for world peace or the protection of the environment, or to lend support to humanitarian organisations – whatever you feel is a worthwhile use of your time. In the thirty to forty years remaining in life after parental responsibilities have ended, you can help to shape society at the local, national, and global levels. Merely spending money, energy and time on matters of no lasting consequence will not impart the same kind of profound satisfaction that comes from sincere efforts to better the condition of the world. Whatever you decide to do, keeping your intellect stretched, and maintaining a satisfying social life is as crucial to your total well-being as your physical health, and will enhance the quality of life in the decades ahead.

To grow older is to grow richer in experience and depth of feeling – this is a well-kept secret known only to older people themselves! Young people may find it hard to believe that life can be better than ever before in the forties and after, but it can be. The anxiety of finding a self-identity is past, the awesome responsibility of raising children is over, careers are generally well-established – why wouldn't these years be more serene and enjoyable? When parents in their thirties are struggling with the intense pressures of jobs, young children, and finances, it may help to bear in mind that smoother times are coming. One day you will 'get yourself back again', and be able to do all the things you have had to put aside in order to give your energies and time for the children. Once they are grown and your responsibilities are lightened, you will feel as if your world has begun anew.

YOU AND YOUR ADULT CHILDREN

If you have done your job well, your children will be ready and eager to face the world. They will not insecurely cling to home, but will want to take the self-confidence and assurance you have instilled in them to begin their lives in earnest. You must let them fly away, but your heart will not be in it. This is one of the hardest parts of parenting – letting go, being unselfish enough to free them for their own lives.

If you have built a strong bond of affection with your children over the years, it will last through distance and time. Years ago, when parents said good-bye to grown sons and daughters who moved to distant places, even across the seas, they knew they might never see them again. We are far more fortunate. In the coming years, communication and transportation systems will continue to improve so that distance will seem even less of a barrier to remaining close than it does now.

You and your children can be connected through letters, telephone calls, visits; perhaps eventually you will settle down near each other. Whatever happens, however, it is the children who must set the pace. If the family has relied on consultation to make decisions together through the years, it may well happen that the young adults continue to seek their parents' views and non-authoritarian advice. When family memories are pleasant ones, the association is more likely to remain close.

With the children gone, the house will seem strangely quiet, but full of love if the husband and wife have kept their own bonds of communication and affection alive. The reward of patience and forgiveness is fully paid now when the couple enters the richness of these years. The major task of child-raising over, the couple has become, in the process of nurturing other lives, almost like one person in thought and feeling.

Eventually most parents become parents-in-law. If you give your children's spouses love and respect, and cultivate the fine art of being uncritical, you will be welcome guests in their homes. It has been said that mothers and fathers cannot know whether they have been good parents themselves until they see what kind of parents their children become. In successful families, the grandparents receive a beautiful compensation when they see that all the love, kindness and sacrifice they have given has been neither lost nor forgotten, but passed on to bless other children and other times.

We wish you well in the exciting task of establishing and raising your family. As fellow members in the larger family of humanity, we appreciate your sincere desire to do your best to love and nurture your partner and children. May your family be full of the loving unity that is the hallmark of the truly successful family, ready and able to take on the challenges of the years to come.

> Note . . . how easily, where unity existeth in a given family, the affairs of that family are conducted; what progress the members of that family make, how they prosper in the world. Their concerns are in order, they enjoy comfort and tranquillity, they are secure . . . Such a family but addeth to its stature and its lasting honour, as day succeedeth day.[108]

Appendix 1

Information for Consultation on Sexuality

This section contains information that may be used in several family consultation sessions focusing on human sexuality. There are two ways of approaching the material. Each person can read it alone, jotting down ideas and questions for future consultation as they come to mind. Or, alternatively, the group can read the material together paragraph by paragraph, discussing each idea as it is presented in the text. Either way, new words and concepts should be fully explained so that everyone will have a common understanding.

ANIMAL AND HUMAN SEXUALITY

In animals, sexual reproduction seems to be strictly programmed. Scientists have observed specific courtship patterns among the various species of birds and other animals. Among mammals, females periodically enter 'heat' or oestrus, which is the state of sexual receptivity, and at some time during this seasonal phase they actively seek to mate. When this phase is over, mating stops and the animals must wait until the next cycle. Mating is almost always followed by the birth of offspring. In matters of reproduction, the so-called freedom of animals does not really exist; there are few choices in courtship and mating patterns for either the birds or the bees! They can only do what they are compelled to do by a predetermined pattern of instincts.

Human beings, on the other hand, do not have periods of heat or oestrus nor are there biological reasons for them to postpone sexual activity until a proper season; this can take place throughout the year. Moreover, with the development of reliable birth control, it need not result in pregnancy. Unlike animals, people can choose if, when, where, and how they want to pursue courtship and mating.

Since humans must use their brains rather than instincts in selecting their behaviour, it is important that they make intelligent, informed decisions that promote their own best interest.

Let us examine some of the choices of sexual behaviour that are available with an open mind, so that we can weigh the advantages and disadvantages carefully. Making any kind of choice should be based on reasoning – it must make sense and stand up under the final test of the question, 'What is really best for me?'

SEX OUTSIDE MARRIAGE

There are some who advocate total sexual freedom. They believe that people should have a physical relationship with anyone they want, whenever it suits them. Their only rule is that the parties be consenting adults. One question that arises from this is: what is adulthood? Is it defined in terms of biological maturity, which starts at about eleven or twelve for most girls? Or is it the age when an individual becomes a completely responsible human being?

Total sexual freedom usually involves little or no emotional bond between the partners; sex then becomes mechanical and often ultimately meaningless. With no emotional commitment, free-for-all sex can be empty, unsatisfying and even boring, according to some studies.[109] Not many people engage in this kind of activity for very long because it does not satisfy the real human need for emotional intimacy. Ironically, people who have over-indulged themselves in promiscuity can eventually be 'turned off' by sex and lose interest in what could, under the right circumstances, be enjoyable for a lifetime.

There are those who seek sex with a great many partners in an attempt to find the 'ultimate' sexual gratification. Other people experiment with various forms of cohabitation, that is, living together without being married. The versions of cohabitation differ in their level of commitment: one form is a loose affiliation in which the two individuals, although sharing the same living quarters, are free to have sex with other people whenever they wish. Another form is 'trial marriage', in which the couple tries to find out if they are suited to each other and can get along on a day-to-day basis. During this time, they are usually physically and emotionally faithful to each other.

Couples who live together before marriage tend to claim that this trial phase results in a more successful marriage. After all, they argue, couples who discover they are incompatible simply would not get married. Sociologists Alfred Demaris and Gerald Leslie have found in their research that this reasoning is faulty. They report that cohabitation before marriage does not assure compatibility; there is no particular advantage in it.[110] Divorce statistics are just as high for those couples who lived together before marriage and those who did not. Another researcher, Dr Marri Gershenfeld, has concluded from her research that cohabitation is not a valid test for marital success because couples tend to hide important aspects of their true selves from each other in order to keep their relationships intact. Dr Gershenfeld studied one hundred couples who had lived together at least six months before marriage and then divorced within five years. Before marriage, the couples had been reluctant to discuss finances, careers and other important topics because they had been afraid that differences between them might mar their relationships. They had spoken and behaved cautiously, avoided criticising each other, and repressed anger before marriage.[111]

Other couples choose cohabitation, not in anticipation of marriage, but because they no longer believe in the necessity of legal marriage. Such couples often view a marriage certificate as a mere 'scrap of paper' and may feel that permanent commitment is meaningless in this age of prevalent divorce. This defeatist attitude ignores the large numbers of happily married couples and may indicate an unwillingness to make the effort to work things out in a permanent relationship. It is easy to find justifications for what is essentially a nomadic mentality. However, if one expects and looks for failure from the beginning of a relationship, it probably *will* fail.

It is true that there are many divorces, but at least people who enter marriage expect it to succeed. How many cohabitation relationships last for a lifetime? We suspect far, far fewer than marriages. Cohabitation may represent insecurity, the inability to make a mature commitment to another human being, and the impossible search for perfection. Clearly, a society peopled by hordes and hordes of cohabitors would be as unstable as sand dunes in a desert. Not much of a lasting nature can be created around the emotional upheavals of ever-forming and ever-dissolving relationships.

SEX WITHIN MARRIAGE

There is an alternative for young people to consider. This is the view that sexual relationships should be confined to couples who have decided to spend the rest of their lives together and made the permanent, public commitment of marriage. On the surface, limiting sexual relations to marriage may sound harsh and restrictive. Some may question the wisdom of this 'puritanical' position and label it as the prudish and unemancipated mentality of a bygone era.

However, there is considerable evidence to support the view that sexual intercourse should be reserved as the privilege of those who are legally bound together in marriage. Free-for-all sex, consented, purchased, forced or otherwise obtained, has negative consequences for society at large. It is true that sexual intercourse is a pleasurable activity, but sex is not simply a harmless form of entertainment, sport or recreation – it can harm the individuals involved through disease, serious emotional trauma, and unwanted pregnancy. Moreover, an irresponsible approach to sexual gratification robs the person of his or her human dignity. Far from being a liberating freedom, sexual permissiveness is a true bondage because the desires of the body control and enslave the mind and spirit. Pleasure is not the supreme purpose of existence.

Morality aside, promiscuous sex endangers public health by spreading venereal disease. The rate of incidence of sexually transmitted diseases such as chlamydia, papilloma, gonorrhoea, herpes, syphilis, and AIDS (Acquired Immune Deficiency Syndrome) has increased dramatically in recent years. In the United States alone, a combined total of millions of new cases of these diseases are added annually to the millions of cases which already exist. The rates in other countries are also increasing.

Young people are often totally ignorant of the effects of some of these diseases until it is too late. For example, men and women who contract chlamydia through casual sex remain unaware of it until the scars resulting from the infection cause them to be permanently sterile – and never to know the joy of having a child of their own. Moreover, recent evidence links genital cancer in both men and women to the papilloma virus. The statistical likelihood of contracting this virus increases directly in proportion to the number of an individual's sexual partners. The cancers it produces are often fatal.[113]

Herpes II has also blighted the health and lives of many millions of people and while it is treatable, it causes much discomfort; law suits involving large sums of money have been brought and won against people who have knowingly passed it on to unsuspecting partners.

The greatest fears about sexually transmitted diseases concern AIDS, which extinguishes the immune system's ability to fight off infections and, at the present time, is always eventually fatal. AIDS has spread all over the globe and has already begun to cause many people to refrain from pre-marital and extra-marital sex. Several international conferences have been held to exchange findings from scientific research; the present outlook is grim – several million people in the world carry the AIDS virus and there will undoubtedly be more by the time you read these words. So far no cure has been found and, because of the mutations of the virus, a preventive vaccine is difficult to develop; it may be decades before one is available.

Government medical expert U.S. Surgeon General Dr C. Everett Koop has been tireless in issuing warnings about this disease. He said that the only way to be completely safe from being exposed to the AIDS virus was to be absolutely certain that your sexual partner has never been exposed to it. He defined this kind of certainty as knowing that someone has had a 'mutually faithful monogamous relationship for the past five years'.

The real story is not told in statistics. We recently spoke to a physician from the Yale University Medical Center and the sadness in his voice was unmistakable, 'We try everything we can to make our AIDS patients comfortable, but with their immune systems destroyed by the disease, they continually catch infections. We fight to get them cured of one infection only to find that they've become seriously ill with another. The worst part is knowing that, after much suffering, eventually each one of them will die.'[114]

But even if there were no possibility of contracting

dangerous and life-threatening sexually-transmitted diseases, sex outside the safety of marriage has other serious drawbacks. Today, in most developed countries, there are many kinds of birth control widely available, with or without a doctor's prescription. In spite of this, large numbers of babies are still being conceived by unmarried people who are either ignorant about or careless of their reproductive systems.[115] In the case of an unwanted pregnancy there are usually three choices, each one causing sorrow and heartache:

- The baby may be aborted, the tiny life extinguished and never permitted to fully experience the physical stage of its eternal existence.

- The mother may go through childbirth and then give the baby up for adoption. Adopted children often grieve over the loss of their natural parents. When grown up, these adopted children sometimes pathetically search for them in the hope of easing their life-long emotional hurt.

- The baby may be kept by the mother. Usually ill-equipped to raise this unplanned child alone, she may harbour hostile feelings towards it and subject it to physical or emotional abuse and neglect. Also, the baby may be seriously ill with a venereal disease from a mother who had many sexual partners. Rarely do these mothers ever attain the levels of education and achievement which would have been rightfully theirs if they had had the foresight and plain good sense to postpone their sexual activity. Even worse, babies born to unwed teenagers sometimes grow up to become the mothers of out-of-wedlock children themselves, and the cycle of poverty is permanently perpetuated.

Aside from the human costs of genuine suffering on the part of both mothers and children, taxpayers can be heavily burdened with their financial support. Money from the public treasury which could be far better spent on job training, education and health care for all citizens must now be spent on the tragic results of what started out as a personal choice in favour of sexual freedom. This type of 'freedom' with all its emotional and financial costs goes way beyond what the human enterprise can afford or should be willing to grant.

Even beyond all these reasons, the ramifications of free sex strike at the foundation of society. The value of human life is eroded and cheapened when sex takes place without the moral and emotional contract of marriage. The activity which can bring into existence a human being with an eternal life should be approached with all the dignity it deserves. The commitment and sanctity of marriage provides the best environment for the growth of a child. When there are two partners to raise children, there are two sources of emotional security, financial means, and loving care, as well as the extended families of both parents to lend additional support.

There is an enormous preoccupation with sex at the present time – it is often graphically depicted in movies, television, magazines, and books. Contemporary society seems to have thrown out any sense of responsibility for advocating sexual restraint. Newspaper articles soberly discuss proposals for setting up birth control clinics in junior high schools for twelve- and thirteen-year-olds. Although the information is necessary, the disheartening thing is the implication that the only choice before us is to try to prevent pregnancy, now that any reasonable expectation of chastity has been abandoned.

Some parents are at a loss to know what to tell their children about sexual behaviour. This lack of clear guidance results in children having to work it out for themselves. They then rely on peer pressures and role models found on television and in movies and the music industry. Obviously, this is not the best way of raising responsible, caring, self-disciplined individuals.

At last some people are beginning to wake up to the fact that sexual freedom is devastating to individuals and society.

> Evidence is piling up that the sexual revolution was a ghastly mistake ... The equation is: the more premarital fornication, the more adultery; the more adultery, the more divorce; the more divorce, the more children suffering from addiction, crime and suicide.[116]

It is time that we study and begin to understand the relationship between the rising rates of pre-marital sex and divorce – if the two are definitely linked, then a young person should seriously weigh the difference between choosing the short-term pleasures of premarital sexual encounters or the long-term happiness of a solid marriage.

Unlike many others, the present authors firmly believe that young men and women are fully capable of leading lives of sexual restraint when they understand that it is in their own best interests to do so. They need not lose their self-respect or contract a possibly fatal disease, or have their youthful talents and career ambitions stifled by an unwanted pregnancy in exchange for a fleeting physical pleasure. They can say no.

It takes courage to be different, to do what a person thinks is right and not go along with others. Friends and acquaintances may try to talk a person out of remaining chaste through disapproval, sarcasm, threats of withdrawing friendship, remarks about immaturity, and a whole list of pressure tactics. Not everyone can withstand them – some are so desperate for approval from others that they sacrifice a very precious part of their being. But those who have the strength of character to make up their own minds and the self-discipline to remain chaste can respect themselves and know that their future marriages will be all the better for it.

We began this discussion by looking at how animals behave sexually. Animal behaviour is not and never will be a standard for human behaviour. Human happiness is best served by having a life-long, loving spouse who intimately shares one's joys and sorrows through the years; these permanently bonded couples can provide a secure, emotionally stable environment for the most important task of all: raising children, *who are the very future of the human race.*

Moral laws and principles make our lives run smoothly and harmoniously. The wisdom of every one of these commands is being tested today and they are being proven to be sound. Without them, personal lives become chaotic, with consequences that are irreversible. According to medical leaders, we would be foolhardy and suicidal as a society not to obey these laws.

Chastity is such a moral law. It can prevent endless heartache and misery. It gives one strength and certitude. It allows us to be in control of our own lives. When we remain chaste, we bring the gift of our unshared selves to marriage, enhancing our physical, emotional and spiritual relationship with our future partner. Chastity creates true human contentment – it is the wisest and most logical answer to the question, 'What is best for me?'

Appendix 2

To Our Readers

We welcome your letters telling us how you applied the principles, ideas, and suggestions of this book to your own situation. Please write to us with answers to some or all of the following questions as well as any other comments you would like to make. Answers from children and adolescents are important too. What we learn from your responses may be used in our future writing and lectures to help other families. If you would like to give examples, please do so. You may want to tape-record your answers instead of writing them down. Unless you indicate otherwise, we will not use anyone's names.

Questions for Parents

1) What did you find useful in learning to use consultation?
2) Have you noticed an increase in speaking and reasoning skills in your children since beginning to use consultation?
3) How often do you use consultation one-to-one? As a family?
4) Do you find that consultation generates more co-operation among family members?
5) How have the attitudes and skills of consultation affected your family life in general?
6) What would you tell other parents in order to help them learn to use consultation in their families? Do you have any suggestions for teaching it to children?

7) How has consultation helped you as a couple?
8) Do you feel that there is a greater awareness of human rights and justice within your family through using consultation? If so, in what way?
9) Do you have a good time together when you consult?
10) How did the suggestions and exercises in the section on 'Communication' help your family? Please tell us about your experiences in using them.
11) What experiences have you had in applying the information found in the other parts of the book: 'Foundations of Child-Raising', 'Drawing Out the Best', 'Psychological Well-being', 'Family Finance', 'Love in Action', 'Problem-Solving', 'Growing into a Larger World', Appendix 1 and so on?
12) Do you feel that the suggestions and advice in this book help prevent problems? If so, how?

Questions for Children and Adolescents

1) Do you feel more included in family decisions through using consultation?
2) Do you feel your parents understand you better now?
3) Will you teach it to your own children when you have a family?
4) What helped you learn the attitudes and skills? (Your answer is very important – it may help many other families.)
5) What parts of the book helped you the most?
6) How should children be disciplined if their parents don't want to spank them or use other harsh punishments? If you can, please give several different ways. Which do you think you will use with your own children?
7) What do you like best about your family?

We sincerely hope that your family is unified and well on the way to becoming experts in consultation. We regret that we cannot give individual advice. Although we are unable to correspond with our readers, we deeply appreciate your sharing your experiences and wisdom with us.

Please write to:　Khalil and Sue Khavari
　　　　　　　　　P.O. Box 17691
　　　　　　　　　Milwaukee, Wisconsin 53217
　　　　　　　　　USA

Notes

All directly quoted material is used with the kind permission of the respective publishers.

1. For a collection of essays dealing with the recent changes in family life see: Arlene S. Skolnick and Jerome H. Skolnick, *Family in Transition*, 6th edn. (Glenview, Illinois: Scott Foresman, 1989). See also James M. Henslin, editor, *Marriage and Family in a Changing Society*, 2nd edn. (New York: Free Press/Macmillan, 1985). For a discussion of the effect of social context on the family and other issues affecting children see: Kenneth Keniston and the Carnegie Council on Children, *All Our Children; The American Family under Pressure* (New York and London: Harcourt Brace Jovanovich, 1977).

2. Ervin Laszlo *et al, Goals for Mankind; a Report to the Club of Rome on the New Horizons of Global Community*, rev. edn. (New York: New American Library, 1977, 1978), p. xiii. Used with permission from E.P. Dutton, Inc.

3. Alvin Toffler, *Future Shock* (New York: Random House, Inc. 1970), p. 416.

4. Roslyn Dauber and Melinda L. Cain, *Women and Technological Change in Developing Countries*, American Association for the Advancement of Science (Boulder, Colorado: Westview Press, 1981), p. xvii.

5. Universal House of Justice, *The Promise of World Peace* with quotations and illustrations compiled by Juliet Mabey and Novin Doostdar (London: Oneworld Publications, 1986), p. 20. See also pp. 22–3 for a chart of the growth of technology.

6. See Ervin Laszlo *et al., Goals for Mankind*.

7. See note 1 above.

8. Eleanor Roosevelt, 1958. Quoted in Ruth Leger Sivard, *Women . . . A World Survey* (Washington: World Priorities, 1985), p. 7.

9. Sivard, *Women*, p. 33.

10. *Ibid.* p. 26. In both the developed countries of the past and the developing countries of the present one-fourth of the deaths of women between fifteen and forty-five have resulted from complications arising from pregnancy and childbirth.

11. For an exhaustive study see: Eleanor Maccoby and Carol Jacklin, *The Psychology of Sex Differences* (Stanford: Stanford University Press, 1974). For a description of ancient egalitarian societies, see: Riane Eisler, *The Chalice and the Blade* (New York: Harper & Row, 1987). For a discussion of the problems of working mothers see: Sylvia Ann Hewlett, *A Lesser Life: the Myth of Women's Liberation in America* (New York: William Morrow, 1986).

12. 'Abdu'l-Bahá, *Promulgation of Universal Peace*, 2nd edn. (Wilmette: Bahá'í Publishing Trust, 1982), p. 182.

13. 'Males and Females and What You May Not Know about Them', *Changing Times* (Sept. 1981).

14. Terri Apter, *Why Women Don't Have Wives; Professional Success and Motherhood* (London: Macmillan, 1985), p. 2.

15. 'Abdu'l-Bahá, *Promulgation*, p. 182.

16. Dana Raphael, *Being Female: Reproduction, Power and Change.* (The Hague: Mouton, 1975). Cited in Marion L. Kranichfeld, 'Rethinking Family Power', *Journal of Family Issues* 8 (Mar. 1987), pp. 42–56.

17. Letty Cottin Pogrebin, *Family Politics; Love and Power on an Intimate Frontier* (New York: McGraw-Hill, 1983), p. 195.

18. 'Abdu'l-Bahá quoted in John E. Esslemont, *Bahá'u'lláh and the New Era*, 5th rev. edn. (Wilmette: Bahá'í Publishing Trust, 1980), p. 147.

19. See Lloyd DeMause, *The History of Childhood.* (New York: Psychohistory Press, 1974), especially the first chapter on the evolution of childhood. The history of childhood and of families in general is a field that was neglected until the awakening of interest in the lives of ordinary people. For a brief overview of the history of childhood and the family see: Elin McCoy, 'Childhood through the Ages', *Parents Magazine* (Jan. 1981).

20. Khalil A. Khavari, 'Marriage and the Nuclear Family', *Bahá'í, Studies Notebook* 3 (1983), pp. 63–84. Also available in Spanish, 'El Matrimonio y El Nucleo Familiar: Una Perspectiva Bahá'í' *Estudios Bahá'ís* 2 (1987).

21. John Naisbitt, *Megatrends* (New York: Warner Books, 1982), p. 1.

22. Alfie Kohn, 'Make Love, Not War', *Psychology Today* 22 (June 1988), pp. 35–8.

23. John Wilkes, 'Murder in Mind', *Psychology Today* 21 (19 June

1987), p. 28. This article reports the study by Dan Archer, *Violence and Crime in Cross-National Perspectives* (New Haven: Yale University Press, 1984).

24. Richard J. Hernstein and James Q. Wilson, 'Are Criminals Made or Born?', *New York Times Magazine* (4 Aug. 1985), p. 46.

25. 'Abdu'l-Bahá, *Selections from the Writings of 'Abdu'l-Bahá* (Haifa: Bahá'í World Centre, 1978), p. 130.

26. Edward E. Jones, 'Interpreting Interpersonal Behavior: The Effects of Expectancies', *Science* (3 Oct. 1986), pp. 41–6.

27. 'Abdu'l-Bahá, *Selections*, pp. 136–7.

28. Elizabeth Hall, Marion Perlmutter and Michael Lamb, *Child Psychology Today* (New York: Random House, 1982), p. 374.

29. Esslemont, *Bahá'u'lláh and the New Era*, p. 152.

30. Khalil A. Khavari and Teresa M. Harmon, 'The Relationship between the Degree of Professed Religious Belief and Use of Drugs', *International Journal of the Addictions* 17(5) (1982), pp. 847–57. Reprinted by courtesy of Marcel Dekker, Inc. See also: S.R. Burkett, 'Religiosity, Beliefs, Normative Standards and Adolescents Drinking', *Journal of Studies in Alcohol* 41 (1980), pp. 662–7; R. Middleton and S. Putney, 'Religion, Normative Standards, and Behavior', *Sociometry* 25 (1962) pp. 145–52; S. Zimberg, 'Sociopsychiatric Perspectives on Jewish Alcohol Abuse: Implications for the Prevention of Alcoholism', *American Journal of Drug and Alcohol Abuse* 4 (1977), pp. 571–9.

31. Jerome S. Bruner, 'Learning the Mother Tongue', *Human Nature* (Sept. 1978). Reprinted in *Annual Editions Psychology 86/86* (Guilford, Conn.: Dushkin, 1986), pp. 134–40.

32. *Ibid.*

33. Paul Chance, 'Your Child's Self-Esteem', *Annual Editions Psychology 86/87* (Guilford, Conn.: Dushkin, 1986), p. 154.

34. *Ibid.*

35. Donna and Roger Ewy, *Preparation for Parenthood: How to Create a Nurturing Family* (New York: New American Library, 1985), p. 124.

36. *Ibid.*, p. 126.

37. Eleanor Berman, *The New-Fashioned Parent: How to Make Your Family Style Work* (Englewood Cliffs: Prentice-Hall, 1980), pp. 78–9.

38. For an in-depth treatment of the general topic of Bahá'í consultation see John E. Kolstoe, *Consultation: A Universal Lamp of Guidance* (Oxford: George Ronald, 1985).

39. Entry under 'Conflict Resolution, History of,' *World Encyclopedia of Peace*, ed. Ervin Laszlo *et al* (New York: Pergamon Press and the Institute of International Studies, 1986), vol. 1, p. 175.

40. Kolstoe, *Consultation*, p. 94.
41. *Ibid.*, pp. 17–18.
42. Rudolf Dreikurs, Shirley Gould, and Raymond J. Corsini, *Family Council.* (Chicago: Henry Regnery, 1974), p. 47.
43. Thomas Gordon, *P.E.T. Parent Effectiveness Training; The Tested New Way to Raise Responsible Children.* (New York: New American Library, 1975), pp. 170–1.
44. Daniel Goleman, 'Parental Influence: New Subtleties Found', *New York Times* (29 July 1986), p. 17 (N) pC1 (L) col. 1 © 1986 by the New York Times Company. Reprinted by permission.
45. *Ibid.*
46. Kolstoe, *Consultation*, p. 53.
47. 'Abdu'l-Bahá, from a letter dated 5 Mar, 1922, quoted in Shoghi Effendi, *Bahá'í Administration.* (Wilmette: Bahá'í Publishing Trust, 1960), p. 22.
48. National Spiritual Assembly of Canada, *Bahá'í Marriage and Family Life: Selections from the Writings of the Bahá'í Faith* (Wilmette: Bahá'í Publishing Trust, 1983), p. 36.
49. This priority of education was outlined many years ago, but is perhaps even truer today: 'Training in morals and good conduct is far more important than book learning. A child that is cleanly, agreeable, of good character, well behaved . . . is preferable to a child that is rude, unwashed, ill-natured, and yet becoming deeply versed in all the sciences and arts. The reason for this is that the child who conducts himself well . . . is of benefit to others, while an ill-natured, ill-behaved child is corrupted and harmful to others, even though he be learned. If, however, the child be trained to be both learned and good, the result is light upon light.' 'Abdu'l-Bahá, quoted in *Bahá'í Education: A Compilation* compiled by the Research Department of the Universal House of Justice. (Wilmette: Bahá'í Publishing Trust, 1977), p. 43.
50. Ewy, *Preparation for Parenthood*, p. 91.
51. Maya Pines, 'Aggression: The Violence Within', *Science Digest* (July, 1985), p. 38. The studies on the relationship between television and aggression in children are discussed in Leonard D. Eron, 'Parent-child Interaction, Television Violence, and Aggression of Children', *American Psychologist* 37/2 (1982), pp. 197–211. For the effects of violence on children, see: Hossain B. Danesh, 'The Violence-Free Society: A Gift for Our Children', *Bahá'í Studies* 6 (Apr. 1979).
52. 'Abdu'l-Bahá, *Selections*, p. 129.
53. For many creative ideas in making toys and playthings, see Jan S. Shea, *No Bored Babies; a Guide for Making Developmental*

Toys (Bear Creek: Bear Creek Publications, 1985) and Fred Rogers and Barry Head, *Mister Roger's Playbook*. (Berkeley: Berkeley Family Living, 1986).

54. Laura Lein, *Families without Villains; American Families in an Era of Change*. (Lexington: Lexington Books, 1984), p .3.

55. For a discussion of historic and contemporary forms of family life throughout the world see: Stuart A. Queen and Robert W. Habenstein, *The Family in Various Cultures*, 4th edn. (Philadelphia: Lippincott, 1974). For a history of the western family which contrasts pre-industrialisation with the nineteenth and twentieth centuries see: Edward Shorter, *The Making of the Modern Family*. (New York: Basic Books, 1977.)

56. For example, a Connecticut statute from the American colonial period reads: 'If a man have a stubborn and rebellious son of sufficient years and understanding, viz. sixteen years of age, which will not obey the voice of his father or the voice of his mother, and that when they have chastened him, will not harken unto them, then may his father and mother, being his natural parents, lay hold on him and bring him to the magistrates assembled in court, and testify unto them that their son is stubborn and rebellious and will not obey their voice and chastizement, but lives in sundry crimes, such a son shall be put to death.' J. Hammond Trumbull, *The True Blue Laws of Connecticut and the False Blue Laws Invented by the Rev. Samuel Peters*. (Hartford, Conn.: American Publishing Company, 1876), pp. 69–70. Quoted in *The Family in Various Cultures*, p. 306.

57. 'Abdu'l-Bahá, *Promulgation*, p. 168.

58. Wayne W. Dyer, *What Do You Really Want for Your Children?* (New York: William Morrow, 1985), p. 55.

59. 'Abdu'l-Bahá, *Promulgation*, pp. 180–1.

60. The following is a list of the ten best child-care books recommended by a panel of paediatricians appointed by the American Academy of Pediatrics. Their choices include books that help diagnose illness, as well as those that focus on children's emotional development This list appeared in the Aug. 1986 issue of *McCall's Magazine*.

    B. Spock and M. Rothenberg, *Dr. Spock's Baby and Child Care*

    T.B. Brazelton, *Infants and Mothers*

    P. Leach, *Your Baby and Child: from Birth to Age Five*

    B.L. White, *The First Three Years of Life*

    S.H. Fraiberg, *The Magic Years*

    F. Dodson, *How to Parent*

    F. Caplan, *The First Twelve Months of Life*

    V. Lansky, *Vicky Lansky's Practical Parenting Tips*

A. Eden, *Positive Parenting*
Ross Laboratories, Ross growth and development booklets.
61. Ewy, *Preparation for Parenthood*, Part 1.
62. Pines, 'Aggression', p. 38.
63. Goleman, 'Parental Influence'.
64. *Ibid.*
65. John Naisbitt and Patricia Aburdene, *Reinventing the Corporation; Transforming Your Job and Your Company for the New Information Society* (New York: Warner Books, 1985.)
66. Goleman, 'Parental Influence'.
67. *Ibid.*
68. Kenneth H. Blanchard and Spencer Johnson, *The One Minute Manager* (New York: William Morrow, 1982.)
69. Esslemont, *Bahá'u'lláh and the New Era*, p. 83.
70. Saf Lerman, *Parent Awareness Training* (Minneapolis: Winston Press, 1980), p. 115.
71. Paul Chance, 'Your Child's Self-Esteem', pp. 153–8.
72. From an anecdote told many years ago on Paul Harvey's 'The Rest of the Story', an American radio programme on the CBS network.
73. Ali-Akbar Furutan, *Mothers, Fathers, and Children: Practical Advice to Parents.* (Oxford: George Ronald, 1980), p. 26.
74. B. Lobel and R.M. Hirschfeld, 'Depression: What We Know'. (DHHS Publication No. (ADM) 85–1318, 1985), p. 38.
75. The following passage is helpful in explaining about revenge: '[Vengeance is] blameworthy, because through vengeance no good result is gained by the avenger. So if a man strike another, and he who is struck takes revenge by returning the blow, what advantage will he gain? Will this be a balm for his wound or a remedy for his pain? No, God forbid! In truth the two actions are the same: both are injuries; the only difference is that one occurred first, and the other afterward. Therefore, if he who is struck forgives, nay, if he acts in a manner contrary to that which has been used towards him, this is laudable.' 'Abdu'l-Bahá, *Some Answered Questions*, rev. edn. (Wilmette: Bahá'í Publishing Trust, 1981), p. 267.
76. Joyce L. Vedral, 'I'm Sorry!', *Parents Magazine* 62 (Apr. 1987), pp. 91–4.
77. D.L. Rosenhan, 'On Being Sane in Insane Places', *Journal of the American Medical Association* 224 (1973), pp. 1646–7.
78. 'Abdu'l-Bahá, *Bahá'í World Faith* (Wilmette: Bahá'í Publishing Trust, 1976), pp. 337–8.
79. For a discussion concerning the spiritual life of children see: Bahiyyih Nakhjavani, *When We Grow Up.* (Oxford: George

Ronald, 1979). For a discussion of child education see H.T.D. Rost, *The Brilliant Stars*. (Oxford: George Ronald, 1979.)

80. Harold Moe, *Make Your Paycheck Last*. Latest edition available by writing to: Harsand Press, N8565 Holseth Road, Holmen, Wisconsin 54636 USA. Also available from the same author and publisher: *Teach Your Child the Value of Money*, 1988.

81. 'The Cash Woes of Women', *Time* (3 Aug. 1987), p. 47.

82. Barbara Cullton, 'Take Two Pets and Call Me in the Morning', *Science* 237 (1987), pp. 156–61.

83. Bahá'u'lláh, *Bahá'í World Faith*, p. 195.

84. Quoted in Elin McCoy, 'Child Labor', *Parents Magazine* 62 (Aug. 1987), p. 99.

85. For a discussion of these stages see Gail Sheehy, *Passages*. (New York: Dutton, 1976) which is partially based on the work of Erik Erikson.

86. See for example: R.B. Zajonc, 'Emotions and Facial Efference: A Theory Reclaimed', *Science* 228 (1985), pp. 15–21; J.W. Jefferson and J.R. Marshall, *Neuropsychiatric Features of Medical Disorders*. (New York: Plenum Press, 1981); and D.B. Barnes, 'Nervous and Immune System Disorders are Linked in a Variety of Disorders', *Science* 232: (1986), pp. 160–1.

87. Suzanne Ouellette Kobasa, 'How Much Stress Can You Survive?' *American Health* (Sept. 1984), pp. 64–77.

88. Gina Maranto, 'Emotions: How They Affect Your Body', *Discover* (Nov. 1984), pp. 35–8.

89. Kobasa, in *American Health*, pp. 71–2.

90. Susan Seliger, 'Stress Can be Good for You', *Annual Editions Psychology 86/87*, pp. 217–21.

91. *Ibid.*, p. 218.

92. Maranto, *Discover*, pp. 36–7.

93. See: P.L. Carlen *et al.*, 'Computerized Tomographic Scan Assessment of Alcoholic Brain Damage and Its Potential Reversibility', *Alcoholism: Clinical and Experimental Journal* 10 (1986), pp. 226–32 and J.L. Johnson *et al.*, 'Assessment of Alcoholism-related Organic Brain Syndromes with Position Emission Tomography', *Alcoholism: Clinical and Experimental Journal* 10 (1986), pp. 237–40.

94. T. George Harris, 'Healers in the Mainstream', *American Health* (May 1984), p. 54. For a discussion on how prayer can create better mental attitudes see: 'Abdu'l-Bahá, *The Reality of Man: Excerpts from the Writings of Bahá'u'lláh and 'Abdu'l-Bahá*. (Wilmette: Bahá'í Publishing Trust, 1966) pp. 15–17. Also printed in *Paris Talks* (Wilmette: Bahá'í Publishing Trust, 1979) pp. 109–11.

95. For a well-researched book on the subject of gender prejudice see Letty Cottin Pogrebin, *Growing Up Free: Raising Your Child in the '80's* (New York: McGraw-Hill, 1980.)

96. For a discussion on the description and origin of racial characteristics see: Grover S. Krantz, *Climatic Races and Descent Groups* (North Quincy: Christopher, 1980).

97. Universal House of Justice, *Promise of World Peace*, p. 53.

98. John Naisbitt, *The Year Ahead 1986; The Powerful Trends Shaping Your Future.* (New York: Warner, 1985), p. 145.

99. For helpful advice by an expert vocational counsellor, see: Muriel Schoenbrun Karlin, *Make Your Child a Success: Career Guidance from Kindergarden to College.* (New York: Perigie/Putnam, 1983.)

100. Howard Gardner, *Frames of Mind.* (New York: Basic Books, 1983.)

101. William G. Dyer, *Creating Closer Families; Principles of Positive Family Interactions.* (Provo, Utah: Brigham Young University Press, 1975), p. 98.

102. Business Subcommittee of the Education Commission of the States Report, '15% of Teens Feared Lost to Society', for the Washington Post Service, published in the *Milwaukee Journal* (3 Nov. 1985).

103. Berman, *The New-Fashioned Parent*, p. 101.

104. Mary Batten, 'Life Spans,' *Science Digest* (Feb. 1984), pp. 46–51, 95, 98.

105. *Ibid.*, p. 95.

106. *Ibid.*

107. *Ibid.*

108. 'Abdu'l-Bahá, *Selections*, p. 279.

109. 'The Revolution is Over', *Time* (9 Apr. 1984), p. 84.

110. Alfred DeMaris and Gerald R. Leslie, 'Cohabitation with the Future Spouse: Its Influence on Marital Satisfaction and Communication', *Journal of Marriage and Family* 446 (Feb. 1984), pp. 77–84.

111. Marri Gershenfeld quoted in 'When Unmarried Couples Live Together' by J. Brothers, *Parade* (20 Oct. 1985).

112. Leslie Roberts, 'Sex and Cancer', *Science 86* 7 (July/Aug. 1986), p. 30.

113. *Ibid.*, p. 32.

114. Paul Khavari, personal communication.

115. 'Births Rise for Unwed Women', *New York Times* (30 July 1986), p. 12 (N) pC4 (L) col 6.

116. L. Sprague de Camp, 'Deciding Morality', *Time* (11 Aug. 1986), p. 11. © 1986 Time Inc. All rights reserved. Reprinted by permission from Time.

Index

ACHIEVING PEACE
BY THE YEAR 2000
John Huddleston

If mankind were to decide to establish peace in the world by the year 2000, what practical steps must be taken now – by individuals, politicians, governments and international agencies – in order to achieve that goal? What options would be open, and how could the concerned citizen contribute to this important process of change?

These are the questions addressed in this highly topical book. John Huddleston, Chief of the Budget and Planning Division of the IMF, presents a penetrating analysis of the causes of war and the role of the superpowers in contemporary politics and puts forward a twelve point plan for establishing world peace.

Of special interest to all those active in the peace movement and the campaign for disarmament, this thought-provoking and timely blueprint for peace is essential reading for anyone concerned about the future of mankind.

ISBN 1–85168–006–3 softcover 128pp £3.50 US$5.95

SCIENCE AND
RELIGION
Towards the Restoration of an
Ancient Harmony
Anjam Khursheed

Over the last two decades, exciting discoveries in modern physics have challenged scientists to reconsider some of their most basic assumptions about the nature of the universe – and of man. It is in the light of these recent developments that Anjam Khursheed, himself a research physicist at the European Centre for Nuclear Research (CERN) in Geneva, reviews the traditional conflict between science and religion in Western society.

Science and Religion is a fascinating and well researched account of that conflict, focusing on man's present predicament and escalating global problems. Of interest to both the scientist and the general reader.

ISBN 1–85168–005–5 144pp softcover £4.50 US$7.50

TO UNDERSTAND AND BE UNDERSTOOD
A Practical Guide to Successful Relationships
Erik Blumenthal

To Understand and Be Understood presents a refreshingly original approach to social life today. Written by an internationally respected psychotherapist in a warm, anecdotal fashion, this book offers down-to-earth, workable advice for successful, loving relationships.

The author brings the reader a new understanding of himself and others based on simple, easy-to-use principles, illustrated throughout with real life examples drawn from years of professional practice. A valuable handbook for all those seeking more aware, understanding relationships in all spheres of their lives.

Erik Blumenthal, a practising psychotherapist, lectures at the Alfred Adler Institute in Zurich, and is currently President of the Swiss Society for Individual Psychology. He is the author of a number of books on child-rearing, self-education, marriage and old age.

ISBN 1–85168–004–7 softcover 160pp £4.50 US$7.50

THE WAY TO INNER FREEDOM
A Practical Guide to Personal Development
Erik Blumenthal

The Way to Inner Freedom is a practical, down-to-earth guide to personal development. Written by an internationally respected psychotherapist in a warm, jargon-free style, this superb book offers a simple, step-by-step programme of self-discovery and self-education.

The Way to Inner Freedom is for everyone seeking the freedom to control their own lives, to develop their inner potential, and to replace self-doubt with confidence, frustration with peace and a sense of purpose. Only you can change yourself; *The Way to Inner Freedom* shows you how.

ISBN 1–85168–011–X 144pp softcover £4.50 US$7.50

THE INNER LIMITS
OF MANKIND
Ervin Laszlo

As a scientist and philosopher, Ervin Laszlo offers in these 'heretical reflections' a brilliant insight into the state of our values, culture and politics, and argues persuasively for the emergence of a new, globally-oriented, environmentally-conscious, spiritually-aware, thinking person.

'This book is a remarkably clear exposé of the problems of contemporary society and of the urgent need for a fundamental reappraisal.'**ALEXANDER KING**, President of the Club of Rome

Considered the foremost exponent of systems philosophy and general evolution theory, Ervin Laszlo is Rector of the Vienna Academy for the Study of the Future, Science Adviser to UNESCO and author of numerous books.

ISBN 1–85168–015–2 hardcover 160pp £8.95 US$14.95
ISBN 1–85168–009–8 softcover 160pp £4.50 US$S 7.95

THE PROMISE OF
WORLD PEACE
The Universal House of Justice

This beautifully produced, sumptuously illustrated book is an unusual mixture of fact, photographs and a plea for peace. In a world beset with escalating global problems it offers a verbal and visual presentation of the need for positive action.

The text, originally written and privately circulated by the governing body of the Bahá'í Faith, represents an analysis of humanity's current predicament and an outline of the attitudes and decisions which need to be adopted to secure world peace. Acclaimed by heads of state, politicians, royalty, religious leaders and philosophers worldwide, its noble and radical appeal to the better nature of humankind has been rendered into forty-five languages.

ISBN 1–85168–002–0 192pp 120 illns softcover £6.95 US$10.95

THE HIDDEN WORDS
OF BAHÁ'U'LLÁH
Bahá'u'lláh

This exquisite collection of meditational verse is perhaps the best known work of the founder of the Bahá'í Faith, written in 1858 whilst exiled to Iraq from his native Iran. For years only a few hand-written manuscripts survived. Now, however, it has been translated into sixty-nine languages, with over 100,000 copies sold worldwide.

With over one hundred and fifty verses, its exquisite beauty, majestic prose and breadth of vision lend this inspiring book a timeless and universal quality – an outstanding contribution to the world's religious literature.

ISBN 1–85168–001–2 cloth   112pp £8.95 US$13.95
ISBN 1–85168–007–1 softcover 112pp £3.95 US$ 6.95

ONEWORLD PUBLICATIONS

Oneworld Publications publishes contemporary books on cultural, philosophical and social issues. We focus on peace and global concerns, personal development, the family, spiritual awareness, religious questions and the Bahá'í Faith. For further information about Oneworld Publications books, please write to the Mailing List Dept at Oneworld Publications, 1c Standbrook House, Old Bond Street, London W1X 3TD, England.

Some Oneworld titles you may enjoy:

SCIENCE AND RELIGION	US$7.50/ £4.50	☐
TO UNDERSTAND AND BE UNDERSTOOD	US$7.50/ £4.50	☐
THE WAY TO INNER FREEDOM	US$7.50/ £4.50	☐
THE HIDDEN WORDS OF BAHÁ'U'LLÁH		
(cloth)	US$13.95/ £8.95	☐
(softcover)	US$6.95/ £3.95	☐
THE PROMISE OF WORLD PEACE	US$10.95/ £6.95	☐
ACHIEVING PEACE BY THE YEAR 2000	US$5.95/ £3.50	☐
CREATING A SUCCESSFUL FAMILY		
(hardcover)	US$18.95/£10.50	☐
(softcover)	US$11.95/ £6.50	☐
THE INNER LIMITS OF MANKIND		
(hardcover)	US$14.95/ £8.95	☐
(softcover)	US$7.95/ £4.50	☐
DRAWINGS, VERSE AND BELIEF		
(Bernard Leach)	US$19.95/£12.95	☐
THE SECRET OF THE STOLEN MANDOLIN		
(Children's fiction)	US$3.75/ £2.25	☐

All these books are available at your local bookseller or library, or can be ordered direct from the publisher. Just tick the titles you want and fill in the form below:

Name (Block letters) _____

Address _____

_____

Send to Oneworld Publications, Cash Sales Department, 1c Standbrook House, Old Bond Street, London W1X 3TD, England.
Please enclose cheque or bank draft to the value of the cover price plus postage & packing:
UK: 15% for orders up to £20 and 10% for orders over £20. Maximum postage £5. OVERSEAS: 15% on all orders.
All payments should be made in US Dollars or Pounds Sterling.